THE WRIGHT MAN:

A BIOGRAPHY

Charles H. Wright, M.D.

THE WRIGHT MAN:

A BIOGRAPHY

Wilbur C. Rich
and
Roberta Hughes Wright

Dr. Charles H. Wright
Died March 7th 2002
@ age 83

Founded Detroit Museum of African American History
in 1965

CHARRO BOOKS of Detroit/Southfield
17344 W. Twelve Mile Road #101
Southfield, Michigan 48076

THE WRIGHT MAN:

A Biography

CHARRO BOOKS of Southfield/Detroit
17344 W. Twelve Mile Road #101
Southfield, MI 48076

Copyright © 1999 by Wilbur C. Rich & Roberta Hughes Wright

First Edition

ISBN: 0-9629468-6-9

10 9 8 7 6 5 4 3 2

Book Design by Charles R. Alexander
Edited by Barbara K. Hughes Smith, Ph.D.

CHARRO BOOKS of Detroit/Southfield

Chapters

Notes

Bibliography

Index

Appendix

ACKNOWLEDGMENTS

The authors wish to thank the many persons who gave encouragement through the years to produce a book about Dr. Wright. Dr. Rich started his interviews as early as 1992. It was not until 1997 that Roberta Hughes Wright joined him as co-author and began to write about her husband.

Knowing that Dr. Rich had moved to Massachusetts and stopped his research and writing, Roberta Wright made a call and suggested that a collaboration might be in order. Dr. Rich, a native Alabamian, had traveled to Dothan early in the 1990s to see the place where Dr. Wright was born and to talk to some of the Dothan folk still around. Roberta Wright was best able to write about events after 1987 when she and Dr. Wright met and to interview him about earlier times. Rich and Wright, however, share responsibility for all of the book.

Some of the friends, colleagues and relatives interviewed: Lovie Page Pinkston; Dr. Hugh Blanding; Dr. N.S. Rangarajan; Dr. James Jay; Dr. Charles Whitten; Robert Shannon; Margaret Dudley; Ronald Hewitt; Eugene Gilmer; Catherine Blackwell; Marguerite Coar Massey; Josephine Harreld Love; Dr. Arthur Jefferson; Rev. Felix James of Montgomery; Anita Kitson and Nadine Battle, Dr. Wright's nieces; David Rambeau; Mayor Coleman Young; Dr. Marion Moore; Dr. Carla Wright and Stephanie Griggs, Dr. Wright's daughters.

A special note about Margaret Dudley, who died while the biography was being prepared. She was so generous with her time, and, being the good school teacher that she was, made some excellent suggestions.

Appreciation also goes to the staff at the Harvard Medical Library, Alabama Archives of History, Alabama State University Archives, Dothan Public Library, Wayne State University Library and Wellesley College Library.

Jean Rich and daughter, Rachel, read drafts of the early manuscript as did Professor Bill Harris. Rich's student assistant,

Carla Sapford, early on, was helpful during part of the project. Dr. Dewitt Dykes, a historian, was most helpful in the discussion of Detroit.

Thanks, also, to Blythe L. Allen for her love and support and for the copy of Maya Angelou's, *Pray My Wings Are Gonna Fit Me Well;* Blythe, Dr. Wright's granddaughter and her brother, Brett W. Allen, repeatedly gave suggestions, as did Dr. Wright's stepchildren, Dr. Barbara Hughes Smith, husband, Joseph W. Smith, Wilbur B. Hughes, III and wife, Adawork Hughes, who also assisted by reading the manuscript.

John Williams shared photos of the Museum's first site and the mobile museum. Robert Shannon located the photo of Jesse Jackson, et al, at the groundbreaking. Monica Morgan photographed the Wrights in formal attire and Lydia Kaplan, of Rhode Island, sent the picture of Wright on the roof at Harlem Hospital. Others, who provided great photos were Mildred Jeffrey; photographer, Larry Smith; Norma and Leonard Davis; and Free Press photographer, Hugh Grannum. Important assistance was received from Nehemiah and Maryhelen Amaker; Mariel Wardell and Brunetta Vinson. Much thanks, also, to Coraleen Cabell Rawls, who did book editing; her suggestions were most helpful. Appreciation is expressed to George Myers and Ron Amos for their support, to Felecia Hunt-Taylor for the photo of Catlett and Mora, and thanks to Verda Gentry of Dothan, Alabama for all her assistance.

It would have been impossible to produce this book without the continued assistance of Charles Alexander. His nimble fingers produced miracles with the computer and his expertise with design and creative ideas provided inspiration to keep this project moving.

And, of course, the authors have unlimited and immeasurable love and respect for Charles H. Wright. We dedicate the book to his nuclear family, to his extended family, to his "babies" and to his many friends.

WILBUR C. RICH

Dr. Wilbur C. Rich is professor of Political Science at Wellesley College. He received his Ph.D. in Political Science from the University of Illinois. Before coming to Wellesley College, he taught at Columbia University, University of Illinois, University of Michigan, University of Wisconsin and Wayne State University. He has held administrative positions with the Illinois Department of Mental Health and the Connecticut Department of Mental Health. He has also acted as a consultant, researcher and program evaluator for a variety of public sector agencies and local governments. His primary areas of research are urban politics, public management and school politics.

He is the author of *The Politics of Urban Personnel Policy: Reformers, Politicians and Bureaucrats* (1982) and *Coleman Young and Detroit Politics: From Social Activist to Power Broker*

(1989). His most recent book is *Black Mayors and School Politics* (1996). In addition, he has also edited a book entitled *The Politics of Minority Coalitions* (1996) and published several articles and reports concerning local government administrative problems. He serves on the editorial boards of three academic journals.

ROBERTA HUGHES WRIGHT

DR. ROBERTA HUGHES WRIGHT (nee Greenidge) is a graduate of the University of Michigan with a Ph.D. in behavioral sciences in education. Dr. Wright's other degrees: Bachelor of Science, Masters of Education, and Juris Doctor were all earned at Wayne State University in Detroit. She is a member of the Bar of the State of Michigan, the Bar of the District of Columbia and has been admitted to practice before the Supreme Court of the United States.

Dr. Wright's mother, Barbara Grace Morris Greenidge was born in Ontario, Canada and her father, Robert I. Greenidge, M.D., a pioneer in medicine and business was born in South America. Dr. Wright was a school social worker with the Detroit Public Schools, a counselor with the Mayor's Employment Project, and the Director of the Detroit Commission on Children and Youth during the administration of Mayor Jerome P. Cavanagh. She was Vice President of Academic Affairs at Shaw College and lecturer at Lawrence Technological University.

Dr. Wright has served on numerous boards and commissions, both state, local and national. In addition, she was elected to the Board of Directors of Home Federal Savings and Loan Association, and was an organizer and member of the Board of Directors of First Independence National Bank of Detroit for ten years. Dr. Wright lists her social clubs, such as The Gazelles, The Sophisticates, and The Contempos (Detroit, Chicago, and New York) as favorites because of the relaxed enjoyment and the camaraderie. However, she is actively involved with Alpha Kappa Alpha Sorority and with the Links, Incorporated-Great Lakes Chapter. Among the awards and recognition received have been Michigan Chronicle Newspaper, Citizen of the Year; *Detroit Skyliner Magazine,* Quality Quintet Award; Alpha Kappa Alpha Sorority Recognition Award; Harriet Tubman Civic and Cultural Award, the NAACP Freedom Award, and the Spirit of Detroit Award.

Roberta Wright has, since her retirement, along with her husband, spent a significant amount of time assisting with bringing attention to Penn Center of the Sea Islands, St. Helena, South Carolina. The Wrights organized the Michigan Support Group for the Center in January 1992 and the group has given the Development Office over $75,000 and has been supportive in many other ways. The MSG's recent project was to furnish one of the beautifully renovated buildings on the grounds.

Dr. Wright enjoys writing and watching the Detroit River from her Detroit apartment or working in her home on Hilton Head Island, S.C. Besides a book of poems, she has published the following: *The Birth of the Montgomery Bus Boycott; A Tribute to Charlotte Forten-1837-1914; Annotated Bibliography of Books of the Sea Islands-South Carolina and Georgia; Detroit Memorial Park: The Evolution of an African-American Corporation;* and *Lay Down Body-Living History in African American Cemeteries,* co-authored by Wilbur B. Hughes, III and published by Visible Ink Press.

Dr. Roberta Hughes Wright, widowed in 1985, is married to Charles H. Wright, M.D., an Obstetrician-Gynecologist and founder of the Charles H. Wright Museum of African American History. She has a daughter, Barbara, who holds a Ph.D. from the University of Michigan, and a son, Wilbur, who has a J.D. from Howard University School of Law. Dr. Wright is a member of Plymouth United Church of Christ of Detroit.

The Wright Man, is a testament to an important and significant history. It is a history of African Americans, a history of strife, struggle, perseverance and diligence. Visionaries often come from humble origins. Ghandi, Martin Luther King, Jr. and Nelson Mandela did not come from backgrounds of privilege and great economic wealth. Their visions and subsequent contributions were derived from the struggles of a people for dignity, justice and equality. Charles H. Wright traveled a similar journey. From a humble beginning in the "Delta" of the South to the top of his chosen profession - medicine - in the North, Dr. Wright's journey was one of struggle and success. Yet, being a successful obstetrician and gynecologist was not enough for Dr. Wright or for his people - African Americans.

During the decade of the 60s, all around the country, African Americans were rediscovering and re-affirming their culture. After visiting a memorial to Danish World War I heroes, Dr. Wright and a small band of "true believers" opened, in 1965, the International Afro-American Museum in three row houses on West Grand Boulevard in Detroit, Michigan. In the first few months, more than 25,000 people visited the "museum" for lessons in African American history and culture. By the end of the first year, more than 125,000 people had walked through the museum's doors. Dr. Wright's vision of creating an institution that would document, preserve and educate the public on the history, life and culture of African Americans through exhibitions, educational programs, research and outreach, became a reality.

Today, the Charles H. Wright Museum of African American History is the largest of its kind in the United States. The museum houses over 20,000 artifacts and archival materials such as the Blanche Coggin Underground Railroad Collection, the Harriet Tubman Museum Collection, the

Coleman A. Young and Horace Sheffield collections. The Museum features four exhibition areas: a 100-foot architecturally ordained glass-domed rotunda, a research library, a 319-seat theater, a café and a museum store.

Charles Wright persevered over the years to make a difference in improving the lives of his people. He understands that we, as African Americans, have a triumphant history, a history which must be honored, revered and most important, preserved. This is a book about living; this is a book about dreaming that should resonate deeply with individuals who care about the search for justice, equality and meaning of life.

Arthur Jefferson, Ed.D
Chair, Board of Trustees
CHWMAAH

Dr. Wright and Dr. Arthur Jefferson, Chair,
Museum Board of Trustees

"Praises Due to the Warriors of Long-Standing"
(for Charles H. Wright, M.D.)

The enduring inspiration of warriors of long-standing
is in their demonstration of how to fight those fights of the righteous
how to endure & subdue those blows of the wicked
remain culturally committed/love that work
& stand tree-top tall in the activist knowledge
that right now is always the time to build.

A warrior of long-standing is subject to be so audacious
he'll spend waking & dreaming moments staying hip to the schemes
steadily demanding equal opportunity, no more/no less
while delivering some 7,000 African American babies into this world
protecting their health with race wisdom & race hospitals
busting open segregated Northern hospital doors for them
while creating a museum to nourish & preserve their lied-on history
& for his next feat he'll turn right around
& start raising much money to save St. Helena Island's
precious Penn Center from the corporate grip
while authoring books of history & culture all along the way.

Warriors of long standing are all the time
re-inventing ways to harness the know-how
to find more ways to make a way out of no way.

In honor of the long-flowing and the on-going
cultural service to the African American state of
Brother Charles H. Wright, MD/ outstanding warrior of long-standing
wearer of many purposeful hats:
unbowed son of segregated Alabama/
healer of the sick/museum founder/ author
savior of sacred slavery-stained sites/
entrenched recorder of Robeson's mighty legacies/
renaissance man/beloved elder
(& this is just the short list of your purposeful hats)
all of them worn with your highly persuasive/ message-sending/
determined/defending/delivering & saving grace.

You made your choice
your life's example says yes-yes to freedom
& no-hell-no to slavery
you enrich us all.

Melvin T. Peters
4/8/98

ix

A loud wail permeated the room; it sounded much like a cry of distress. A few masked men and women stood nearby in various stages of concern. The slap had been firm and purposeful; and, the indignant response was immediate. Those in attendance either felt relief, or joy, or perhaps it seemed like just a routine to someone. To Dr. Charles H. Wright, the obstetrician-in-charge, it was a time of satisfaction, a fulfillment, another baby was born. This was a significant baby; Dr. Wright knew that all of his babies were significant and would make it in the world. In addition to this, his thought was that he had followed his dream that started back in 1953, when he left Harlem Hospital in New York, with the OB-GYN letters after his name. But mixed with the joy on this day in 1986, was a feeling of sadness. Dr. Wright had set the date of his retirement from practice. He knew that life would be different. This was to be his last delivery. But, of course, there had been a significant delivery in 1965. And in 1998, that baby had grown up and even was given Dr. Wright's name—it became the Dr. Charles H. Wright Museum of African American History.

From left: Dr. Roberta Wright; Wilbur B. Hughes, III; Dr. Wright; Hon. Brenda M. Scott; Dr. Barbara Hughes Smith; and Joseph W. Smith at press conference

From left: Owsley Spiller, Judge Willie Lipscomb, Dr. Wright, Robert Shannon, Norman Dillard, and Dr. Clarence Stone

And, so it was. On Monday, March 30, 1998, a press conference was held at the Museum to announce its renaming as the Dr. Charles H. Wright Museum of African American History. The Detroit City Council had voted previously, unanimously, for the name change, and, of course, Mayor Dennis Archer had given his approval. It was on Thursday,

The Wright Man

March 28 that the Board of Trustees of the Museum (Dr. Arthur Jefferson, chair), approved the name change. Dr. Wright's friends, Robert Shannon, Norman Dillard, Owsley Spiller, Judge Willie G. Lipscomb, Jr., and Dr. Clarence Stone were in attendance at the Board meeting. They and scores of former volunteers and friends, for many months had encouraged and supported the renaming and the Hon. Brenda Scott led the way.

The press conference received attention from all of Detroit's print media as well as radio and television coverage. Betty DeRamus, of the Detroit News, entitled her three-column article: "Renaming Museum is a Fitting Tribute to Dr. Wright." With Dr. Wright as Betty's gynecologist, she was able to write a "no holds barred" timely and reflective story. (See Appendix for complete article.)

Dr. Wright was highly exuberant, in his laid back manner, by the tribute, and was pleased that he was around to enjoy it. He quoted Yogi Berra, saying, "You can't be aware of it, unless you are aware of it."

To understand Charles Wright's character and career, and how this all came about, it is necessary to examine his origins in Dothan, Alabama. The town takes its name from the Palestinian village where Joseph's brother plots to kill him (Genesis: 37:24). It is the seat for Houston County, the heart of the "so-called" Wiregrass region, located in the southeastern section of Alabama about eighteen miles from the Chattahoochee River, that marks the eastern border with Georgia. The railroad and U.S. 241 and U.S. 84 highways connect surrounding towns to Dothan. A system of red dirt roads crisscrosses the county, linking village and sparsely settled areas. Although it is the center of Houston County's social and political activities, Dothan has remained a small, unpretentious town.

Settled in 1840 by Scotch-Irish squatters, Dothan became known for farming and turpentine brewing, the main economic activities for the settlers, some of whom grew wealthy and established small plantations. As Black slaves were brought to the town to work the plantations, two Dothans developed, one Black and the other white. Charles Wright grew up in the Black Dothan. The making of the Black community took several generations, each of which contributed significantly to history and culture.

The Black community of Dothan was divided into four separate communities or enclaves: Frog Town, Pine Street, Baptist Bottom, and the East Side (next to the Acid Plant Hill). The Virginia Carolina Guano Fertilizer Plant belched out foul smelling and polluted air over the East Side. The Black poor had to endure living near the plant, but the Black bourgeoisie could afford cleaner enclaves.

Although Charles grew up in a working class family, he played with the children of the Black middle class. He grew to admire the achievements of this class. At the top of the Black economic pyramid were men such as Will Hawk and Monroe Page, funeral home owners. The funeral homes prospered because of the popularity of burial insurance among Black people. The business did not depend upon white support and required little initial capital.

By 1935, Black Dothan had a Black physician, Dr. Dasher, and a dentist Dr. D.V. Jemison. Mr. C.C. Walker was an insurance salesman and the long time Sunday School superintendent at First Baptist Church in Baptist Bottom. Charles Wright remembers Mr. Walker as well dressed, owning a nice car and living in a beautiful house. The sidewalks on his street were paved. Nevertheless, the prestige and wealth of these Black gentlemen did not translate into social standing in the general community. The Black physicians, undertakers, and ministers constituted Dothan's tiny Black bourgeoisie. For example, Monroe Page lived in a big house on a street with a number on the door (a sign of status some Blacks did not enjoy). He also had a gardener. His daughter, Lovie Lee,

The Wright Man

recalled that "some whites called Papa, Mr. Page."[1] Although the Pages lived within sight of whites and were wealthy by Dothan standards, they were not treated as equals by whites. Negroes, regardless of wealth, could not escape the caste system.

Race relations in Dothan clearly reflected the Old South's segregation, which whites worked hard to maintain. One of the unintended consequences of rigidly enforced social separation of the races was the creation of a relatively self-sufficient Black community. Dothan had its Black businesses, and for a short period, Blacks had their own newspaper, *The Voice of the Negro*, evidence that the town had its share of literate Black people and enough cash resources to support this enterprise. Although the paper did not have many advertisements, it was able to support itself through subscriptions. The paper discontinued publication before World War I, but Blacks still had oral networks linking the small hamlets that portrayed Dothan as a place to find non-farm work.

LAURA AND WILLIE WRIGHT

A native Alabamian, Willie Perry Wright, Born in 1892, came to Dothan from Ozark, Alabama, the seat of Dale County, known chiefly for hog raising. Willie had come from a family of fifteen brothers and two sisters. Although there was a high infant mortality rate in the Old South, large families were not uncommon in rural America as children were needed for the laborious life of sharecropping. Times were always tough for Blacks who were born on the farm and into large families. Children in such families never had a carefree childhood, as they were expected to be in the fields at an early age. Many were pushed out of their birth home once they reach the age of employment. Schooling was barely extended beyond the literacy stage.

Born in 1898, Laura Florence moved to Dothan from Batesfield, Alabama, about sixty miles away in Barbour County.

The village of Batesfield is near Eufaula, the county seat. The only industry in Eufaula was the Cowikee Cotton Mill. Cotton raising and picking were practically the only jobs available to Blacks. Laura came from a family of fifteen children, and they were expected to rise by dawn, to chop or pick cotton, pull potatoes and milk cows. She came to Dothan, in part, to escape the harsh life of sharecropping and to find a job. It was also common for Black families to encourage children to leave once they reach a certain size or age. At the age of 13, Laura went to work as a domestic for a white Dothan family.

Laura lived with the white family until she met Willie Perry Wright. As the first Black chauffeur in Dothan, Willie was a celebrity in town. Willie would bring her presents during the courtship and in 1914 she married Willie who, then, was a driver for one of the town's most successful white physicians and owner of the local infirmary, Dr. Earl Moody. Laura at 16 years of age was big for her age, about 5' 9 inches. Willie was 22 years old. "After a brief courtship, they married."[2]

Laura and Willie lived on Pine Street in the heart of the Negro section. Pine Street was an unpaved, hilly, red-mud-packed thoroughfare. During the summer, red dust would get into the house and into everything, including the clothes. The house had a permanent red haze and looked much like others on the block but this house had a porch, which ran across its entire front. The house was lighted by kerosene lamps and heated by a pot-belly stove. The family drinking and washing water came from a well and there was a nearby outhouse. Charles Wright and his siblings were born and reared in this moderate three-room dwelling.

Pearl, the eldest, was born in 1915, Charles in 1918, and Robert Wright in 1921. With this small family, the Wrights were able to lead a relatively middle class existence. The second child, Charles Howard Wright was born on September 20, 1918. Dr. Page, a white physician, delivered him.

The Wright Man

Charles was born in the midst of a Spanish flu epidemic. By October 8, Mayor James Grant ordered all public places, churches and schools closed for fear of spreading the disease. The ban lasted for almost a month. Luckily, the Wright family was not affected by this epidemic.

During Charles' early years, America was undergoing several important social and economic transformations. World War I was raging and drafting soldiers from towns like Dothan. The Nation had undergone its first major "Red Hunt" (i.e., communists) and was poised to pass the 18th Amendment (Prohibition). Unlike his parents, Charles was born into an urban nation. The 1920 Census found that the urban population had surpassed the rural one. Dothan's population had grown to 10,034.

While the Nation was changing, life in Dothan went on as usual. This tranquillity permitted young Charles Wright to enjoy the wonders of childhood. A slender, brown-skinned boy, he remembers running through the dirt roads in the Black community, falling in the dirt, and getting red clay circles on the knees of his overalls. Charles also remembers his chinaberry-filled popgun, which he used to shoot at imaginary foes and sometimes at his peers. His weekdays were spent doing chores and attending school.

The church played a very important part in the lives of the Wrights. They were Baptist and held strong religious beliefs. On Sundays, young Charles dressed up for Sunday school, morning services and evening Baptist Young People Union, BYPU. There were vacation bible school sessions and summer revivals. The church left a strong impression on young Charles' life.

In the Wright family, the children were the stars. Willie and Laura were strict disciplinarians, but loving parents. Laura was the family pace setter, who made most of the family decisions. She was also responsible for discipline, which meant an occasional thrashing. Although she was still a teenager when she gave birth to Pearl and Charles, she was extremely self-reliant. When Willie took a job as brakeman on the Atlantic Railroad, she had to run the household, care for the kids and take care of the family business.

The Wright children were admonished to know their place vis-a-vis whites. Young Black males had to be careful around whites at all times. When Charles received roller skates he knew that almost the only place in his community with paved streets was in the white section of town. He skated there, but he was always fearful that the whites would try to stop him or try to hurt him. No one ever did, but this pervasive fear was common for Black children. In a child's eyes, whites were aliens who were ready to hurt Black people.

When his father was away, Charles had to perform several chores; but, he made spending money by selling the *Pittsburgh Courier,* the leading Black newspaper in the Nation. The *Courier* contained news of the so-called Negro world; one could read about Marcus Garvey, Jack Johnson and W.E.B Dubois. The paper became Charles' source of Black history and his salary provided him with money to buy candy. Charles also raised bees and pigeons. The pre-teen years of the Wright children seemed happy. Charles retained only one bad memory from those years. He remembered going into his sister Pearl's playhouse kitchen against her advice and "ate her spoiled cucumbers." He became sick and, thus, has never eaten cucumbers again.

During the twenties and thirties, Blacks rarely visited a doctor for routine ailments. Charles took home remedies for illnesses, such as hog huff tea, rabbit tobacco, Epsom Salt, Three Sixes, etc. The Black community had folk medicine brought from Africa, other medicines perfected in slavery and still others borrowed from Native Americans and European slave masters. Not many Blacks were Christian Scientists, yet all believed prayer could help heal people in many cases. Sometimes a prayer was all they could afford.

The Wright Man

PEARL GOES TO SCHOOL

The first traumatic experience of young Charles' life was the separation from his sister, Pearl. At the age of 14, Pearl finished the ninth grade and left Dothan to attend Alabama State Laboratory High School in Montgomery. This was an ambitious move by the Wrights, since they, themselves, never finished grade school. In 1929 the Nation was poised for its worse depression, but Laura Wright wanted more for Pearl than the opportunities she had at age 14. She did not want Pearl to work at a domestic job or marry early. Charles was eleven at the time and could not understand why his big sister had to go so far away to school. Later, Charles deduced that boarding school was "necessary" to keep girls out of trouble (pregnancy). Nevertheless, he missed his sister.

Alabama State Laboratory High School was located on the Alabama State Teachers College campus. In 1928, it became an accredited high school. By the 1930s Laboratory High was considered an elite school for Negroes. Most of the students were the children of Alabama State Teachers College for Negroes faculty and of local Negro gentry. Pearl received a work scholarship and worked as a clerical worker in the principal's office. Pearl was allowed to go home for Christmas. Described by her brother as beautiful, Pearl, a 5'5 woman, was later selected as Miss Alabama State, in 1937, an honor that was bestowed upon the campus' most attractive female student.

With Pearl out of the house, an intense sibling rivalry developed between Charles and Robert. Although they had the same parents, they possessed totally different personalities. For example, Robert was a good ball player and Charles was not. Robert had a ball and bat; his rule was that he never played "out" which meant that he was always the batter. Basketball and tennis were among Robert's favorite sports. He was not considered studious but did well in school. Charles recalled, "We walked to school together but had different friends. My friends were boys with whom I exchanged books and magazines. Robert was an easy going type and sought to get out of schoolwork and household chores."[3]

Because Willie's job required him to be out of town all week, Laura was the parent-in-residence. Charles always *felt that* his brother, Robert, was her favorite. To Charles' dismay and over his protestations, she would do Robert's work in the family grocery store. However, his mother recognized the sharpness of Charles' mind and his ambitious spirit. When Charles was 8 years old, she gave him a birthday party, "My first and only," said Wright. A parent of one of the other little guests approached Charles and asked what he wanted to be when he grew up. Before Charles could answer, his mother said, "Charles is going to be a doctor." His life's course was established from that moment.

SON OF A RAILROAD MAN

Willie P. Wright provided a different role model for Charles. Willie was a farm boy who became a man during a time when a Negro male could not show aggression toward whites. He was certainly not the kind of individual whites would call an uppity Negro. Considered to be a quiet man, it took quite a provocation to stir him to action. In Dothan, provoking Black males carried little risk for whites.

Charles remembered being hurt by a white man at Stough's Drug Store. The family had a charge account at the store (i.e., a standing credit account). The white man kicked him and Charles ran home crying. He reported "Daddy went to Stough's and the proprietor offered him a strong apology in my presence. Daddy protected me."[4] In the South, such protective behavior by Black fathers was considered a brave act. Many Black fathers would never challenge a white man or would choose to overlook the incident. Some would even blame the child for not avoiding trouble with town whites. This incident created a special bond between father and son. Charles enjoyed fishing with his dad and maintained a good relationship with him, despite his frequent "railroad" absences from home.

Charles also remembers handling another white provocation on his own. A white store clerk tried to cheat him. He had gone to a store to buy a side of pork weighing 8 and half pounds at 13 cents a pound. The clerk weighed the meat but overcharged him. Young Charles protested and the clerk got angry. The owner of the store intervened in the ensuing argument, and decided that Charles was right. To save the face of the clerk, he told Charles he would give him a discount. The discount came to exactly the amount Charles had figured in his head. This incident was important in Charles' life, it taught him that he must stand up for his rights, and that whites were fallible.

Willie lost his railroad job during the 1929 Depression, but became successful as an insurance salesman and head of the Peoples Insurance Company's Dothan office. Insurance salesmen usually went door to door, weekly, collecting small installments on the premium. It was a job that allowed Willie to return home at night.

Willie P. Wright, a self-taught man, learned to read Greek so he could read the Greek version of the Bible. He became a preacher while Charles was in college. This surprised Charles, because his mother seemed to be the more religious of his parents.

LAURA OF DOTHAN

Laura Florence Wright was a deeply religious woman, who believed that God was present in Dothan—and that He did not like ugliness, sins or mistreatment. She had a reputation for being a talkative and assertive woman with an independent streak. Charles remembers an incident in which his mother defied the local police, practically unheard of for a Black woman in those days. They had been looking for a person who they believed had run into the Wright house. Laura assured the police that the man was not in the house. The policemen did not believe her and wanted to search the house. Laura, ironing Charles' clothes at the time, threatened to put the hot iron in their faces, if they did. The police retreated. Laura was not afraid of anyone and taught her kids to defend themselves. Charles remembers his mother, Laura, as a "club woman." She was a member of the Ladies Aid Society, the Eastern Star and a woman's group in the church. "She was also a good cake maker," says Charles.

> She was good at baking cakes at Christmas time. Every child had a favorite, mine was coconut, Pearl's was chocolate, and Robert's lemon cheese. The house favorite was a lane cake that used ingredients of the fruitcake for the icing of a layer cake. When she sent one to me at school, the line outside my door was noisey and quite long.[5]

Laura was not content just being a housewife and a mother. In 1935, when her children were 14, 16, and 17, she and Willie decided that Blacks needed a grocery store in their neighborhood, and opened one. With a small amount of capital, she started the Wright Grocery. It was a one-room store where she sold everything including bread and canned goods. Although she had no experience as a merchant and had little education, she became a dedicated business women. She would get out of bed and go next door, just to sell vegetables, eggs, butter, etc. Some Blacks resented the store. Many did not "trade" (i.e., shop) with the Wrights. They would shop at the white store three blocks away. Charles recalls, "they would walk by and wave a loaf of bread at us."[6] In a small racially divided town, this type of behavior among Blacks may have been their way of showing their resentment and jealousy toward the Wrights. Whites rewarded this behavior because it discouraged Black entrepreneurship and perpetuated the idea that white merchandise was better.

The store had no painted sign outside, but it was called the Wright Grocery. "I was fastidious about the store and

The Wright Man

wanted everything neatly arranged, no paper on the floor, etc. Robert couldn't care less. We had words about that. We didn't sell cigarettes, but boys would come in with a penny to try to buy a cigarette. Some people had charge accounts. Mama, despite her scant education, kept the account and made change with no trouble. She was a sharp trader with the farmers from whom she bought vegetables, eggs, butter, etc." In the family store, Charles learned about capitalism, the value of money and how to deal with customers. Seeing his mother conduct business proved to be a good learning experience for him. Watching his mother's tenacity, he learned that once a person made up his mind to do something and persevered he/she could accomplish anything. This is the lesson that guided his life. He was acutely aware of the advantage of being one's own boss.

Charles' childhood in Dothan was facilitated by supportive neighbors and relatives. He had a favorite uncle, a Mr. Gulley, who married his father's sister, Chanie, but later divorced her. Mr. Gulley was Charles' confessor. Uncles who act as surrogate parents were quite common in the rural South. He would greet Charles by asking, "What going on?" They would talk about philosophy, God, and being young. He was a special person because he allowed Charles to verbalize his dreams. Charles could be a doctor, a leader, a savior or just a boy with his uncle. Charles saw more of Mr. Gulley than he did of his father. Mr. Gulley remained a friend to Charles after he left Dothan for college.

THE EDUCATION OF YOUNG CHARLES

Charles' first three years of school were spent at the Bernard Boys Arithmetic School in Baptist Bottom. The school had about thirty students and charged 50 cents tuition a month. Many families brought eggs, milk and other food in exchange for the tuition which they couldn't afford. The schoolmaster was Professor Abner Jackson, a thin and wily

1890 graduate of the Tuskegee Institute. Tuskegee, founded by Booker T. Washington, was a "normal" school with a strong agricultural, vocational and industrial education curriculum.

Abner Jackson was Dothan's link to the Tuskegee legacy and to Booker T. Washington's philosophy of economic self-help. A reclusive man with ill fitting clothes and a gold watch in his vest, Professor Jackson dressed like the Black preachers of his day. He was an intellectual and entrepreneur. Professor Jackson sold the *Pittsburgh Courier*, NAACP's *Crisis* magazine, and books in order to supplement his meager teacher's salary. Professor Jackson, the prototype of a stern schoolmaster, was well read, assertive and demanding. He understood that reading was fundamental for learning beyond what was taught in school. Charles and classmates were expected to read aloud with regularity and to recite their multiplication tables from memory. Students knew that if they neglected their studies, punishment would be swift and painful. "If you messed up, he would knock you down." Charles and his classmates feared and admired the Professor.

Abner Jackson was very important in Charles' early life and education in that he taught him intellectual discipline, encouraged him to take learning seriously, and taught him the penalties of poor preparation. It was from Jackson that Charles learned the values of memory, good study habits and preparedness.

Professor Jackson sacrificed all that he possessed to buy the little frame schoolhouse in Dothan, Alabama. His two prior schools had been burned to the ground, in the rural regions of nearby Barbour County, by white men who opposed the education of African Americans.

He used a small back room in the schoolhouse for sleeping, cooking, etc. Since his students were, primarily males, and he was best known and remembered for his mastery of mathematics, the school was named: The Bernard Boys Arithmetic School.

The tuition was raised to $2.00 per month, if you could afford it, or a dish of gingerbread cookies. The professor sold his own books such as *Webster's Blue-Back Speller* and a complicated mathematics textbook. Their prices were negotiable.

Blackboards, in the early days, were black, enameled, cheesecloth. When he could afford it, Jackson bought slates and chalk. A dust-filled rag was used as the eraser.

The truly, amazing story of Professor Jackson is recounted in Wright's unpublished manuscript, "The Wiregrass Sage."

Professor Jackson set out to teach, and teach he did. He "made" his students learn how to solve difficult mathematical problems and insisted that they learn how to pronounce and spell everything in the *Blue Back Speller*. His students were regularly chosen, above all others, to spell or read, or count change. People in a bank or grocery store, etc, who needed assistance, would look around for one of the professor's students.

Professor Jackson's discipline was earth-shattering, figuratively and literally, writes Wright. Often students had to stand, stiffly, in line, before being allowed to go to the out-house. Some, who waited too late, did not make it.

Sometimes an emergency arose at lunch-time. Occasionally a student failed to retrieve the lunch he or she had pitched into the front corner of the room, upon arrival. The culprit was usually one of the several cats that roamed, freely, through the classroom.

The cats were sneaky, but, even when seen, no one dared disturb the peaceful tranquility of Professor Jackson's classroom to deny one of his feline friends a lunch. They never pilfered Richard Small's lunch. They were too intelligent and knew that he brought collard green sandwiches to school, every day.

Professor Jackson weighed only 140 pounds, but whenever he swung at a student near the back of the line, Wright always hoped that he was not in the standing line. The students all went down, to the floor, like dominoes. The professor ended class on Friday afternoon with the warning, "If you cut up in the BYPU, on Sunday, I'll cut down on the BUT, on Monday."

"We believed that Professor Jackson would know if we did not behave or if we were quiet in church," said Wright. He was held in high regard by the community, in general, especially, the African American community.

When North Highland Public School students neared Professor Jackson's school, enroute to and from their school, all their loud, playful jocularity ceased. After passing the Jackson property line, the tempo increased to its original level.

The winter of 1925 was unusally severe in Dothan. Pearl Wright came down with pneumonia and had to leave Professor Jackson's school. After she recovered, Charles' parents had a big decision to make. They removed both Charles and his sister from Professor Jackson's school and sent them to the all-Negro Southeast Alabama High School (a private school). That school was certainly not top-rated. Two years later, brother Robert attended the same high school. For a total of 18 years the Wright children attended this almost non-existing school, rather than attend the Dothan public schools.

HIGH SCHOOL IN DOTHAN

Attending high school during the Depression was a trying experience for young Charles. The Southeast Alabama High School was in a four-room school building with four teachers, no heat, no indoor plumbing and no library. In the winter, Professor Edward Lee, the principal, searched every day to find

The Wright Man

wood and coal to keep the pot-bellied stove burning. Although the teachers were dedicated, they had few teaching materials. As a result, Black students were taught only the basics.

Professor Lee fought to keep the school open. He worked on the edge of a shutdown every day. His most difficult problem was meeting the next payday. There was simply no money to pay the teachers. Despite a small tuition, the amount did not cover teachers' salaries. Professor Lee was required to raise money to keep the school open. When students got behind in payments, teachers had to be boarded in their homes to make up for the tuition. The lack of a salary and other uncertainties caused a rapid turnover of teachers in Charles' school.

White officials in Houston County were indifferent to the plight of Negro schools. The schools got some financial assistance from the Baptist churches, but none from the city. Charles and his schoolmates were acutely aware of the struggles of Lee and others, but they had to make the best of it. These adult examples taught them the value of education and the self-help requirements of it.

No student appreciated the struggle more than Charles, the high school's most exemplary personality. Charles felt that something was missing from his education, he sensed their limitations when his teachers could not answer his questions. He understood he was far ahead of his fellow classmates, but that was not enough.

Charles graduated from high school in 1935 at the age of 16, and was determined to be the physician his mother had predicted. His profile as a high school graduate with ambitions of being a physician fits that of early Black doctors.[7] Charles' high school provided him with no high school biology or calculus. But he could read, "figure," and retain material with the best students. These qualities served him well when he faced the new competition of college.

The opportunities for Black medical students changed greatly while Charles was growing up. During the year of his birth (1918), Leonard Medical College in Raleigh, North Carolina closed. Also discontinued was the Medical Department of the University of West Tennessee, Memphis (1923). The Flexner Report, which very few folks in Dothan had ever heard of, standardized medical education and forced most commercial medical schools to close down because of inadequate curriculums. By the time Charles would graduate from college, only two Black medical colleges existed. Aside from the few seats available in white institutions, a Black medical aspirant faced heavy competition for admission. This was especially true for most Black southerners, who went either to Meharry College in Nashville or Howard University Medical school, in Washington, D.C.

So, as we see, Charles Wright emerged from Dothan, with its separate racial communities, a fiercely self-reliant and independent man. In shortchanging his high school education, Dothan made him aware that knowledge was power. Dothan's racial apartheid failed to kill his spirit. Instead of saddling him with an inferiority complex, his experience in the small town helped him to develop an incredible amount of self-confidence. He outgrew Dothan's provincialism. He left Dothan respecting none of its leading white citizens or institutions. Charles' memories of his hometown were exclusively of the Black community.

Charles grew up in a vacuum of mainstream culture. In Furman Roger's history of Houston County he observed, "Entertainment of all types has been extremely limited in Dothan throughout its history. Until 1939, Dothan had no public library worthy of mention." He concluded, "Dothan is the perfect example of the distressing cultural lag in Alabama,"[8] Nothing in his childhood would have appeared to nurture an interest in culture or prepare him to excel at college. No one knew at the time that this skinny Black teenager who left Dothan with a small suitcase in hand would someday become one of the major cultural figures of Detroit.

The Wright Man

Charles left Dothan and joined his sister, Pearl, at Alabama State to start the first leg on his journey to become a doctor.

Wright at March 1998 press conference. From left: Maggie Porter, Willia Miller, Kathy Bradfield, Dorothy Mottley, Bedia Thomas, Ida Drewery, Mariel Wardell, Ruth Cook, Dr. Nellie Brodis, Ruth Stephens, Tinnie Morman, Dr. Roslyn McClendon, and Roberta Bass.

Dr. Wright, 1988, visiting the professor's grave; Insert: Professor Abner Jacksoon

The Wright Man

Wright visiting Pine Street birthplace, 1988

Wright now allowed inside Dothan library

When Blacks from rural Alabama came to Montgomery to attend college, they escaped the cotton fields, potato patches and the white man's kitchens. They could trade a cotton sack for a one-room schoolhouse after receiving a teaching certificate at 'Bama State. It was the ultimate step in social mobility. One could move from dressing in overalls to shirt and tie within a generation. The grounds of Alabama State contained those magical buildings that turned a country bumpkin into an urbane adult.

Alabama State Normal School and University for Colored Students and Teachers College was founded in Marion, Alabama by George N. Card, a white man, in 1874. William Burns Patterson, also white, succeeded Card in 1878, and sought to move the school to Montgomery in 1887. Patterson met with Black congregations at Old Ship AME Zion Church and Dexter Avenue Baptist Church and received a pledge to raise $5,000, ensuring that the school would be located in Montgomery. The doors of the Alabama Colored Peoples University were opened on October 3, 1887, at Beulah Baptist Church. Private donations kept the school open, until the state approved funding for the school, in the same year.

Charles and classmates were never told of the humble beginnings or the Black church nexus with their school. They were introduced to the Patterson legend. President Patterson had reportedly stood outside the state capital passing out flowers in order to lobby state legislators to create a Negro normal school for training teachers. Patterson was president of

Alabama State Teachers College from 1878 to 1915. In 1882 Patterson also organized and became the first president of the Alabama State Teachers Association. William Patterson, a white man, acting in both capacities, was one of the anomalies of a segregated South.

Alabama State was very innovative for the times. It operated Laboratory High School, an elementary school for teacher training, and was the headquarters for the teacher association. Alabama State College was the chief source of teachers for central and south Alabama. Because there were so few other occupations opened to Negroes, Alabama State became the college for some of the best Black high school students in the state. Students found a faculty of men and women who were among the most highly educated Blacks in the country. The college fostered a sense of responsibility in its students. Many students arrived from small towns and after graduation dutifully returned to these Alabama towns, while others scattered themselves across the nation.

Charles and his classmates underwent a social transformation. According to Charles' lab mate Hugh Blanding, "the College helped mold them into dignified personalities."[1] The school became a symbol of an aspiring Black middle class denied entry into occupations, other than teaching. However, the social transformation was not designed to politicize this nascent class. The school never formally challenged white legislative control or any other symbol of white power.

Charles Wright arrived at Alabama State when Harper Council Trenholm, son of second Black president, George Washington Trenholm, had been president for over a decade. Born in Tuscumbia, Alabama in 1900, young Trenholm graduated from Morehouse College in 1920, with a Bachelor of Philosophy in Education and then received a Masters degree from the University of Chicago. The young Trenholm was in graduate school when he was called back to Montgomery upon his father's death. He was acting president for a brief time, and was then appointed permanent president, as it turned out, for life. He was 25 years old, the youngest Negro college president in the country.

President Trenholm was a man of which legends are made. He gained fame by organizing the first summer school for teachers. Over 2,000 teachers attended this in-service training program in 1928. The young president, a tall light-skinned man with autocratic bearing, suffered from diabetes and poor health during most of his tenure. He worked extremely hard to maintain a college for Negro teachers in the face of a hostile and miserly white legislature. White legislators supported him because he reportedly never asked for anything except for enough money to run the school. Rumors surfaced that the frugal president would return unused funds to the state treasure. This action endeared him to the state legislators but made him an object of ridicule in some portions of the Black community. He led an aloof lifestyle and decided, single-handedly, most of the administrative recruitment and development policies of the institution. Yet, he was the most respected Black man in the city.

CAMPUS LIFE

The campus was compact, allowing students to reach all buildings within five minutes. Black college students lived in a completely Black environment in which they rarely saw or spoke to whites. There were no white students or faculty. Several Black-owned retail and service establishments were located near the campus. Students did not have to interact with white people unless they went downtown to shop.

During Charles' undergraduate years, the campus consisted of seven brick buildings and eight frame structures of Georgian and modern design. (There was one hollow-tile structure). There was no official college quad or student center

The Wright Man

on the 47 acres. Patterson Hall, erected in 1924, was the center of the campus and was used for administration and classrooms. The small cluster of buildings was still an imposing structure for a young man from Dothan who had spent most of his life in one-to-four room school housing. The faculty and curriculum were also impressive for its era of segregated normal schools.

This tiny campus, surrounded by multi-family homes and one of the city's largest public housing facilities, would be Charles' environment for the next four years. At the center of the campus stood Bibb Graves Dormitory for women. Resplendent with its clock, the dorm faced South Jackson Street that connected the college to the downtown area. The male students lived in Trenholm Hall. Kilby Dining Hall was located across the street from the academic building. All resident students ate there. The John William Beverly Hall was completed the year Charles graduated (1939).

Charles lived in Trenholm Hall with roommates, Noah Purifoy, Wiley Bolden, and Felix James. The small dormitory room had one double bed and two twin beds. For this tall wiry young man, these were very tight quarters. Cooperation and negotiation among roommates was imperative. Charles remembers that after the second breakfast bell, he and his roommates managed to dress, including neckties, and leave the room in five minutes. This was a feat and a challenge, but he always made it, often in less than five minutes.

Campus life was routine; classes were held from 8-5 p.m. The social life revolved around sport teams and fraternities. There was college rush week where the freshmen were sorted out for membership in Greek letter organizations. This was a serious activity in Black colleges. Charles joined the Omega Psi Phi Fraternity, and became a "Q," the nickname for the fraternity. Pledging involved hazing, rituals and branding. Joining a Black fraternity was a sure way to be involved in the campus social life as fraternities created instant friends or "brothers." Brother Charles became vice Basileus and then Basileus (president) of the chapter.

Charles was also active in the YMCA, the George Washington Trenholm Debating Society, the Pan-Hellenic Council and Tau Sigma Rho Scientific Society. Otherwise, his campus life was somewhat self-contained and self-restraining. However, Charles was a frequent visitor to the local churches. He also was a Sunday school teacher at college vespers (religious services). During Charles' college days, every student was required to attend vespers, where seats were assigned.

Blessed with a sharp analytical mind and boundless curiosity, Charles perceived his classes as a challenge. Fascinated by academic competition and the attention it brought to him, Charles was probably a better student than he needed to be. He remembered that his only academic competitors were Wiley Bolden of Mobile and Ms. Mildred Motley of Montgomery. Throughout Charles' undergraduate days, he didn't try to hide his academic prowess. He was once described by a classmate as the "only man who could take a calculus examination with a fountain pen."[2] How ironic that Charles' trusted fountain pen got him into trouble when he tried his hand at journalism.

CHARLES WRIGHT AND THE BAMA BRIEFS

Charles' peers recognized his writing ability and recruited him for their student paper, the *'Bama Briefs*. As a budding journalist, Charles attacked the job with gusto. Writing was a task he found intellectually stimulating and fun, and it allowed him to inform his fellow students of the happenings of the day. Charles was not particularly political, but he became indignant about race problems. He agreed with those who took pride in being called "Negroes," not coloreds. Although the local papers repeatedly referred to local Negroes as "coloreds," students insisted on calling each other "Negroes." The local paper resisted, in part, because Negro had to be capitalized and whites with a lower case "w." In a racist society such distinctions are important.

Although the South was stagnant, the world was changing in the late thirties. Hitler's Nazi party, after governing for three years, became the bane of the world. Newsreels exposed the world to the rise of the Third Reich. Charles wrote a *'Bama Brief* editorial which criticized the Germans for persecuting the Jews; the Italian dictator, Mussolini, for invading Ethiopia; and southern whites for their treatment of Blacks. The latter comment got him into more trouble than the first two.

This kind of commentary was considered fortuitous and was immediately condemned by the college administration. Alabama State was not a paragon of free thought nor was it a defender of First Amendment Rights. "Nice" 'Bama State students were not expected to say such things. The president of the college saw to it that they did not say such things. Paternalistic and pro-administration, the faculty considered any student political commentary as a threat to their way of life. No one defended Charles' constitutional right to write or freedom of the press. (See full article in Appendix.)

Because of his anti-segregationist statements, Charles was removed from the student paper. Firing Charles was designed to set an example for other students who challenged the system. But it had the opposite effect on Charles. He discovered that he had hit a raw nerve with the administration. He knew that he was right, just as he had been at the meat market in Dothan. If Charles had not been an honor student, he may have been asked to leave school. In the 1930s, college administrations could arbitrarily dismiss students without fear of lawsuits. The threat was not lost on Charles; he quickly abandoned his journalist hat for a lab coat.

CHARLES AS LABORATORY ASSISTANT

Charles got his job as lab assistant after failing as a cook in the dining hall. Most of the food Charles prepared was returned uneaten. He was asked to look for another school job. He took a job as lab assistant for Professor Henry Van Dyke. This move proved to be not only the perfect job and learning experience, but the gateway to the future.

Van Dyke was a quiet and rather rigid man who came to State from Western State Teachers College in Michigan. Graduating in 1927, and obtaining a Masters degree from the University of Michigan in 1933, he was an instructor at the State Normal School before coming to Alabama State, where he taught chemistry and other pre-medical subjects. Like most Black college teachers of his time, he never completed his doctorate. However, most science teachers were accorded the title of "Doctor."

Charles worked for Van Dyke for three years. Van Dyke took a personal, almost paternal interest in Charles' education. He was an exacting and demanding academic mentor. Charles' responsibilities included checking the laboratory experiments at the end of the day, and making chemical reagents for students to use. Charles, who was the senior assistant, with Nelson Preyor and Hugh Blanding, set out equipment for the science students. In addition, Charles did some substitute teaching for absent professors and graded papers as well.

Charles learned the wonders of science, testing, re-testing, observing and recording. Lab assistant employment was a good job for him because he loved and was obsessed with details. Professor Van Dyke would not tolerate second rate or sloppy work. According to Hugh Blanding, Van Dyke insisted that everything had to be in its place, even window shades had to be at an even level. He recalled Van Dyke saying, "I want to go in the room where the chemicals are stored in the dark and pull out a bottle and know it was the right one" (Blanding,

1992). The students nicknamed Charles "Van Dyke" because of his attention to details.

Charles became president of the science honor society, Tau Sigma Rho, a group sponsored by Professor Van Dyke. During his tenure as president, Charles organized a trip to Tuskegee Institute to visit the laboratory of Dr. George Washington Carver, the botanist. The group was greeted by Dr. Carver in his laboratory.

Charles graduated as valedictorian of his class in May of 1939. Despite working closely with Van Dyke and accumulating a sterling academic record, Charles was not ready for medical school. He had taken only a small number of science courses, and those were not given in modern college labs with the best equipment. Van Dyke recognized these inadequacies and set up a summer course to teach his star student physical chemistry after Meharry denied him admission, but promised to keep a "slot" open in the freshman medical class, if he took and passed the summer course. After the summer tutoring, Charles was finally ready to be admitted to Meharry Medical School.

MEHARRY: MECCA FOR BLACK PHYSICIANS

The Meharry Medical College was founded by pre-Civil War Northern white abolitionists who wanted to train Blacks for careers in medicine. A medical school was relatively easy to create since all an entrepreneur needed was a faculty, local physicians and hospital facilities. Most schools went bankrupt, however, because they were under-funded. At the turn of the century, there were several Black medical schools, but only Meharry and Howard University survived the financial pressure of medical education. Meharry survived, in part, because it was affiliated with the African Methodist Episcopal Church (AME).

When Charles was accepted to Meharry, it was an extremely exhilarating experience for his family. He was the toast of his neighborhood, family, and peers. As they beamed with pride, his parents saw for Charles, opportunities America had not been willing to give them, at Charles' age. His admission to medical school was a symbolic triumph over the poor schooling in Dothan, and the shortcomings of a teachers college.

In September of 1939, Charles took the "L & N" train (later called the Southwind), to Nashville, Tennessee. The Southwind was a favorite of Black folks since it traveled through Montgomery to Chicago. Intercity trains were carefully segregated so that white folks would not have to pass through the colored sections of the train. Sometimes partitions were erected so that whites did not have to look at Black passengers. Blacks got the first car on the train, meaning that cinders got into their eyes. Since they were often forbidden to use the dining car, many Black passengers carried their own trusty supply of fried chicken. A Mason jar, full of sweet water, was also a must. The white, and often officious conductor, followed by a Black train porter, punched Charles' ticket and left him to the sometimes swerving ride. This was his second train trip outside Alabama. In 1925 the Wright family, with the help of railroad passes available to Willie Wright and all railroad employees, went to Newark, New Jersey to visit Willie's brother. The ride to Nashville was a long one for Charles, through the mountains of North Alabama passing cities such as Birmingham and Huntsville.

Charles' first task after arriving at Nashville's Union Station was finding a place to live. He had received a list of boarding places that took in medical students. Charles was determined to find the most reasonable rate. He found a good rate at Mrs. Ann Thomas' home, a three-bedroom house that boarded six other medical students. Meals were eaten at Ann's Place, a local restaurant that billed students monthly.

Blacks in Nashville represented over a quarter of the population (28.3%), and they were concentrated in separate

The Wright Man

communities and neighborhoods. The principal business streets were Cedar, Fourth Ave., North Jefferson and Jo Johnson. Nashville had four Black hotels and a successful Black entrepreneurial class.

THE STATUS OF BLACKS IN MEDICINE, CIRCA 1939

A few white colleges began admitting Black medical students in 1939 and the Black hospital movement was in full swing. Daniel Hale Williams, a giant in Chicago's medical circles and founder of Provident Hospital, had died eight years earlier, but the hospital was still critical to the development of Black physicians. In 1940, according to Arnold Rose, the famous sociologist, there were 3,500 Negro physicians in the United States. They comprised about 2.2% of the total number of physicians (Rose, p. 111). Apprehensive about the opportunities for Negro physicians, he opined:

The prospects of the Negro physicians are becoming increasingly uncertain because of the growth of all kinds of public health facilities. This trend cannot fail to take the low-income clientele away from the private practitioner, and this, of course, means that the Negro doctor may lose nearly all his patients unless he is given a place in the new public health system.[3]

Charles wasn't worried yet about patients, changes in public health policies, Blacks who preferred white physicians, or his financial prospects; he had arrived at his medical Mecca. He didn't come to "worship" medicine at the shrine but to study it.

MEHARRY, SHRINE AND STARTING PLACE

In 1939, the Meharry campus consisted of 3 brick buildings and a library. The main building housed the disciplines of medicine, dentistry, pharmacy and nursing.

Hubbard Hospital, named after the first president of the school, was located on the grounds as well. Meharry was a free-standing college and was affiliated with several Black hospitals and infirmaries. Although members of the school administration were white (Dr. Edward L. Turner was president), the school had a good staff of Black teaching physicians. Among them were Matthew Walker, and John Henry Hale, Professors of Surgery, and Julius August McMillan, Professor of Gynecology. The college followed a policy of hiring its top students as teachers.

The faculty at Meharry also included Dr. Rafeal Hernandez (Class of 1925). He taught courses in anatomy, histology, and neurology. Dr. Daniel Rolfe taught physiology. Harold West, Ph.D taught chemistry, and later became the school's first Black president. Occasionally, white teachers from nearby Vanderbilt University lectured at Meharry. The best known faculty member was John Hale who was Chief of Surgery. Matthew Walker, his successor, gained fame because he set up a clinic in an all Black town, Mount Bayou, Mississippi. With the help of Rev. P.M. Smith and the International Orders of Twelve Knights, and Daughters of Tabor, they started a hospital, which used Meharry students.

Charles attended his first classes and was surprised at the quality of knowledge of his fellow students. Of the fifty-five incoming medical students at Meharry in 1939, only 50 completed the first year. The only female was Eleanor Makel. No one from Alabama State had ever been accepted to Meharry. Charles had a lot to prove. He also knew that he did not have an insider status like the people from the more prestigious colleges like Morehouse, Howard University and Bluefield State. He slowly realized the weakness of his education. Most of the material he learned was new to him. He discovered the subtle class system in medical school. The progeny of physicians were at the top of the social pyramid.

The Wright Man

All freshmen at Meharry took basic sciences. This class included both dental and medical students. For some with a pre-med background, the material was quite familiar, but for others it meant hours and hours of reading. In the first years of medical school the basic science courses tested Charles' mettle. Charles' summer training with Professor Van Dyke proved to be a useful experience. Physical chemistry was called "physiological chemistry" at Meharry. The course analyzed the relationship of chemistry to diseases. But Professor Van Dyke never taught Charles embryology. This proved to be Charles most difficult course. At the end of each term, students were required to take final examinations, part of which were oral. Charles answered all of the questions, and Dr. West was astonished by the performance of this student from a teacher training college. The student from Alabama State made his peers take notice of him.

The first year in medical school was devoted to the basic sciences. The curriculum included anatomy, physiology and biochemistry. It entailed tremendous amounts of reading and memorizing parts of the body, formulas and medical terms. They had to learn where the parts were and how they worked. This part of the curriculum suited Charles because he enjoyed reading books and testing himself on what he retained.

During the sophomore year, students were taught pathology, bacteriology, and pharmacology. Charles got a chance to see medicine in action, as he underwent a tonsillectomy at Meharry. In those days before antibiotics, the tonsils were removed. This surgical procedure was occasionally botched by general practitioners. But Charles was in capable hands and made a good case study for his fellow students. This was the first medical treatment Charles had ever received. This was common to Southern Black males from the rural South. They were generally very healthy as the result of homeopathic medicine. Charles also had dental work done at the Meharry dental school.

At the end of the sophomore year, the students with the highest grades were allowed to do research. Only six out of fifty were chosen and Charles was among them. During his first year Charles got his chance to dissect cadavers in anatomy. Young medical students anxiously anticipated the moment of dissection. Classmate Emile Nash, who was a whiz at memorizing muscles and bones, helped Charles study.

In his sophomore year, Charles received a letter from his sister, Pearl, telling him that the family store in Dothan was not doing well and that he would have to work to help pay for his schooling. Pearl's husband, Joseph Battle, had a friend in Detroit, Joe Webster, who could help get him a job on a boat called the "Greater Buffalo." It traveled from Detroit to Buffalo, New York via the Detroit River and Lake Erie and carried passengers and cars. The second year, he worked on a boat called "Greater Detroit."

During the summers of 1941 and 1942, Charles worked on the boats as a bellhop, secretary to the captain, and as the ship's unofficial manager of medical emergencies. As a bellhop, he made certain that the incoming passengers could readily locate their rooms, and, of course, their luggage. Although the bellhops did not work in the bar, often they were asked to serve drinks to the passengers.

During the second summer, especially, Charles was given the additional job as secretary to the captain. The additional pay was much needed. Charles' duty was to keep a complete list of the workers. Then each time a member of the crew boarded or left the ship, Charles had to record the time and date. Also, since the captain knew of Charles' medical studies, he put him to work as unofficial manager in charge of medical emergencies.

The money Charles earned was used to pay for medical school. Charles did not gamble, drink or smoke. His only vice was an occasional movie. He did not have any girl friends in Detroit, and he went dutifully back to Nashville, by-passing the gambling joints and saloons.

The Wright Man

During Charles' second year, Meharry College ran into financial troubles. This prompted *Time* magazine to write a story about the white Meharry brothers, and the money they donated to start the school. At this time, Dr. Edward Turner was president. The Rockefeller General Education Board decided to phase out their annual contribution of $160,000 to Meharry, which was a major share of the revenue needed to operate the school. However, president of the Board, Abraham Flexner, famous for his report which reformed medical education, announced that the Board would donate $3,700,000 to the $800,000 endowment if the school would raise $2,300,000.[4] The successful fundraising drive had several famous sponsors such as Wendell Wilkie and Eleanor Roosevelt.

Wright's classmates included Clarence Greer, who was one of the very few students with a car. His roommate was Rupert LaCaille, from the West Indies, who lived in Harlem. Studying together, they shared their triumphs and failures. One night LaCaille got so frustrated at a poor grade that he broke up a chair and threw it in the pot-bellied stove, much to his landlady's distress. Another classmate was Emile Nash, an excellent student from Rust College in Holly Springs, Mississippi. Emile and Charles had a lot in common and they would learn from each other. Rupert LaCaille taught Charles about Harlem politics and life in the big city. Many students had more preparation than he did because they came from prestigious schools and medical families.

During Charles' stay in Nashville, he became interested in local politics. In 1943, Nashville was in the middle of municipal reform. After a Public Administration Report was published, which called the Nashville City Council too large, the number was reduced from twenty-seven to seven. It appeared that there was a possibility of electing the first Black city council person. Z. Alexander Looby, a lawyer who taught medical jurisprudence at Meharry, campaigned for the job and lost. Charles had an opportunity to work in his first political campaign. Looby later emerged as one of the first Black politicians in the fifties.

This was Wright's first venture into local politics. Local Black politics in the forties was part of the civil rights movement and a part of the struggle for community recognition. Black politicians usually confined their campaigning to the Black community. They spent most of their time trying to convince their constituency that it was safe to register to vote.

Campus life at Meharry was similar to Alabama State, although Nashville was about twice the size of Montgomery. In order to see a movie, Blacks had to sit in the loft of white theaters. On Sunday, Charles attended Chapel at nearby Fisk University, a small coed liberal arts college known nationally as the home of the Jubilee Singers. Charles represented Meharry at the Student Christian Union, which consisted of Meharry, Fisk and Tennessee State chapters.

Being a medical student was supposed to attract women, but women at Fisk were accustomed to medical students. Charles did not have the time or money to attract the Fisk women. His one lady friend, Lillian Thomas, a teacher in the local school, later married his landlady's son. Charles would go with his colleagues to 18th and Jefferson Street and watch "Black Nashville" parties. They were sometimes joined by students from Tennessee Agricultural and Industrial State Teachers College, which was located on close by Centennial Blvd. There wasn't much time for social life as academic life consumed most of Charles' life.

The final two years of medical school were devoted to clinical medical education. During these two years Charles Wright began the slow process of learning to be a doctor. Donning the traditional white coat, the student is exposed to all types of medical procedures and treatment modalities. Most of the student's time is spent in hospitals observing and

The Wright Man

recording. It was learning by watching and taking notes, and it helped Charles to understand his place at the bottom of the medical hierarchy.

On June 6, 1943, Charles Wright graduated from Meharry Medical College. His mother, father, and Uncle Louis attended the ceremony. He was ranked number six in his class. This was no small feat for a young man from Dothan who had not seen a library nor taken a science course until he entered Alabama State. Charles Wright became Doctor Charles Wright.

Although this was a joyous moment for Charles and his classmates, it was tempered by the realization that racism in medicine and hospital discrimination would be a permanent part of their professional life. This came home to the newly minted MDs as they applied for internships. Only Homer Phillips in St. Louis, Missouri and Harlem Hospital in New York City offered such opportunities to Black medical school graduates.

THE STATUS OF BLACKS IN MEDICINE, 1940'S

In 1941, there were 110 Negro hospitals in United States, 70% of which were privately owned. Black physicians began to protest their exclusion from hospitals and medical schools in the mid-forties. In December of 1943 Sydenham Hospital, which was a private hospital in Harlem, announced it was integrating its staff and board of trustees. Members of the Medico-Chirurigical Society of Washington, D.C. filed a suit against Gallinger Municipal Hospital in 1945. Three years later, Howard University faculty and students were allowed to use their facilities. In spite of these changes, it was not until 1952 that the medical society of D.C. began to admit Black doctors. Black physicians, all across the nation, protested their exclusion from local hospitals. World War II was very important to the acceptance of Black physicians in the Armed Services. But the

Armed Forces were segregated until 1948, when President Truman signed an executive order integrating all of the services.

As his school days ended, Charles realized that he had never left the Black community. He had never competed with whites in a classroom situation and had heard only a handful of white professors lecture. However, he felt good about his training and now he wanted to test it in New York. In 1943, young Dr. Charles Wright, with his newly minted Doctorate of Medicine, took a train to Harlem, the capital of Black America.

Alabama State had a profound effect on Charles Wright's vision of life chances. After his critical article in the *'Bama Brief,* he gained a new respect for the power of words. The written word could literally shake the foundation of a venerated institution like Alabama State. Wright also realized that hard work could overcome any deficit he had in his education.

Meharry and Howard University graduates founded the National Medical Association (NMA) in 1895 as an alternative to the American Medical Association, which did not accept Black physicians until the 1950s. Here again were examples of institution building.

Meharry was a different experience for Wright. This was the first time in his life that he didn't dominate his peers academically. With his science teacher's background, he held his own, but his class was full of bright people. Everyone had to work hard, as medical education requires a tremendous amount of reading and memorizing.

Meharry socialized Dr. Charles Wright into the professional community of physicians. Harlem Hospital provided him an introductory lesson. He learned much from listening to stories of the scions of senior Black physicians. Although he was now twenty-five years old, all of his schools operated in an environment of financial uncertainty. The lessons of these struggling Black institutions would be,

The Wright Man

arguably, the most important of his life. The fiscal crisis of Meharry taught him that institutions could survive for a time on volition. None of his experiences at medical school, however, would fully prepare him for Harlem, New York.

Charles Wright - 1938

Class of 1939 visiting Alabama State College for 50-year reunion

The Dutch settled in the section of Manhattan called Harlem. With the turn of the century, the area evolved slowly into an enclave of Black immigrants to New York. During the 1920s, Harlem developed a reputation as the center of Negro cultural life, a place where a young man could learn a great deal just by being there. Most of the New York Negro literati and entertainers kept apartments in Harlem.

Most Meharry graduates went to Homer Phillips in St. Louis or Provident Hospital in Chicago. Very few went to Harlem Hospital. Charles Wright's roommate, Rupert LaCaille convinced him to seek an internship at Harlem Hospital. Wright's sister, Pearl; husband, Joe Battle; and daughter, Nadine, lived in the Bronx. The young Dr. Wright decided to serve his internship in New York.

Harlem Hospital, founded in 1887, was located on 120th and East Avenue. In 1907, it was replaced by a new 250-bed hospital built on 136th street and Lenox Avenue. Harlem was a multi-cultural community until the turn of the century. In the hospital's early years, the staff was dominated by foreign-trained white physicians. Black nurses and aides were on the staff, but no Black physicians were appointed until 1919, when Dr. Louis T. Wright, born in Atlanta and trained at Harvard University, was appointed to the staff. The first Black intern, Ira Cowen, was appointed in 1926. When Cowen's appointment was announced, the white chiefs of gynecology and obstetrics resigned. White physicians at Harlem held a very low opinion of Black physicians, regardless of their training or medical school.

Dr. Charles Wright arrived in Harlem on June 28, 1943 and his internship began on July 1, 1943. During this time there were many Jewish physicians working in the hospital. Among these were Henry Falk, chief of Gynecology, Charles Posner, Chief of Obstetrics and Waldo Fielding, Charles' fellow resident. Many war refugees from Europe came loaded with their socialist ideologies and attempted to recruit young Black men to their various causes. Wright never joined any organizations, but was intrigued by their intellect.

The working environment at Harlem reflected the social structure of the Black community. It was by no means the best teaching hospital in the city, but it was among the few hospitals that provided adequate opportunities. When Charles Wright arrived at the hospital, Louis Wright had been promoted to chief of surgery.

BLACK INTERNS AT HARLEM

The competition among interns at Harlem Hospital was intense. Like Alabama State and Meharry, everyone at Harlem seemed first-rate. The staff represented the cream of the crop of the nation's Black medical colleges. The place was a hotbed of brilliant young people, both Black and White all struggling to emerge on top. Charles liked the intensity of the competition and of being in a major medical facility. Charles did research and wrote papers for medical journals during his internship. He found that interacting with people from different backgrounds was an exhilarating experience.

An intern is on duty around the clock, and is the low man on the hierarchical totem pole. Rose Coser observed that the intern would be the "proletarian" in the hospital were it not for the fact he does not think of employer-employee relations, but of the "medical fraternity." He tends to perceive his internship as a rite of passage.[1] So it was with young doctor Charles Wright. Life at Harlem allowed him to observe the idiosyncratic behavior of attending physicians and the medical caste system.

Wright, always the amateur historian, began to study the history and sociology of the hospital. He interviewed nurses because they had so many stories about the mistakes certain doctors had made during their internship at Harlem. They alerted young Dr. Wright about senior doctors on the staff who could cause problems for him. In the process the nurses became his teachers. Burling et al summarizes the unusual role of interns.

> Since the internee's status in the hospital is an ambiguous one—part student, part staff member, part donor of services—his relationship to the other staff members and other hospital employees are often rather ill-defined. Although he is at the bottom of the staff pyramid, he is already intensively trained and is soon to become a full-fledged specialist. One might say that his real status is a latent one. His relations with nurses are generally good and rewarding. More and more, internees and nurses work as partners. The internee is not old enough or experienced enough to dominate the nurse, even though he may "show off" from time to time. The typically warm, often light and humorous bond between them is strengthened by the fact that an alert nurse may save the beginning doctor from serious mistakes.[2]

Wright lived on the second floor of an eight-story building called the Women's Pavilion. The quarters were shared by interns, residents, and other staff members. The hospital gave him a uniform and paid him $35.00 a month for a salary. He had no car, no credit and no knowledge of the city. The subway cost a nickel, and he used it to go to his sister's house in the Bronx where he baby-sat for his niece, Nadine.

Interns at Harlem were rotated through the various services. They would spend a month or two on the medical ward, surgery, OB-GYN, and other medical specialties. Interns also worked in the clinics, and in the emergency room. The emergency room was always the most fascinating part of a physician's training. On Saturday night people were rushed to the hospital suffering from cuts, gun shot wounds and broken bones. Black males were often victims of violence as they sought to establish themselves within the Harlem enclaves. Sometimes interns had to stay up all night patching up people. The nurses in the emergency room were the best ones in the hospital. They walked the interns through the process.

Charles Wright's supervising physicians were Italian, Jewish and Black. Among them were Louis Hill, Vincent Merendino and Vaughn Mason. Interns were expected to examine the patients, write histories, describe what they saw, and assist residents. They were coached and evaluated by first-year residents and by head residents. The Chief of Services evaluated head residents. The pecking order was quite apparent at Harlem. Interns knew their place and if they didn't, residents would remind them of it.

Wright's medical training was going well, but the country was in the middle of WWII, and doctors were needed for the battlefields. The military wanted all newly trained interns to go directly into the military. The hospital had reduced the intern and residency training period from a year to nine months. During the war the entire medical training period was reduced by 25%.

As Charles Wright and his fellow interns approached the end of internship, they had to decide what they wanted to do—if they didn't obtain a residency, the military would draft them. Wright was not eager to go to war or to join the segregated military. Black physicians were routinely sent into the infantry, and after basic training they were assigned to Black units. Some were sent to Europe and others were sent to stateside facilities. The U.S. Army was highly segregated and it reminded many soldiers of the deep South. Maurice Davie, a sociologist, recognized that service in the War was very difficult because of the continuing racial crisis in the states. He concluded that, "more than any other war in which the United States has engaged, the Second World War magnified the Negro's awareness of the disparity between the American profession and practice of democracy."[3] Charles was quite aware of this disparity and did not like the way Negro physicians in uniform were treated. In order to avoid the service he had to find a residency quickly.

Wright sought a residency in surgery, but Harlem only offered such training to Black doctors with medical or political connections. Dr. Wright learned another lesson, "It is not what you know, but who you know." Obtaining a respectable residency in surgery or obstetrics-gynecology seemed to be out of his reach. White hospitals, in the North and South, were not interested in recruiting Black residents. There were still segregated wards for Black patients. Most Blacks received their medical care in their homes or the doctor's office. As a result, many Black graduates of medical schools became general practitioners with inadequate or no hospital affiliation.

After failing to get a residency in surgery, Wright applied for a nine-month residency in pathology. Harlem accepted his application on the condition that he would get a draft deferment. The hospital wrote to the Army Procurement Officer in Washington to secure a deferment for Charles. Hearing nothing from the Army, Charles started an investigation of his own. He discovered that the Office of Procurement was located at one place in Washington and the Army Surgeon General was in another. "If orders were written by the Surgeon General before the Office of Procurement requested deferment, the Surgeon General wouldn't change any orders. They would tell the Office of Procurement that deferments aren't available and send you into the Army."[4]

Charles decided to write to the Surgeon General's office, himself, and inform them that the Office of Procurement and Assignment had a request from Harlem Hospital for him. His letter fell into the hands of a Major who was curious enough

The Wright Man

to call the Office of Procurement to confirm that Dr. Wright had been asked for. The request was confirmed, and Wright was deferred. Wright took his papers to the hospital administration and obtained his residency. His fellow interns were upset because they had not thought of this maneuver before their draft orders were in the mail. Several interns made long-distance calls to Washington, to no avail. "Draft orders were coming in like rain."[5]

Dr. Wright triumphantly and dutifully began his training as a pathologist, not the most glamorous specialty in medicine. The image of the county coroner comes to mind, as most medical students do not enter medical school aspiring to be pathologists. Yet the work they do is essential.

Wright's pathology internship started April 1, 1944. He began studying gross pathology, microscopic pathology and general pathology. He became quite proficient at autopsies. The chief pathologist, Dr. Rothman, supervised Charles' work. The young Dr. Wright supervised the blood bank. His job was to make sure there was always enough blood available for transfusions. The blood had to be typed and matched to ensure compatibility.

THE OTHER SIDE OF HARLEM

The Harlem of the 40s was somewhat reminiscent of its famous Renaissance in the twenties. Black writers, artists and intellectuals added a certain zest to life in the enclave. Harlem was alive, and Blacks were dancing, singing, and praying for their liberation. Hollywood was busy making what was called "passing movies," such as *Lost Boundaries* (1949) and *Pinky* (1949). It also made *No Way Out* (1950), which starred Sidney Poiter as the first Black intern in a white hospital, *Home of the Brave* (1949) and *Showboat* (1951). Harlem residents were debating the roles of the actors of these movies, because race images were changing. The debate would be another learning experience for Charles Wright. Life in Harlem also had a darker side, captured by *Time Magazine*:

"To the night lifers, Harlem, the Negro metropolis, is a glittering island of creepjoints, honky-tonks, jive halls. But for the 245,000 inhabitants jammed into 230 narrow city blocks, Harlem is a virtual pesthole. The TB mortality rate is ten times higher than the rate in the more prosperous sections of New York City. It is not uncommon for Harlem doctors to be stricken. Confined to a tuberculosis sanatorium at present is a brilliant, contentious skull surgeon, Louis Tompkins Wright, considered by many the outstanding Negro physician in the U.S."[6]

The article went on to highlight the work of Dr. John Baldwin West, and his work against TB in the Central Harlem Health Center. He had a staff of 200 which was able to X-ray 250,000 people. The Center had one of the largest outreach programs in America. They were also able to significantly lower the infant mortality rate from 100 per 1000 to 52.[7]

Meanwhile, the war continued and more Blacks were drafted. While Black soldiers were leaving for Europe and Harlem was growing in notoriety, many famous performers walked its streets. The legendary Apollo Theater was at it peak. Most of the new Black talent auditioned there and played it when they came to New York. Mr. Fishman, the manager at the Apollo, had an arrangement with Harlem Hospital that allowed interns and residents free admission to the Apollo. He wanted a doctor in the house in case of an emergency. Charles Wright took the opportunity to see performers and enjoy his hours off.

When he was at the hospital, he returned to his more serious face. Dr. Wright was involved in hospital activities and was appointed to the editorial board of the hospital newspaper. He began writing about racial discrimination in the hospital. He claims that he was unaware that hospital administrators

The Wright Man

were reading the staff's little newspaper. Subsequently, he was called in and told to submit future articles for pre-publication review. Wright resigned from the newspaper, and never wrote for them again.

All of the frustrations of Black New Yorkers somehow centered in Harlem. Just as Harlem was the cradle of Negro culture, it was also the caldron of racial tensions. In the summer of 1943, Harlem had a major race riot. The resulting violence tested Dr. Wright's mettle as an intern. The riot happened six weeks after the Detroit riot. It started because of a rumor that a white policeman had killed the Black soldier, Robert Bandy. Black people protested the killing by taking to the street. They surrounded the 28th Precinct headquarters and demanded answers. People used bricks to break windows and the riot got out of hand. Looting and vandalism followed and six people lost their lives. More than 100 people were injured. "Most injuries came from looters being cut jumping through broken plate glass windows," to steal furniture and were cut by the glass. Many were cut several times and were losing blood.[8]

Harlem Hospital became the center of medical care. People with all types of injuries were brought to the emergency room. The Pathology Department helped supply blood for individuals who were shot and cut over the three days of looting. One patient had been accidentally shot by a machine gun and the whole calf of his leg had been blown off. He required many pints of blood before being stabilized. Charles worked very closely with the emergency room staff during this crisis. Professor Capeci, the historian of the riot, called the medical assistance "commendable."[9] He described the strategy of the medical operations:

"Medical authorities, no doubt with major instructions, were tactful as well as competent. In order to prepare Harlem Hospital's surgical wards for possible emergency use during the evening of August 3, patients were evacuated to Bellevue. The evacuation was in a manner to avoid exciting. . . rumors that might trigger another outburst. Eight, four-stretcher ambulances from six hospitals participated in a shuttle service, in which no more than two vehicles were loaded at a time. The ambulances were routed through quiet areas, traversing only a very small section of the area in which the disturbance was taking place."[10]

Charles had never experienced anything like the riot before. Blacks in Dothan, Montgomery and Nashville (and even Detroit) were militant but none of these cities experienced this type of violence. The rage that exploded had been building for years. The vandalism was directed toward the property belonging to white owners. Arna Bontemps, a Rosenwald fellow at the University of Chicago, took a different view of the riots. He concluded:

> ". . .Harlem did not riot against white people. Harlem rioted against Harlem. True, it ravaged the shops and businesses of the owners who get their living in Harlem but do not live there. Likewise, beyond dispute is the fact that the mob went for the symbols of exploitation and oppression, but that was not its deepest impulse. Harlem was trying to commit suicide. It was trying to uproot and destroy its ghetto existence. Harlem was sick of muggers and cultist and zootsuits. Harlem was horrified and disgusted by the fruit of the beautiful years, and in a moment of confusion and frustration it rioted against itself and tried to wipe the slate clean."[11]

World War II gave birth to a new type of militancy among Negroes. The so-called "new Negro" was not afraid to challenge the racial norms of the country. The times had changed. Hitler's racism in Europe helped to illuminate the racial contradictions in New York City. Attitudes at Harlem Hospital were not changing fast enough to keep up with its patients. Blacks were routinely denied jobs on the housing staff. The next year, 1944, Councilman Adam Clayton Powell raised the issue of hospital integration again. Once again the hospital dragged its feet.

The Wright Man

At the end of his nine months, Charles, in need of more training, began searching for another residency in pathology, and found one in the Cleveland City Hospital. He wrote a letter to the chief pathologist, Dr. Howard T. Karsner. Karsner had written a textbook entitled, *Human Pathology*, and was reported to be a good teacher. After reviewing Charles' credentials, Karsner accepted him as a resident. Leaving Harlem and New York meant leaving his sister, Pearl, his new niece, and fellow physicians and nurses, many of whom had become close friends. Charles had mixed feelings about leaving, but he had to go to Cleveland, otherwise his deferment would expire.

CLEVELAND, OHIO: HERE I COME

Charles Wright arrived in Cleveland on a cold New Years' Eve in 1945. Cleveland was a city very different from the Big Apple. Located on Lake Erie, the city was home to many European ethnic groups. The groups were divided by the Cuyahoga River, which ran through the city. The 1940 Census found that 84,504 Negroes lived in Cleveland and they comprised 9.6% of the city population. Most of them received their medical services at Cleveland City Hospital. This institution had a very different history than Harlem Hospital. Cleveland City had accepted its first Black intern, Dr. Frederick D. Stubbs, as early as 1931. City hospital was called a "bright spot" in an otherwise gloomy picture for the training of Black physicians. Along with Homer Phillips Hospital in St. Louis, Cleveland City was considered a likely place for a Black medical student to get an internship (Pringle and Pringle, 1948). As the largest hospital in the city, and one of the largest in the nation, it possessed the entire array of medical and surgical services, a pediatrics unit, a mental hospital, an infectious disease hospital, and a pathology unit.

Although Wright was an experienced resident in pathology, he would learn more about the field from Dr. Karsner. Dr. Karsner, a professor of pathology at Western

Reserve University, had written a textbook, which was considered the standard at the time. Karsner was considered a very strict and difficult person. He wanted all the "T's" crossed and the "I's" dotted. This type of teacher must have reminded Wright of Professor Jackson, his teacher in Dothan. Charles spent his next nine months concentrating in pathology. His first paper entitled, *Addison's Disease: Report of a Case and an Analysis of Autopsied Cases of Tuberculosis of Adrenal Gland,"* was completed at Cleveland Hospital and published by *Ohio State Medical Journal* in 1946. He knew that he needed one more year in pathology to become eligible for the Pathology Boards. Since he did not know anyone in the city, he spent most of his time at the hospital.

During his stay in Cleveland, Charles began to interact with foreign residents from Latin America. Many of these residents knew very little English, and were trying to learn the language while completing their residencies. Most foreigners were ignored by the other residents, many of whom were white Southerners. Charles took an interest in them, and revived his interest in the Spanish language that he developed as an intern at Harlem Hospital. Few doctors at Harlem spoke Spanish, making communication difficult with Puerto Rican patients, a growing percentage of the hospital population. Wright had promised himself that if he got the opportunity, he would learn the language and his Cleveland residency permitted him to interact with Spanish-speaking physicians. They taught him Spanish and in return they learned English. Wright bought Rosenthal's *Spanish Self-Taught,* and studied it religiously. Since he did not know many people in Cleveland, he spent his off-hours pronouncing Spanish words, learning the grammar and building his vocabulary.

One day, Dr. J. Sweat, a resident from Mississippi, noticed Charles' command of the language and asked why he was spending so much time learning Spanish, "when all you have to do is put an 'o' after the English word and you have Spanish." When Charles related the story to his South

The Wright Man

American friends they were quite amused. To them it reflected the contempt of the *gringo* for their language. Spanish became a vocation, a second language, for Charles and a way to occupy his idle time. It introduced him to another culture and provided a frame of reference that became a major influence on the rest of his life.

Near the end of his stay in Cleveland, Charles discovered that he had a cousin, Mary Alice Florence, in the city. Her parents were also from Batesville and Eufaula, Alabama. This new relative gave Wright a life outside the hospital and an opportunity to spend time in the Negro section of the city.

Cleveland had its attractions as did his hospital specialty of pathology. But Charles Wright's heart was never in the city, nor was he attracted to pathology as a life work. "Pathology was chosen to stay out of the Army. I knew that pathology would be useful no matter whether I finally became a surgeon or a gynecologist." At the end of his pathology residency at Cleveland City Hospital, he left for Detroit. "After having spent so much time in Detroit as a medical student, I thought it was the place I belonged." His summer jobs in Detroit had addicted Wright to life in the Motor City. The idea of returning to Dothan was not even a fleeting thought for the young physician as he packed his bags for Detroit.

After sojourns into New York and Cleveland, Charles was 28 years old, with no specialty and no family of his own. Detroit seemed full of opportunity for a young physician. By 28, he had been a censored journalist, a campaign worker, an intern in the Big Apple, a resident in pathology and a language student. Now Charles Wright, M.D. had to settle on a life as a cogwheel of the profession, a general practitioner. When asked why he unhesitantly selected Detroit, he cites "the comfort level." His classmates, James Robinson, M.D. and Clarence Greer, M.D. had always made him welcome in their city. Whenever he visited the city the Greers fed him and treated him like family. He liked Detroit.

Charles emerged from Harlem, New York a more urbane person. He had traveled to Montgomery, Nashville, New York, and Cleveland, but he never really left the Black community. At Harlem Hospital he tried journalism again, but he didn't fare any better than his days at Alabama State. He narrowly escaped induction into the service and was forced to study pathology. Harlem Hospital was his first taste of bureaucratic life, and he did not like it. Yet, he was becoming stronger in his faith in the capacity of Black people. Harlem convinced him to reach out to other cultures. In Cleveland he began to reach out to the Spanish culture. Charles had grown substantially since early life in Dothan.

Professor Rich interviewing Dr. Wright

The Wright Man

Driving west to Detroit, Charles reflected on his strange sojourn from Dothan. He arrived in Detroit on June 19, 1946. It was an interesting year in the Motor City, the UAW had just completed a 113-day automobile strike against General Motors. American industry, particularly Detroit's, was at the peak of economic potential. The city, with its mosaic of immigrants, was in a surge of affluence. A man could make a living with his hands or his mind. All one needed was a willingness to work hard. In his trusted $200 Hudson's Terraplane (car), Dr. Wright was ready to take his chances in Motown.

Charles would be one of many Meharry graduates who decided to establish a practice in Detroit. Detroit had a reputation as a lunch box town, a working man's city. Steven Babson put it well: "Few places in America boasted a more self-confident, combative working class than the Motor City."[1] The infectious confidence of Detroit residents had grown on the young doctor from Dothan. Many Black residents were immigrants from Alabama and Mississippi, and Charles felt comfortable with them. Charles knew instinctively that this lunch box town offered more room for growth. One did not need a fancy pedigree to be somebody in Detroit; one just had to work hard.

CHARLES IN WARTIME DETROIT

Detroit as a residence easily won out over larger cities such as San Francisco, Los Angeles, Chicago and Boston. How did Detroit lure Charles Wright? Charles respected the strength of the city's economy and its peerless union history. Members of the Black professional class knew that they could prosper because the unionized working class could support them. The 1940 U.S. Census showed Detroit as having 160 Negro physicians. Even with this unusually large number, the city was a good place to start a practice because Negro workers had good jobs on the assembly line and could afford to pay for medical care.

Wartime Detroit's Black population, 149,119 or 9.2 % of the total population, seemed to be on the threshold of economic breakthrough. The automobile industry made most of the tanks and airplanes for the war effort, and money was to be made everywhere. Capeci reported that a cab driver could make $25.00 on a weekend night and a laborer at General Motors made $41.24 weekly.[2] By wartime standards, these were good wages, and in the Black community they were phenomenal.

Despite the robust economy, Detroit was no emerald city. The city had a history of job and housing discrimination. There were the so-called Negro jobs in the foundries. Unionized white workers had a monopoly on the high paying skilled jobs, and their leaders worked to keep the racial status quo on the floor. Black trade unionists fought to be accepted as equals. Most neighborhoods of Detroit were segregated along racial lines. When Charles Wright arrived, Negroes had very little political power in city government and very few Black teachers taught in the public school system. Although there were no blatant racial signs, for Blacks, Detroit was just "up South."

The Wright Man

Those who would challenge that characterization had only to look at the housing situation for Negroes. In the mid-forties the city was deluged with people looking for work in the automobile industry. Negroes had to compete with fellow newcomers: Polish, Irish, Lebanese and Italians for living space. The traditional Black neighborhoods could not accommodate every new family that wanted to live in Detroit. Negroes were forced to live in segregated projects such as the Brewster Housing Project on the eastside. Those who moved into white neighborhoods ran the risk of having their home damaged by "white mobs."[3]

Despite Detroit's history of tight housing space and pathological ghettoes, Charles had an affinity for the place. Many of the Blacks living there were fellow immigrants from the South. He was keenly aware of the need for doctors. A good general practitioner could make a good living taking care of the automobile workers and their families.

HANGING OUT HIS SHINGLE

Having taken the medical license examination in November of 1946, Dr. Wright was ready to see patients. However, he needed an office in a good location to build a practice. He heard through the physician's grapevine that an office was available on Caniff and Oakland Avenues. Betty Cain Harris' physician husband had died and the office was empty. Charles, having saved $300.00 from his $65.00 per month salary as a resident, decided to rent the office. Dr. Harris' old office had two little rooms each with examining tables. The new Dr. Wright's first three patients were walk-ins. On his first day in practice, he saw three patients and collected $17.00. Slowly patients began spreading the word that another doctor was in Dr. Harris' old office and the practice grew. Soon he began taking care of patients from all over the neighborhood. As a general practitioner, Dr. Wright began to treat aches and pains, sew up lacerations, and deliver babies. All types of patients with ailments and diseases came through his door. Some of the patients had complicated ailments and were sent to the few specialists that were available. Patient referral is the network that connects the physician's community together. The Meharry connection was also an important network for Dr. Wright. Black physicians needed to connect with each other because they were discriminated against by white colleagues and health institutions.

Black physicians did have full privileges at Receiving Hospital, the city's largest hospital. Receiving had some Black nurses. Private hospitals such as Grace and Harper tolerated Black doctors only if they had white patients. Of the other city hospitals, only Herman Kiefer employed a Black physician. Many Black patients received care at the Black-owned hospitals, some of which had the reputation of not having adequate equipment. When necessary, Dr. Wright treated his patients at Black-owned hospitals, such as Burton Diagnostic, Kirwood and Parkside.

Dr. Wright was a busy man because Blacks in Detroit were not healthy. Capeci reports that health conditions in Detroit for Blacks were terrible. The infant and maternal mortality rates were 50.8 per 1,000 for Blacks and 3.6 per 1,000 for whites.[4] Even worse were the tubercular death rates, where Blacks had seven times the death rate as whites.

The practice on Oakland Avenue went well. The years 1946 and 1947 were good ones for him. Accordingly, he decided he wanted to own his building. Along with Dr. James Robinson, he purchased a building on West Grand Boulevard. Most Black physicians rented their offices. This puzzled Wright because the advantages of ownership were so apparent to him. Wright knew what some physicians refuse to acknowledge, that is, providing medical care is a business, and the general practitioner is a small businessman. Dr. Wright had learned about being a small businessman from his mother in a grocery store in Dothan. As a new physician in town, Wright was also successful as a small businessman.

The Wright Man

His personal life was another matter. Still a bachelor, Charles dated quite a few of the city's lovely young women. As a successful general practitioner, he could afford to take them to nice places. Considered one of the city's most eligible Negro bachelors, this tall, brown man got his share of social invitations. The wives of physician friends often set him up with single women. However, none of them struck him as a potential wife. He was thirty-two and looked forward to settling down with the right woman.

MEETING LOUISE LOVETT

Charles Wright met Louise Powell Lovett on a blind date arranged by a mutual friend, Jean English. Louise, a Chicago librarian, was visiting Detroit for the holidays. She and Charles attended a 1948 Christmas party together and afterward they went to the Black-owned Gotham hotel, and had dinner in the Ebony Room. As well-dressed waiters swirled around them, they talked about Nashville, Fisk, his work, her work, and their lives. After dinner, Charles took her to the train station and she went back to Chicago. Louise struck him as special. Louise Lovett was somehow different from the women in Nashville, Cleveland, New York and Detroit. She was a librarian in Chicago and a graduate of Fisk University. In many ways, she matched the stereotype of Fisk women: beautiful, culturally sophisticated and light-skinned. While at Meharry, Charles had visited Fisk several times, but few of the women he met had made a particular impression on him. Louise had been in the Alpha Kappa Alpha sorority and very active on campus. Although their time in Nashville overlapped, Charles and Louise had never met each other on the Fisk campus.

Charles decided that he wanted to see her again. It was clear to him that she was extremely well read and matched his need for intellectual company. He was anxious to know more about her. He found himself visiting the Windy City and seeing more of Louise. Although located about 250 miles from

Detroit, it did not seem too large a stretch to maintain a courting relationship. By Charles' own description, his car was "pretty rickety. We met midway in Michigan sometimes."

Louise's life in Chicago was very different from Charles'. As the daughter of public school teachers, Albert and Zelda Lovett, she had lived in a city with a relatively large and politically connected Black population. Chicago's Black community was more politically developed than Detroit. During Louise's childhood, Blacks in Chicago had elected Black Congressmen Oscar Depriest and Arthur Mitchell. Many Black politicians were incorporated into the Democratic political machine.

In the early fifties, Chicago already had an established Black middle class living in integrated neighborhoods. The Black middle class in Chicago contained several second- and third-generation college graduates. As a second generation middle class family, the Lovett's were well connected to the Negro social structure of Chicago.

The long-distance relationship evolved into a serious one, and Wright proposed after less than two years of courtship. In February of 1950, he married Louise Lovett in a large wedding. The couple took a train and honeymooned in Mexico. At last, Wright got a chance to use his Spanish.

On returning to Detroit, they were ready to begin housekeeping. Now a married man, Charles had to make some adjustments. While he continued his private practice on the first floor of his West Grand Blvd building, he had to convert three rooms on the second floor into an apartment sufficient to accommodate his wife. Charles' marriage to Louise represented a critical passage in his life.

As the Wrights settled into their cramped quarters, Detroit was experiencing a new surge of immigrants. Blacks from the South were still migrating to Detroit looking for work. In 1950 Detroit was the fifth largest American city, with a population of 1,838,517. The greater metro area now encompassed 2,973,019 people. Dr. Wright and his peers were able to make a decent living, but they were not respected by their white colleagues. They were indeed second-class citizens of medicine.

THE STATUS OF BLACKS IN MEDICINE; CIRCA 1950

In 1948 the issue of the color line in medicine was again receiving attention in the media. The *Saturday Evening Post* lamented the state of medical care for Blacks and the dearth of Black physicians.

> Only 4,000 Negroes are now practicing medicine, as compared with 176,000 white physicians, and it is estimated that more than 5,300 more are needed to care for the increasing Negro population. The national average today is one colored doctor to every 3,337 Negroes, although the accepted minimum standard is one to 1,500. In Mississippi the ratio is one to 18, 527...[5]

> . . .The present rate of output of Negro doctors is just about replacing the ones who die or retire. And the number of deaths and retirements will increase, because a large percentage of Negro physicians are more than fifty years old.[6]

The article elaborates on the racism experienced in white medical school admissions. Conditions had not improved much since Charles was a medical student. Harlem Hospital was slowly becoming an all Black facility. By 1950, fewer and fewer whites were receiving care there. The rigid color line in medicine now extended from medical college admission offices to hospital wards. Charles and his peers spent time commiserating about this discrimination, but they were unable to do anything about it. As a general practitioner, Charles was not in a position to demand privileges. If he were a specialist, things might be different.

RETURN TO HARLEM

Charles still hoped to become an obstetrician gynecologist. The idea of another residency and becoming a specialist never left his mind. Soon after he returned to Detroit and two months after his wedding, Dr. Vaughn Mason, an old friend from Harlem Hospital, visited Charles. Dr. Mason was attending the National Medical Association conference being held in Detroit and they reminisced about the good old days at the Hospital. During their conversation, Dr. Mason asked Charles if he was still interested in a residency in OB-GYN. Charles said, yes. "I will close my practice tomorrow and move." Wright had become interested in the specialty as a result of working during his rotation with Dr. Helen O. Dickens. Dr. Dickens had worked at Harlem between 1943-1944, during Wright's internship. She recognized his potential in the field and was the first to suggest that he should go to Meharry or Harlem for further training.

Shortly after the Vaughn visit, Charles received word that his application for a residency in OB-GYN at Harlem had been accepted. The doctor, who had been slated to take the position, got sick, so suddenly there was an opening. Charles had to be ready to start on July 1, which left little time to convince his new wife and close a thriving medical practice.

The decision to return to Harlem Hospital was one of the most important decisions in Charles' life. But this time he was no longer a bachelor. Telling his friend, Dr. Mason, that he was willing to drop everything was different from telling his new bride that they were moving. Louise was furious. This was his first serious disagreement with his new wife. Charles discovered that marriage meant sharing aspirations and plans. In the course of the courtship, he had never told Louise that he wanted to be a specialist, nor had he consulted her before agreeing to go. The new bride was just beginning to make friends in Detroit and the city was quite close to Chicago by train. She had settled in with friends from Fisk, and another move would be extremely difficult for her. Being given short notice was to be the first burden of the doctor's wife. Moving, trauma, and long hours are all a part of a physician's lot and thus a part of his wife's as well. For an ambitious young physician, a residency at Harlem was the chance of a lifetime, even if the pay was only $150.00 a month. Becoming board-certified would mean enjoying great prestige in the medical community and privileges in white hospitals. Once considered an expert in his field, he would be consulted by colleagues and would receive many other perks denied to the general practitioner.

The health of Black babies remained a major problem throughout the nation. In 1945, Davie reported that the infant mortality rate for Negroes, in 1945, was 56.2 per 1,000 births, which was considerably more than the rate of 35.6 per 1,000 for white infants. The robust wartime economy did not close the gap in the rate of Black infant mortality (Davie, p. 234). Davie reported that two-fifths of Black babies were delivered by midwives and in the South the number was as high as four-fifths. Ninety-eight percent of white babies were delivered by physicians, and eighty percent of them were delivered in hospitals (235). The next five years saw no appreciable decline in the infant mortality rates. Thus, Charles was entering a specialty which was badly needed in the Black community

LEARNING THE SPECIALTY

When Charles returned to Harlem Hospital, Dr. Dickens was no longer there. The head of residents in OB-GYN was Dr. Morris Leo Bobrow. His teachers in obstetrics were Dr. Vaughn Mason and Dr. Charles Posner. When Charles accepted the residency, he became a medical student again. He began studying gynecology, a sub-field of medicine that deals with the diseases and hygiene problems of women's reproductive organs. His second specialty was obstetrics. The public thinks of OB-GYNs as physicians who do Cesarean

Sections and deliver problem babies. Actually the specialty is a complicated sub-field of medicine.

As a resident in OB-GYN, Dr. Wright was confronted with the poor health of Black and Puerto-Rican women. All types of complications were encountered as some mothers gave birth without any pre-natal care. There were mothers who were drug or alcohol-dependent, fathers who were not involved with the pregnant mothers, and very young women having children. A resident's job is to monitor the women during and after delivery, which is seldom routine. Even for veteran mothers, the birth of a new child is always different. The joy and anticipation of a new life usually generates enthusiasm in the delivery room. Obstetrics is often the most positive wing of the hospital and Charles enjoyed his specialty.

The specialty was changing even as Charles Wright was learning it. New medicines and technologies were being introduced and he had to keep up with the research reported in journals. Charles learned about the new research in trophoblastic growths, Pyclonephritis, Rubella, and ectopic pregnancies. Treating women as patients was both a science and an art to Wright. He was part counselor, part nutritionist, and part basic physician for the health of mothers and babies. In Dr. Wright's own words,

> At that time most women were only receiving the lower level of gynecological care. Black women were receiving less. I knew the level of care could be improved. In Obstetrics an additional person is involved. Obstetrics involved the most important part of the baby's life, the first five minutes after birth. You must get the baby started on all cylinders.
>
> . . .Both clinical and hospital work were required. Caring for patients and training interns and new residents. Much time was spent in operating rooms and delivery rooms and preparing for seminars. I also had to attend meetings outside the hospital.[7]

The Wright Man

Charles developed an enthusiasm for his new line of work. This residency at Harlem was quite different from his tenure as a pathology resident. Delivering babies was much preferred over conducting autopsies. When Charles returned to Harlem Hospital he felt more in control of his life, and he knew what he wanted to do. Those nurses and staff who knew him as an intern saw a different man, and interns came to watch and learn from him. Charles would move from assistant resident to head resident over the course of his three years. Some of the faces in Harlem were the same, but now he was at a higher tier in the hospital's internal politics.

While Charles Wright was there, there were five Dr. Wrights at Harlem Hospital, a fact that became confusing. Dr. Louis Wright was a powerful administrator at Harlem. Yet he was a man who was admired. In 1929, Louis Wright became the first Black physician to be appointed police surgeon. Feared by the house staff, the chief's demands, orders, and criticisms were laced with profanity. He swore at subordinates including Charles. The only physicians who were safe from Louis Wright's attacks were his two daughters, who were also physicians employed at the hospital.

It was during this time at Harlem Hospital that Wright met Dorothy Mottley. She was a senior nursing student and after graduation , she worked primarily in ICU emergency. Mottley, still a close friend, and one of only about three people who call him "Charlie," remembers that, "Charlie had the reputation of being one of the finest residents to have come through Harlem Hospital."

"As chief resident," she states, "he taught his residents to be caring, loving, and efficient. Two of his very close friends, Drs. Johnny Gilchrist and Jimmy Hubert, admired him greatly and talked of him years later." However, any physician who has ever worked as an intern or resident under Wright's supervision will tell you it was not easy. If you were a few minutes late, say 6:10 a.m. instead of 6:00 a.m., you would get the good afternoon, Mr. treatment. Yet, they unanimously agree that all that he taught was highly beneficial to them and well worth the "abuse."

A DIFFERENT HARLEM

During Wright's absence from Harlem, the neighborhood surrounding the hospital had changed. The Harlem of the fifties had become a predominately Black enclave. New Black immigrants were joined by Puerto Ricans and those from the West Indies. The Wrights lived in Brooklyn. Louise struggled to adjust; she worked in Manhattan, at New York Public Library's Main Branch, in the reference division. She enjoyed her work and stayed at the library until she became pregnant. Dr. Wright commuted from Brooklyn to Harlem for three years. These were long rides on the A-Train of the IND subway, holding the iron and leather strap with garment workers on one side and Wall Street professionals on the other.

Harlem had changed during Wright's six years absence. Rev. Adam Clayton Powell, now a congressman, clearly dominated the political scene. Wright attended his Abyssinian Baptist Church, located on 138th Street. The young Rev. Powell had started his political life by standing on a soapbox at 125th St. and 7th Ave, and delivering his political messages. Elected to the Congress in 1944, Powell was running for reelection and Charles received his second chance to work in the Powell campaign. These were heady times for Powell, as he projected himself as both the savior of Harlem and gadfly of Congress. His flare for life and his independence, some say arrogance, made him a much admired man among the denizens of Harlem.

This new stay at Harlem Hospital represented many things to the Wright family. Charles' first daughter, Stephanie, was born on September 18, 1952 at Harlem's Sydenham Hospital. She was delivered by Dr. Vaughn Mason, Charles'

The Wright Man

mentor. As the residency ended, the family began to make plans to return to Detroit.

RETURN TO DETROIT

Charles was anxious to return to his adopted city, Detroit. He quickly picked up the pieces of his practice and started his practice as a specialist. The return was different for Louise. As a newcomer and a young physician's wife, Louise had to work her way into the inner circle of the social set. As a Fisk graduate, she had helpful alumnae contacts, but she had to establish herself in the physician's community. Working in the gift shop at Kirwood Hospital and as president of the Meharry Medical Society Auxiliary she developed a reputation of her own. She made her mark as a volunteer.

Charles was never interested in the social structure of Negro society and was uncomfortable in many social circles. In deference to him, Louise remained an outsider, not by choice but as a reaction to the no-nonsense posture her husband had assumed in the community. The Wrights found themselves socially isolated. Charles' daughter, Carla Wright, remembered: "We were fringe people."[8]

Charles did not think of himself as a "fringe person," but his alienation from the ostentatious proclivities of his adopted middle class made him suspect in the medical community and among other Black socialites. Many saw him as highly principled, serious and not much fun, as he didn't drink or gamble. Charles never joined the Cotillion Club. He was faithful to his fraternity and Alumni Club but he was always more involved with his own research projects.

Charles H. Wright - 1950s

Dr. Wright and wife, Louise Lovett Wright

The Wright Man

In 1954, the U.S. Supreme Court declared separate but equal schools unconstitutional, but stated nothing about hospitals. In the South, hospitals were segregated by law but in the North they were segregated by custom. After returning to Detroit in 1953 and reopening his office in the basement of 1549 West Grand Blvd and West Warren, Dr. Wright found city hospitals still closed to Blacks. This was the same year the Detroit Medical Society honored him as the "Physician of the Year." But being physician of the year couldn't protect him from the humiliation of segregated hospitals in Detroit. Most of his patients went to Black-owned hospitals. Nevertheless, Dr. Wright began his OB-GYN career as one of few Black physicians with admitting privileges at a white hospital.

The exception for Wright has a curious history. In 1955, Wright was certified by the American College of Surgeons and the American College of Obstetricians-Gynecologists. Yet, board certification did not automatically grant hospital privileges for Blacks. Blacks who applied for the privilege were usually refused at hospital committee level.

Wright, who knew the power of letter writing, asked Dr. Henry Falk, formerly Chief of Gynecology, at Harlem Hospital to write a letter to Woman's Hospital recommending him for a staff appointment. Dr. Wright's credentials were accepted at Woman's Hospital (Hutzel). Woman's was one of the few white Detroit hospitals granting privileges to Blacks. Dr. Marjorie Peebles Meyers, an internist; Dr. Horace Bradfield; Dr. Thomas Love; and Dr. James J. McClendon, general practitioners also had privileges at Woman's Hospital. In Dietrich Reitzer's study, he found that Negro physicians who wanted hospital affiliations usually got them through white recommendations. A Black physician could generally get an appointment either by studying under a white doctor in medical school, or through contacts with influential white physicians.[1]

Although the appointment at Woman's was significant, most of Charles' patients would not benefit from this affiliation. Most continued to be treated at Black-owned hospitals such as Parkside, Kirwood and Burton Mercy Hospitals. Specialists are more dependent on hospitals in their practice. This type of practice is also dependent on referrals from general practitioners.

In his research, Dietrich Reitzer found that most Black physicians preferred referring patients to other Blacks rather than to white specialists; the older physicians also welcomed young Negro specialists.[2] However, Charles disagreed with Reitzer's research. "Maybe Reitzer found this to be true. I did not. Some Black doctors never referred patients to Black specialists."[3]

Becoming a specialist was a personal triumph for Charles Wright. However, it was quickly overshadowed in his house by events in the South. That year (1955) marked the beginning of the Montgomery Bus Boycott. Charles Wright had been an undergraduate student in Montgomery and knew many of the actors in unfolding civil rights events. After Mrs. Rosa Parks, a seamstress, refused to give up her seat to a white male bus rider, she was arrested. Blacks refused to ride the bus for an entire year, using car pools and church vans to ferry people around the town. Many domestics walked to work to the Cloverdales and Normandales of Montgomery. Also, a new name in civil rights history emerged, that of Rev. Martin Luther King, Jr., pastor of the Dexter Ave Baptist Church and president of the Montgomery Improvement Association (MIA). The city that called itself the Cradle of the Confederacy rocked with the tune of "We Shall Overcome."

The Wright Man

The summer of 1955 was also a year of shock and dismay for most Blacks in Northern cities. Emmett Till, a teenager from Chicago, was killed in Money, Mississippi for making a flip remark to a white woman. This incident reminded Black males everywhere of the danger of living and traveling in the South. Dothan, Alabama is larger than Money, Mississippi, but not by much. The analogy was never lost on Charles Wright.

Wright kept abreast of events in the South through friends and relatives. The plight of civil rights workers became the daily topic of discussion for Wright and his colleagues. While consolidating his practice and becoming a father for the second time, Wright became more intensely aware of the discrimination in medicine in Detroit. In 1956, Dietrich Reitzer conducted another study of Negro physicians in fourteen cities for the Rockefeller Foundation. In Detroit, Reitzer found that there had been a 21.2% increase in the number of Black physicians since 1946. In 1956 there were 160 Black physicians in Detroit, 52.6% under the age of fifty, including Charles. The city had 17 board-certified Black physicians.[4] With one of the largest numbers of Black physicians in the nation, Detroit became the center of the struggle for recognition of Black professionals by the medical establishment and the end of de facto segregation at white hospitals.

The irony of the struggle for privileges at white hospitals was that if they were granted, the need of Black hospitals would diminish, if not be eliminated. These venerable institutions had sustained Black physicians for decades. When other hospitals refused their credentials and their patients, Black hospitals welcomed them. The association with these facilities reinforced friendships and created network opportunities. Would Black physicians continue to refer patients to Black hospitals or would Black patients choose to go to a Black hospital once the white ones became available? The dilemma reminded Charles of Black people who used to dangle loaves of bread that they had purchased from the white merchants as they passed the

Wright's small grocery store. No one would contest the fact that the larger, better-equipped white hospitals could provide more modern care, the issue was the plight of the Black hospitals in those changing times.

BLACK HOSPITALS IN DETROIT

The Negro Hospital Movement was a reflection of the reality that medicine was one of the most segregated professions in America. Vanessa Gamble, a historian, cites the 1895 founding of the National Hospital Association (NHA) as a result of the need for facilities to treat Black patients. Organized to be the functional equivalent of the American Hospital Association (AHA), NHA never had the prestige or authority of its counterparts. Yet, Black hospitals and infirmaries grew as more Blacks migrated to northern cities. Prominent Black physicians owned many of these facilities. Local physicians would use these facilities for those patients who needed special care or around the clock medical and nursing supervision.

These facilities were critical to nursing care in the Black communities. Physicians needed an adequate theater in which to practice medicine and patients needed a place to go for proper medical care.

Detroit possessed an illustrious Black hospital history as outlined by Dr. Wright. By 1917, Detroit's African American physicians had finally accepted the futility of attempts to gain admitting privileges in the existing hospitals. They opened the 20-bed Mercy Hospital. By that time, Harper, Grace, Ford, Providence, Herman Keifer, and Receiving hospitals were already in full, but racially restrictive, operation.

Thus the victims of racial oppression began what proved to be a 75-year effort to survive its ill effects, at a time when they were sick and most vulnerable. While seeking survival, Detroit was given the ubiquitous title "The Black Hospital Capital of the U.S.A.," by many who were disposed to be unkind.

The Wright Man

The project began when twenty-five to thirty of Detroit's African American physicians met in 1917 to form the Allied Medical Society. They sought to maximize their meager resources by becoming affiliated with the NMA, which was organized 22 years earlier for the same reason.

The physicians' immediate goal was to establish their own hospital. A husband and wife physician team, Drs. Daisy and David Northcross, were members of the group and had just fled from the Ku Klux Klan in Montgomery, Alabama, where they had practiced together in their own "Northcross" sanitarium.

This couple brought with them much-needed medical and administrative experiences that were helpful in the preliminary discussions about hospitals. It soon became apparent, however, that a joint venture between the Northcrosses and the other African American physicians was not possible, so the Northcrosses chose to go it alone. They established Detroit's first African American hospital, Mercy Hospital at 73 Russell St. near the Detroit River, later moving to 688 Winder Street between St. Antoine and Hastings.

After Mercy General Hospital was launched in 1917, the remaining members of the Allied Medical Society met with a bi-racial committee of community leaders and formed a subsidiary group to seek health care provisions for Detroit's expanding African American population that already exceeded 20,000. Instead of attacking the racism of the hospitals, the group elected to form the Dunbar Hospital organizing board of trustees and worked hard to create an acceptable, segregated alternative—the Dunbar Hospital.

Dunbar Hospital's first board of trustees included John Dancy, executive director of the Urban League; John Lyle; William C. Osby (who in addition to leadership roles in the NAACP and Urban League, served as general manager of the Dunbar Hospital through the mid-1920s); Alice Stone; and

Charles Webb. As president, Osby led the board's first, citywide financial campaign.

Dr. Babcock, a Grace Hospital administrator and a national authority on hospital building and management, spent many helpful hours with Dunbar's and, later, Parkside Hospital's management team. Fred Butzel, one of Detroit's most generous contributors to African American causes, often came to the hospital's rescue in times of need. Aided by Trustee John Dancy, who was a member of Senator James Couzen's Community Affairs committee, the Dunbar trustees were able to gain the congressman's attention when hospital matters became urgent.

The trustees and staff acquired a three-story dwelling at 560 Frederick Street (now 580 Frederick), which had been built in 1892 by Detroit jeweler, Charles W. Warren. They occupied it in 1918 and converted it into Detroit's first non-profit, African American general hospital. When fully operational, Dunbar could accommodate 27 patients. Although the administrators did boast of a "well run" operating room, no facilities for obstetrical deliveries were mentioned.[5]

The trustees chose two of Detroit's most prestigious African American physicians to direct the medical affairs of Dunbar Hospital, Dr. James Ames and Dr. Alexander Turner. A 1922 photo of physicians, posing on the building's steps, includes: Drs. Joseph Wills, James Ames, James Young, Parker Gamble, George Bundy and Albert B. Cleage. Others were Drs. Lloyd Bailer, Ed Carter, Robert Greenidge, John Miller, Leo Welker, Charles Greene, Frank Raiford, Emmett Morton, and Herbert Sims.

By 1924, Dunbar Hospital had outgrown its space at 580 Frederick. The members of Allied Medical Society and trustees of Dunbar Hospital acquired an adjacent building, adding space for offices, a reception room, a medical library, nurses quarters and boosting the bed capacity from twenty-seven to forty.[6]

The Wright Man

Dr. Ames continued as medical director of Dunbar Hospital for several years, but other staff doctors shared the position as well. His many political and social obligations were demanding on his time, but medicine remained his highest priority.

Upon first glance it appeared that all of Detroit's hospital doors were completely closed to African American physicians. However, Dr Greenidge's archives revealed a lone birth certificate which stated he had delivered a male child to Mayme and Charles Diggs in Woman's Hospital on December 2, 1922.

When confronted with this finding, some of Woman's (currently Hutzel) senior obstetricians were highly skeptical that such an event could take place in 1922 at that facility. Others dismissed the rumor as a Greenidge fabrication. Spurred to further study, Dr. Greenidge's great granddaughter, and Dr. Wright's granddaughter and early editor, Blythe L. Allen, discovered that:

> Dr. Charles Hollister Judd, a European American, had been a generous, brave, and exceptional member of Woman's Hospital's OB-GYN staff. He had allowed Drs. Greenidge and Bundy (the former St. Matthews Episcopal priest) to enter the "back door" of Woman's obstetrical unit and deliver babies on several occasions. Although only Dr. Greenidge's name appears on the Diggs' child's birth certificate, Judd/Greenidge does appear on the delivery room sheet for the date of the delivery.

Insofar as the hospital was concerned, aside from the delivery room sheet, this clandestine delivery of Charles Diggs, Jr., who later became a U.S. Congressman, was a non-event. It is not too difficult to imagine two young enterprising African Americans—one a doctor (Greenidge) and the other an undertaker (Diggs)—putting their heads together to plan a proper hospital delivery for the businessman's first born.

Dr. Greenidge, the father of co-author, Roberta Greenidge Hughes Wright, was and is one of Dr. Wright's heroes. Dr. Wright included Greenidge's history in his book, *The National Medical Association Demands Equal Opportunity: Nothing More, Nothing Less,* and rates him with Paul Robeson, Rosa Parks, Nelson Mandela, and some of his other heroes. This is a partial account of the story as written by Dr. Wright.

Robert Isaac Greenidge was born in British Guiana, South America in 1888, and was a British subject until he migrated to Battle Creek, Michigan in 1909. Dr. Wright's book includes details regarding the country, the slave trade and Dr. Greenidge's early life. He also writes of his schooling and his religious affiliation. Dr. Greenidge, in his diary, reveals that "one Sunday evening I visited the Adventist meeting in Georgetown and was, in some way, transformed into a new man."

After working many jobs but feeling restless and unsatisfied, Robert made the decision to go to the United States. It was no accident that he chose Michigan and chose to work in the Battle Creek Sanitarium. First, he had requested a letter of recommendation from his employer at the *Argosy* newspaper. When efforts to dissuade Robert from departing failed, his employer bade him farewell with a very supportive letter to any future employer.

Like the management of the *Argosy,* the Church officials had learned to respect and trust Robert and they sent an equally glowing letter of recommendation to the Kellogg Sanitarium in Battle Creek, Michigan. So, armed with referrals from the business and the church, Robert left British Guiana and arrived in Battle Creek in July 1909. His arrival was anticipated by "The San" as Guiana church officials had made plans for him to live and work there. Robert did not have much money, but his self-confident stride, knowing smile, and no-nonsense approach to life, portrayed sufficient self-esteem to make up for the shortfall.

The Wright Man

In addition to being one of the most well known Adventists in the country, Dr. Henry Kellogg was also a celebrated surgeon and a great humanitarian. He attracted patients from across the nation and his apparent lack of racial prejudice set him apart from most of his contemporaries.

It was fortuitous that Robert spent his first two years in close, if not direct, contact with Dr. Kellogg. Before his arrival in Battle Creek, he had manifested, neither by word nor deed, even a latent interest in medicine as a career. Yet, upon leaving Battle Creek, two years later, he seemed drawn toward medical school, from which he obtained a M.D. degree in 1915.

When his bubble of hope, the Florence Crittenton Home, burned in his face years later, he entered into a phase of community entrepreneurship that was reflective of Dr. Kellogg's Battle Creek activities. These acts helped in part to save his sanity.

During his first 10 years in the U.S. (two with the Kellogg Sanitarium; four in Wayne State University Medical

School; and four years practicing medicine), Dr. Greenidge had never come face-to-face with the brutal American residue of chattel slavery. Always quiet, reserved and dignified, he couldn't remember ever having been called a derogatory term, not even in jest.

Without seeking the advice of his colleagues, Dr Greenidge decided to try his own hand to strike a blow for freedom and justice for African American womanhood and her offspring. He sought and kept his own counsel for a venture into unknown and dangerous territory.

Fortunately, Dr. Greenidge left a paper trail that describes his most embarrassing, painful, and unforgettable 30-minute journey backward into bondage; a voyage all African Americans are forced to take, sooner or later.

This narrative is preserved in a series of revealing letters that expose the soul of one of the world's worst evils, the illusion of white supremacy. The letters were all authenticated by the signatures of their authors: M. Louise Hood, superintendent; Wayland D. Stearns, vice president of the Florence Crittenton Home; Percival Dodge, assistant secretary of the Detroit Community Union; and John Dancy, the executive secretary of the Detroit Urban League.

A careful reading of these letters and other pertinent data provides a brief glimpse of racism at work, protecting the prerogatives of white supremacy. In preparation for what proved to be one of the most memorable series of events of his life, Dr. Greenidge did what he thought was careful, preliminary research, which revealed that:

The Administrators of Detroit's Florence Crittenton Home, an obstetrical hospital, had never granted staff privileges to an African American physician. This, even though the hospital received a portion of its operating funds from the Detroit Community Union, a public fund.

Miss Hood had sent invitations to all the European American physicians in the vicinity soliciting their obstetrical patronage. In strict conformity with the racist policies of the Crittenton Home, Hood went out of her way to make sure that no African American physician was solicited.

Dr. Greenidge made a handsome contribution to The Detroit Community Union, selected a test case, and bided his time. On the morning of February 28, 1925, the chosen patient called to inform Dr. Greenidge that she was in labor. Although not acquainted with the hospital's layout, he directed the patient to the Florence Crittenton Home without notifying the hospital staff. He arrived at the hospital soon after the patient did and somehow found his way to the Obstetrical area without being accosted.

Before he could completely disrobe and don his cap, mask, and delivery gown. Supt. Hood was notified that an unidentified Black man had invaded their space. She sped to the scene and, undeterred by Dr. Greenidge's medical credentials, ordered him out of the hospital. The resident had already examined the patient, having arrived earlier. She was found to be in early labor, therefore delivery was not anticipated for several hours.

Supt. Hood, now playing before a full house, pressed home her two demands while pretending that Dr. Greenidge was not in the room:

"Dr. Greenidge must leave the hospital, forthwith! If he elects to do so, he can take his patient with him.

If she remains for delivery, it will be done by the resident who will take charge of and manage the delivery and provide post-partum care."

The prospect of discharging the patient from the hospital for a home delivery did not seem a very attractive option to the doctor or the patient. Greenidge was aware that all eyes of his expanding European American audience were on him, expecting a reply. The few African American employees present were speechless and obviously embarrassed and uncomfortable.

Fortunately, the patient's husband intervened and transferred his wife to the resident's care. As quickly as possible, Dr. Greenidge gathered up his possessions, glanced at his watch and departed, a far different person than he had been upon arrival, 30 minutes earlier.

For the rest of his life, wherever he went, Dr. Greenidge was able to tell his audiences not just the hour, but the minute when he was finally forced from the status of South American immigrant to that of "North American hostage." Whenever Dr. Greenidge relived that scene, he could never recall the exact details of how he escaped from that hostile event, though he did remember that the time was 11 a.m., and the date, February 25, 1925.

Down, but not out, Dr. Greenidge fought back. His first quest for relief was a letter to his friend, John Dancy, recounting the events and charging the hospital with racial discrimination. Dancy sent a letter of inquiry and a copy of Dr. Greenidge's letter to Percival Dodge, at Detroit Community Union, the funding source.

Dodge wrote to Stearns, who asked Hood for the details. Her reply was clear; straightforward and devoid of any hint of embarrassment or guilt.

The Wright Man

> *Whenever a colored patient has made application for admittance, she has been informed that it will be necessary for her to enter under a white physician, usually our resident physician.*
>
> *In August, we notified a large number of Wayne County physicians that we would be glad to have them bring patients to our hospital. A very careful check was made that no colored physicians were in the list.*
>
> *Whenever a physician desires to make reservation for a patient and the supervisor of the hospital or the superintendent receives the call, it is understood, and has been has been the custom, that any physician not known is asked the question if he or his patient is colored and answered accordingly.*
>
> *Mrs. Matthews entered the hospital at 7:05 a.m. Her baby was delivered at 12:05. You note there were five hours for her to be removed from the hospital.*
>
> *Upon returning to my office, I called Mr. Norton and discussed the matter with him, being assured by him that, inasmuch as it is not the policy of the Home to permit colored physicians to bring in patients, I was told that I was justified in maintaining that policy and not to worry!*
>
> *I do not feel that it is in good taste to accuse Dr. Greenidge of trying to put something over, but I must confess that it is significant that he was too wise to call either the supervisor of nurses or the superintendent.*
>
> *To my knowledge, only the Woman's Hospital receives and permits colored physicians to bring in and attend patients, aside from the two hospitals for colored people—the Dunbar and the Mercy.*
>
> *Yours very truly,*
>
> *M. Louise Hood*
> *Superintendent*

Stearns sent Dodge a copy of Hood's letter, with this closing statement:

Miss Hood, in my opinion, explains the matter satisfactorily, and I trust that after reading her letter you will consider the matter closed.

Mr. Dodge passed the ball back to Dancy, whose letter had initiated the exchange, for final disposition:

Dear Mr. Dancy:

Enclosed is a letter from Mr. W.D. Stearns of the Florence Crittenton Home and a long explanation by Miss Hood. I am passing this correspondence on to you to take up with Dr. Greenidge, if you feel that advisable, or handle in anyway you see fit. My only hope is that you will be able to satisfy Dr. Greenidge so that he will still remain a friend of the Community Fund.

Yours very truly,

Percival Dodge
Assistant Secretary

The only one who showed any remorse was Supt. Hood who wondered how well she had served the hospital's interest during this racial crisis. She was congratulated on her performance as the hospital's enforcer of its racist policy. When reassured that she was "justified" and need not worry the matter, for her, was closed.

Whether Dancy transmitted the "Guardians of Status Quo" dismissal message to Dr. Greenidge or not, is unknown. I could not find that any of the other principals ever gave this matter a second thought. Even Mr. Dancy failed to mention this face-off in his book, *Sands Against the Wind*. On the other hand, it was one of Dr. Greenidge's most unforgettable and painful experiences and is recounted in many of his written speeches.

Since only Dancy expresses any sensitivity about Dr. Greenidge's mistreatment, the establishment left it up to him to apologize "only if you think it advisable."

Even to the end, Dodge reminded Dancy that he was in charge by issuing to him the final directive: "My only hope is that you will be able to satisfy Dr. Greenidge so that he will still remain a friend of the Common Fund!"

The Wright Man

Dodge's final statement in this incredible exchange is highlighted to signify its importance as a technique used by white supremacists to retain absolute control. They must induce losers to continue to play their game: because they are convinced that theirs "is the only game in town." The fact that this assignment was passed on to Dancy informed both Greenidge and Dancy that the matter was closed.

It is understandable that Dr. Greenidge was never the same following that traumatic episode. His enduring feeling of vulnerability never allowed him to confront, head-on, the European American establishment again. Instead, he picked his self-esteem up from the floor, dusted it off, checked himself in the mirror of public opinion and took off in another direction.

It was at this time that Dr. Greenidge's creative entrepreneurship was aroused, forcing him to concentrate on developing those latent resources already existing in the African American community. He wasted no time weeping about the past.

It was at this time that his community interests broadened and took on characteristics similar to those which had been manifested by Dr. Kellogg in Battle Creek, who showed a strong interest in helping people that extended well beyond the field of medicine.

After the embarrassment at the Crittenton Home, a different Robert emerged.

In June 1925, just four months after the Crittenton episode, Dr. Greenidge attended the first meeting that led to the establishment of Detroit Memorial Park Cemetery which is Michigan's oldest African American corporation. He went on to help create Great Lakes Mutual Insurance Company, Victory Loan Association and Home Federal Savings and Loan Association. The East Side Medical Laboratory at 4839 Beaubien was his own, private creation.

Like Detroit Memorial Park Association, Inc., Home Federal Savings and Loan Association still serves the community. The continuing success of these ventures is a tribute to a medical pioneer from Guyana who saw racism at its worse and dealt with it under his own terms.

Following Florence Crittenton's unchallenged ejection of Dr. Greenidge from its premises, it became abundantly clear that the African American physicians had no alternative but to meet this challenge themselves. Their most viable option was to try to improve the quality of care being provided at the 40-bed Dunbar Hospital.

Unfortunately, events at the hospital took a downward turn that eventually led to its transfer to a new site at Brush and Illinois streets and a name change to Parkside Hospital. It was their forlorn hope that a new name and a few cosmetic improvements in the hospital's amenities would bolster the public's sagging perspective of it.

Soon after it opened, Dunbar Hospital's administrators had entered into an agreement with the officials of Receiving Hospital to accept the city's overflow patients for hospital care at a per diem rate less than Receiving's—an arrangement that served the best interest of the hospitals, but not the patients.

"Insofar as I have been able to determine, stated Wright, only African American patients were transferred from Receiving's new, efficiently operated facilities to the understaffed Dunbar. There was no follow-up by the Receiving Hospital staff after patients were transferred to Dunbar. During my four years as a general practitioner, with Parkside as my main hospital, I don't recall that any patients were ever returned to Receiving Hospital because of deterioration in their conditions. Nor did I ever encounter a European American patient who was transferred from Receiving to Parkside."

The Wright Man

For a brief time, Dunbar/Parkside Hospital officials were reported to have convinced an accrediting agency that the hospital was qualified to train interns. Dr Joseph Dancy, John Dancy's brother, is said to have been its first intern. However, the accreditation of Parkside Hospital for internship training was never officially recognized.

The hospital remained a source of contention throughout the nearly forty years of its existence. Instead of being rebuilt for African American management, as proposed by one faction of the Medical Center Authority, it was torn down in 1962 to allow the Medical Center Authority to build Receiving Hospital, on that site as originally planned.

Thus, Dunbar/Parkside Hospital, Detroit's African American community's second venture into hospital administration, bowed out gracefully as did Mercy General.

By mid-century, the stubborn refusal of the medical establishment to abandon its policy of racial segregation caused many African American physicians to seek their own private solutions to this thorny hospital problem. They built and operated more small, private hospitals in Detroit, than elsewhere in the country.

The best remembered of these later institutions were: Bethesda and Edith K. Thomas Hospitals, at 535 E. Garfield and Haynes Memorial Hospital, at 73 Palmer; which were all owned by the Drs. Alfred Thomas, Sr. and his son, Alfred, Jr., Good Samaritan Hospital, by Dr. B. McKenzie; Fairview Sanitarium, by Drs. Greenidge, J.J. McClendon, and Rupert Markoe; Kirwood, by Dr. Guy Saulsberry; Mt. Lebanon, by Dr. C.W. Preston; Trinity Hospital, by Drs. Chester Ames, Harold Johnson, and Frank Raiford; Wayne Diagnostic (later Burton Mercy), by Dr. Dewitt Burton; and Boulevard General, which along with Burton Mercy, Delray and Trumbull General Hospital, formed Southwest Detroit Hospital.

In the 1930s, Dr. Robert Greenidge established the Eastside Medical Laboratory on Beaubien Street to serve as a training and service center for Black physicians. He would read and interpret X-rays and offer physicians advice for treatment. Dr. Wright frequently mentions that Dr. Greenidge always took time to speak with young physicians and provided assistance whenever possible. He enjoyed his many talks with Dr. Greenidge.

Greenidge summarized the purpose of the lab: "We opened the lab to provide a place for doctors to have tests performed on their patients and to do X-ray diagnosis as a specialist.[7]

Meanwhile, Blacks in Detroit grew less patient with their segregated city. Although they could sit in any seat on the bus, buy a meal almost anyplace and stay at hotels, Blacks were virtually very isolated from whites. This was particularly apparent in health services as they were denied admission to the city's leading hospitals. Charles and his fellow physicians saw the practice as an affront to the entire Black community and disrespect for their credentials. They fought exclusion, individually, and as a group.

In 1956, the Detroit Commission on Community Relations published a report outlining the segregation in health services. It stated that 103,742 of the 354,905 total patient admissions were in hospitals with a segregated bed policy.[8] Of the 160 Negro physicians in Detroit, only 25 were affiliated with so-called white hospitals. Charles and his partner William Bentley were exceptions as they had affiliations with Grace and Mt. Sinai hospitals. But for many of their Black colleagues, white hospital privileges were not yet available.

White owned Detroit hospitals were some of the finest institutions in the nation. Hospitals owned by Blacks did not have the facilities of the famous white hospitals such as Henry Ford, Harper, Detroit Receiving and Hutzel. William

The Wright Man

Beaumont, located in a suburb, was and is also a major hospital facility. Outstanding hospital facilities were made possible because of the wealth generated by the automobile industry and its workers. Unlike their Black counterparts, these facilities were in the position to take advantage of the efforts of state and federal grants to improve hospital services.

INTEGRATING DETROIT HOSPITALS

The refusal of Detroit's private hospitals to accept Black patients provided a symbol that some whites needed to feel superior. White immigrant workers who worked on the auto assembly line could get hurt or sick with no question about their admission to hospitals. This discriminatory practice was maintained officially by hospital administrators, and unofficially by the lower level staff (admission clerks and nurses). Admission clerks would routinely challenge Black patients and physicians at the hospital door or over the telephone. This form of institutional racism was applied to all Blacks, regardless of education or income. But as Reitzes found, Blacks resisted their exclusion from these facilities.[9]

Although Dr. Wright's patients had good jobs and were good citizens they could not even use the city's health facilities without being hassled. This became a critical problem as more and more Blacks streamed into the city. In the 1950s, their numbers increased 100% as Negroes began to move away from the Eastside and into other neighborhoods. Despite their takeovers of Detroit neighborhood blocks, middle class Blacks were still victims of the color line.

Charles Wright had to confront the institutional racism in white hospitals. He felt obligated to do so as a physician sworn to provide the best care for his patients, but also as a Black man, to whom it was a question of justice. On his rounds at white hospitals, Dr. Wright found empty beds after being told there were no vacancies. Charles Wright, the doctor, and Charles Wright, the Black man, could not stand by while Black patients were treated unfairly. Black patients' lives were as valuable as whites. Black infants were being denied the latest technology for pre- and post-natal care. Nurses and admission clerks would routinely turn Black patients away. Those who were admitted were segregated from white patients, just like in Mississippi. The only difference was that there were no Colored entrances or official Colored wards. When the room clerk denied admission to his patients because of "no beds," Dr. Wright would check for himself by making impromptu ward rounds with a nurse in tow and Dr. Wright states, "Usually I found an empty bed in a semi-private with a white patient in the other bed."[10]

He remembers several occasions when a Black patient was in the hallway outside the semi-private room with an empty bed. The nurse was asked to verify that she did have empty beds. Nurses would telephone ahead, to the other wards: "Dr. Wright is making rounds, today. If they could arrange a quick coffee break or some other reason for an immediate departure, they (nurses) would not be found on the ward."[11] For a young Black physician who grew up in Dothan, Montgomery and Nashville, these familiar Jim Crow practices made a mockery of everything he was taught in college and medical school. For a trained obstetrician such as Dr. Wright, these exclusionary practices were reprehensible and unacceptable.

White physicians were not sympathetic to the plight of their Black colleagues. Many supported the ban on Black admission to hospital staffs. Indeed, white physicians justified their actions by insisting that Black doctors were less well trained, less competent and less professional. Regardless of being board certified or having a reputation of being a first class physician, Black physicians were routinely denied privileges. Many, particularly those trained at Wayne State and Michigan State, watched less qualified white classmates get positions at local hospitals that were denied to them. This practice

The Wright Man

reinforced the idea that Blacks were receiving second-rate health care from professionals who were not respected by their white counterparts.

The struggle of Black physicians for recognition and hospital admitting privileges became a significant part of the overall fight for equal rights for Blacks in Detroit. Although physicians represented the backbone of bourgeoisie in the Black community and could afford the best of everything, they were routinely humiliated by the underlings of the medical establishment. A few Black physicians denied that these practices interfered with their work. Most were furious, but did not have the financial or political resources to challenge the status quo. Sociologists called this "status inconsistency."

In a small paper by Wright entitled, "The Progress of Negro Medical Specialists in Detroit," it was reported that there were fifty Black specialists in the city, in the 1960s.

Approximately one-third of these doctors were trained in those few Detroit area hospitals that offered residencies to them. Only one was trained in a private, general hospital! Opportunities for residencies in this area have been available to the Negro doctor in the City, County, Veterans, and Children's hospitals only. More recently, Providence and St. Joseph Hospitals have accepted Negroes in their residency programs. The majority of Negro specialists, therefore, were trained outside Detroit.[13]

The paper reported that doctors were leaving Detroit because of the lack of residency opportunities. Dr. Wright, as a member of the Detroit Medical Society (DMS), became involved in the struggle against hospital policies. In 1956, ninety-five of the 160 Negro Detroit physicians belonged to the AMA. However, most were active in National Medical Society and the DMS. Reitzes quoted an interview with a Black physician who criticized the Wayne County Medical Society (WCMS) as not doing enough to integrate the city hospitals.

He stated that in WCMS, "all business is conducted by the council and, lacking Negro delegates, questions of discriminatory policies and practices within the profession do not come up for discussions."[14]

The DMS, first called the Allied Medical Society, founded in 1919 by a group of seven Black physicians, served a variety of purposes for the Black physicians. Among them were social, clinical and political activities. DMS was also a philanthropic organization supporting many diverse Black causes. Primarily, it promoted the interests of its members, which were mainly issues of competence, ethics and networking in the field of medicine. There was a variety of elements that held the group together; school ties, fraternities and business partnerships.

The Detroit Medical Society, the NAACP, and the Urban League were all opposed to the discriminatory practices within hospitals. Along with Charles, some of the other prominent physicians in the fight were Lawrence Lackey, president of the Detroit Medical Society, Ethelene Crockett, Remus Robinson and D. T. Burton. Delegations were sent to Harper, Grace and Mt. Carmel Hospitals to protest the discriminatory policies. At the time Harper had one Black physician, Grace had six and Woman's (Hutzel) had seven. The delegation demanded hospital privileges and when they were denied, they sought explanations. This action constituted the doctors' version of sit-ins. However, some of the local hospitals remained adamant about denying them privileges.

The hospital segregation issue began to infiltrate municipal politics. In 1956, the Chicago City Council passed an ordinance prohibiting racial discrimination in Chicago hospitals. If Chicago, a city in the hands of the Irish political machine could pass such an ordinance, why couldn't Detroit? In 1957, Attorney William Patrick became the first Black person elected to the City Council. The City Council of Detroit was elected at-large, meaning that all candidates must run in all precincts, citywide. Patrick's victory was the culmination of massive efforts by the Cotillion Club, the NAACP, the UAW, Black labor leaders and local churches. The election of Patrick was a major political breakthrough in Detroit politics. Many Black physicians, through the Cotillion Club and Detroit Medical Society, took an active part in Patrick's campaign. This type of political involvement carried a long tradition in the Black health provider community, but the Patrick campaign was, in part, a recognition election for physicians.

Patrick proved to be a good ally for DMS. He introduced non-discriminatory ordinances before the City Council. His white colleagues, under pressure from the hospitals, refused to support the ordinances. A City Council refusal went against the grain of the changing national attitudes toward Black civil rights. Even President Dwight Eisenhower supported a mild civil rights bill. Anti-discrimination provisions for public accommodation were not to be included in a civil rights bill until the mid-sixties. Many whites felt that they should not have to share a hospital room with Blacks, and that Black physicians should not treat them. The hospitals had the support of the white community behind them.

In 1959, the National Medical Association met again in Detroit. The keynote speaker was Thurgood Marshall, the famed NAACP lawyer who had argued successfully the Brown v. Board of Education case (1954). Discrimination in public accommodations like hospitals was highlighted as a critical item on the civil rights agenda. The DMS membership, now 170 strong, began to arm themselves to change the status quo. Dr. Lackey outlined the goals of the DMS. They demanded: (1) Harper Hospital to admit at least a dozen Negro physicians to its staff; (2) Grace and Woman's hospitals to increase their Negro physicians to a more representative number; and (3) the city to assign officials to see that their recommendations were carried out.[15]

The big political breakthrough for Blacks came with the election of Jerome Cavanagh. In 1962, Cavanagh upset Mayor Louis Miriani, who had been backed by the UAW and most of the business community, and he became the youngest mayor in Detroit's history. The election of Cavanagh was a watermark in Detroit's political history. The fruition of years of coalition building among Blacks, the efforts of the Cotillion Club and liberal white leaders, and the Cavanagh victory was the undoing of the white conservatives on the City Council. Coming as it did after the 1960 Kennedy election, Blacks were included in the inner circles of city politics for the first time. The story of Cavanagh can be described as Detroit's Camelot.[16] Robert Conot described the new mayor as the "personification of the American success story: overalls to pinstripes in one generation."[17]

The Cotillion Club formed the Committee to End Discrimination in Detroit's Hospitals, and met with Dr. Joseph Molner, Detroit's Health Commissioner. The committee included Congressman Charles Diggs, Dr. Thomas Batchelor, Dr. Roland Chapman, Leonard Proctor, William T. Matney, Herman Glass, Cassius Pendleton, and Damon Keith. In the two hour session with Molner and his staff, the Black spokesmen tried to convince Molner of the existence of racism at the Herman Kiefer Hospital. Molner claimed that patients requested the ward's segregation. However, Molner pledged to stop the practice; although he did not. Black physicians Thomas Batchelor and Ethelene Crockett, who had been active in the Cavanagh campaign, elicited a promise from the new mayor to fire Dr. Molner. Dr. Molner was then called by Cavanagh and fired over the phone. With the support of the new administration, the struggle to fully integrate the hospitals took a new turn.

In 1963, Dr. Wright began to use the pen as a weapon against racism. Having learned the power of letter writing at Harlem Hospital, Charles wrote to U.S. Senators Phillip Hart

The Wright Man

and Patrick McNamara, complaining about the discriminatory practices at the city hospitals. He also wrote to Congressman John Dingell. Wright observed:

Certainly, there is no question that such an expansion is needed in our community. There is some room for doubt, however, if the total public will benefit from this large outlay of public funds.

. . .You should know already that for the past several years the local Negro doctors have fought hard for equal opportunity in the (medical development) corridor hospitals Grace, Harper and Woman's. The results have been only marginal, at best. Of these, Harper Hospital has remained the hardest core of unresponsiveness toward the acceptance of qualified Negro physicians (private correspondence).[18]

Woman's Hospital wanted to expand its facilities and needed federal funds to do so. The Hill-Burton Act prohibited discrimination in hospitals. Senator Hart announced the approval for a large grant for renovating the Hancock Street building of Woman's. Charles wrote the Senator that the money should be withheld because Woman's Hospital officials were in violation of Hill-Burton. In response, Senator Hart sent copies of Charles' letter to local hospitals and to Michigan state health officials. Mrs. John Failing, president of the Board of Trustees of Woman's, responded with a letter to Senator Hart. She denied that the hospital engaged in these practices. Charles recalled, "the challenge stirred up a firestorm but patient segregation ended, at Woman's Hospital, the day after Senator Hart's letter arrived.[19] The City Council had the authority to prohibit discrimination in hospitals in the city, but was reluctant to exercise it.

In the same year, Michigan Congressman John Dingell and Senator Jacob Javits introduced an amendment to the Hill-Burton Act eliminating the separate but equal provision in state laws. Although rejected by Congress, the federal court held that the separate-but-equal clause was unconstitutional. Confirmed by the U.S. Supreme Court in 1964, the legal foundation for hospital segregation was eliminated by the Department of Health, Education & Welfare regulations. In the same year the American Medical Association passed a resolution against racial segregation in hospitals.

These steps represented a major victory for Black physicians. Doors, which were once closed, now opened. Their patients were at last treated as first class citizens. Their white colleagues, although apprehensive, were forced to accept them as colleagues and competitors. Admission clerks and nurses were no longer gatekeepers for Black patients. Ironically, the integration of white hospitals led to the gradual demise of Black hospitals. Many Black physicians who had utilized Black institutions quickly switched their patients to white facilities. As a result, there were bitter feelings over this change within the Black medical community. It took years to heal this division in the DMS.

In 1963 Lawrence Lackey, president of the DMS, wrote an essay in the *Journal of the National Medical Association* praising the efforts of physicians in integrating the hospitals in Detroit. He noted that Black physicians had been active in civic affairs for years. Dr. J.J. McClendon had been president of the NAACP from 1937-1945. At that time 80% of NMA members were life members, and for years physicians had raised money for civil rights activities in the South. Black physicians had also run for public office, and had served, effectively, in them.[20]

With the hospital fight over, many physicians sent their patients to the best facilities available. Black hospitals began to lose their appeal for many patients. Detroit was slowly becoming a true marketplace for health care.

FREEDOM TO PRACTICE MEDICINE

In 1959, Dr. Wright and a fellow physician named William Bentley attended an OB-GYN convention in Boston. As they drove back to Detroit together, they ran into a snowstorm and had to stop in New Jersey at Charles' parent's new house in Teaneck, New Jersey. This delay allowed the two men to get to know each other. They discovered that they had similar problems in their practices. In 1960, the two men entered into a partnership. The Wright-Bentley partnership enabled both men to stabilize their practices financially and organizationally, and allowed them to pursue non-medical activities.

Medicine and OB-GYN were changing, as was Charles. In 1963, ultra-sound was invented, which made it possible to examine unborn babies. The drug DES (diethylstibestrol), once thought to be a cure-all for morning sickness, was declared a cancer risk by the Food and Drug Administration. Biomedical research, however, continued to create new technology and treatment strategies.

The Wright-Bentley office kept pace with these changes as they saw ever-increasing numbers of patients. Although Wright was busy with his own practice, he didn't hesitate to become more active in teaching medicine. In 1969, Charles became a clinical professor at Wayne State University School of Medicine. As a part-time teacher, Dr. Wright published eleven medical journal articles; he had always enjoyed writing.

Dr. Wright's involvement with academic medicine would lead him to another medical partner, Dr. N. S. Rangarajan, a South Asian, and graduate of India's University of Madras Medical School. Wright met Dr. Rangarajan, a resident at Highland Park General Hospital, before both became affiliated with Wayne State University. Rangarajan recalls that Charles intervened after one of the Highland Park staff physicians made a derogatory statement about Rangarajan. The young physician confronted the senior physician about the remark. Rangarajan probably would have been fired if Charles had not posted a note on all the bulletin boards noting the incident and admonishing people to treat others fairly. Charles was quite aware of the prejudice against foreign physicians as he had observed it at Harlem and at Cleveland. Rangarajan recalled "the white medical community had problems with anyone other than themselves."[21]

After his residency, Dr. Rangarajan became a faculty member at Wayne State University. Although being also voted the best teacher in OB-GYN, and voted medical director of the department, he discovered that he was being paid $8,000 less than his white subordinates. Again Dr. Wright intervened to help Dr. Rangarajan. This time it was a fight with Dr. Thomas Evans, the Chairman of OB-GYN at Wayne State. After being confronted with the discrepancy in pay, he indicated that Rangarajan, being Indian and foreign, did not deserve equal pay.

Dr. Wright offered Rangarajan medical partnership in 1972. Dr. Evans called Charles and informed him that he would not allow Rangarajan to work for him. When Dr. Wright prevailed, Evans tried to remove Rangarajan from the hospital's staff. Unable to carry out that threat, Dr. Evans removed Dr. Rangarajan from the medical school faculty. As a result, even when Dr. Rangarajan was in the hospital covering one of their private patients, he was not allowed to take care of other patients. On some occasions, the patients and residents were forced to await the arrival, from home, of the staff doctor. The Wright partnership carried the fight to Hutzel's board and the Medical School's faculty. The controversy continued from 1972 to 1982, when Evans was fired.

Dr. Rangarajan credits Dr. Wright with teaching him how to deal with patients. Whenever a patient complained about Rangarajan, Wright would bring the patient and the doctor to his office to discuss the matter. When older patients came to

Wright's office, he would see them but not charge for the visit. He also opened his office on Saturday for patients who came from out of town. So, Dr. Wright developed his practice largely through word-of-mouth. Former patients would recommend their family members to him. The more popular he was, the more his workload increased. "Charles was always a patient advocate. He influenced me by example." said Dr. Rangarajan. "He would say take good care of the patients and they will take care of you." Dr. Rangarajan characterized Dr. Wright "as a very serious person with grit."[22]

As we have seen, the segregation of white and Black physicians and hospitals in Detroit was almost absolute. Black and white physicians saw a few patients in common, but rarely worked together on medical teams. An admitting clerk could refuse a bed to Black patients with serious medical problems. White physicians supported these practices even though they knew Black facilities lacked the modem equipment some patients needed. The overthrow of this system was more than a triumph for a profession, but really a victory for all Black Detroiters. The end of segregated white hospitals became the deathblow for Black hospitals. It was a bittersweet victory.

The positive aspect of Black hospitals was that they were a source of pride for many users. Featured in Black newspapers and magazines as models of Black entrepreneurship, they were touted as a source of community pride. Detroit had enjoyed the reputation of having the best of such facilities. These institutions competed for the loyalty of the Black physicians. Doctors who ran these facilities were the superstars of the Black medical community.

In May of 1977, Dr Joshua Williams traced the history of Black hospitals in a speech delivered to National Medical Association. The speech ended with this statement:

> The perception of the depth and breath of the turn-about in opportunity for professional development of Black physicians may be warped by the vision of the one who

perceives. One who was here between 1936 and 1966 may be too close. One who has arrived since 1967 may be viewing from too far. Never-the-less, all can rejoice that the profession is alive and well and thriving in Detroit.

. . .the history of Black Medicine in Detroit is inseparably bound to the history of the Black Hospital. This is the historical fact of the 30 years between 1928 and 1958. It will never be true again.[23]

These Black hospitals were very important for Dr. Charles Wright. However, he realized that in the long run desegregated hospitals would be better for all patients. As the years went on, his passion for history and art grew more intense. As his medical practice and partnership became more secure, he wanted to travel and learn more about the world. He wanted to become more connected to the international community. Becoming a patron for African students allowed him to achieve this goal.

The Wright Man

Robert Isaac Greenidge, M.D.

CHAPTER SIX
AFRICA AND THE AFRICAN
MEDICAL EDUCATION FUND

During the late fifties and early sixties, Black physicians in Detroit were able to earn considerable sums of money. The Korean War had re-stimulated the expansion of the automobile industry, and Black assembly line workers were working a lot of overtime. In general, people could afford to see a doctor. Physicians, with their newly acquired disposable income, were able to reach out and give something back to their community. Many contributed to community churches, charities and Black colleges.

Dr. Wright supported philanthropic and humanitarian efforts in Detroit. Having grown up within the Baptist church, he felt obligated to help the unfortunates. Aside from contributing to the church, he could afford to contribute to the NAACP, the Alabama State Alumni Club, and his fraternity. For Black professionals, it was good public relations to contribute to local churches and organizations. Besides, most gifts were tax-deductible.

What distinguished Charles Wright from some of his physician cohorts was his willingness to go the extra mile and offer advice to many struggling Black organizations. Fascinated with new ideas, people and history, Wright read as much as he could about any cause that struck his fancy. He continued to read more history, particularly African history. As he read he became a Pan-Africanist, a person who believed that Black people everywhere should maintain their spiritual ties with the land of their ancestors. Although Detroit had a history of Pan-Africanism activism, the assertion of a linkage between the "dark" continent and Negroes was fraught with perils. Trying to make a psychological connection with Africa was replete with conflicting images. In 1963, Harold Issac tried to capture this conflict with his phrase "the hazy presence."[1] He observed, "Down through the generations Africa has persisted as a hazy presence in the universe of Negro Americans, an image now receding, now advancing, taking on different shapes, occupying different places in Negro mental landscapes."[2]

In European history, Africa was seen as "a savage, heathen land awaiting a tardy redemption on which even Negro slavery in America could be seen as a deposit."[3] The White man's burden was to Christianize and industrialize this lawless and primitive land. For Blacks of Charles Wright's generation, with little education about Africa and years of Tarzan movie, the image of the continent may have been that of "an ancestral land, dimly known, forgotten, denied, or thrust away both as a place and as a memory, dark, torrid, dangerous, a deeply unwanted piece of oneself."[4] The more Wright read, the less he believed these two images. He believed that Negro Americans needed more than a romantic and spiritual linkage to Africa, they needed to forge a new material linkage.

In the late fifties, colonialism in Africa was on the decline. After years of plundering the continent for its resources, European nations could not continue to finance their empires.

Having divided Africa into French and English-speaking nations, Europeans had installed their language, culture and surrogate leaders. But this did not pacify educated Africans who wanted independence. The leaders that British and French had hoped would rule under white tutelage turned against their mentors. Africans wanted freedom to rule themselves. This rejection of paternalism came as a shock to some whites and Blacks. Many Anglophile and Francophone Africans stayed in Europe or migrated to the United States. However, some returned to their native countries to lead the growing resistance to colonial rule.

In 1957, the Gold Coast (Ghana) became the first African nation to be granted independence. Dr. Kwame Nkrumah, a Black man educated at Lincoln University, a historically Black college in Pennsylvania, became president. Many prominent Black Americans attended the inaugural ceremonies. Dr. Martin Luther King, Jr. (fresh from the victory in the Montgomery Bus Boycott and now the de facto leader of American Blacks) and Vice President Richard Nixon, a man expected to run for president in the next election, were present. The two men were photographed together in *Jet,* a small magazine which reached the hands of most Black Americans. This event changed for American Blacks the image of their African brethren.

The rise of independent African nations gave new hope to Black intellectuals in America. African independence juxtaposed with the civil rights movement provided new aspirations to those who lived a life of the mind. How could the nation refuse to serve African diplomats at southern lunch counters? Would these Africans, with their diplomatic passports and immunity, be treated better than Black Americans? Was America ready to operate in a world of color? These social contradictions were repeatedly discussed in the Black press, pulpits and barbershops.

Nkrumah, was aware of the power of the Black community. Lincoln University, an all-male college, had provided him with rich contacts with the Black middle class. He knew their capabilities and vulnerabilities. He had lived among professional Blacks and had invited them to help build Ghana into a modern nation. Many, including Dr. W.E.B. DuBois a leading Pan-Africanist, historian, and the former editor of the *Crisis,* the media organ of the NAACP, took him up on the offer. Others followed and new linkages were established.

The reborn nations of the continent had nation-building agendas. Black Americans were now a welcome part of the Diaspora and rejoiced in seeing African diplomats and

The Wright Man

presidents. On television they saw African cities, faces like theirs, and the sheer beauty of the land. Africa was not the jungle continent of Tarzan, whites on safaris, and wild animals that they had seen depicted in the media.

Most young African leaders wanted to quickly rid the continent of all symbols of colonialism and get on with industrialization. "Modernization" became the code word of the time. They wanted to build their own factories and organize their own trade markets. No one knew at the time how difficult this would be. Everyone assumed that these new nations would modernize quickly. There was every reason to believe that Africans would create these modern states themselves.

Africa had mineral and oil resources with which to take a great leap forward, economically. But it was also a continent in need of capital and skilled manpower for development. Independence created as many problems as it solved. No one anticipated the elevated expectations that accompany independence. The people became more aware of their ethnic differences and of their poverty. Old ethnic rivalries emerged and the national boundaries that had been drawn by Europeans for administrative purposes now became permanent ones. Religious and ethnic groups, called tribes by the Europeans, had been incorporated in these boundaries. These boundary lines masked lingering divisions and conflicts within these new nations.

When the colonials left, they took everything with them that was not nailed down. The new Black leaders had the trappings of power, but few resources with which to govern. Wright and his peers knew that these new nations were in desperate need of health providers. The Europeans had left them with few health professionals and rather primitive hospital facilities. Hospitals in Africa were not equal to Black hospitals in the United States. Modernizing these facilities was beyond the resources of the newly formed governments.

Dr. Wright, along with other physicians, had sent books to African medical schools. No one thought that this was enough and Charles wanted to do something about the need for physicians. He decided that raising money for African students to attend medical school in the United States would be a vehicle that could increase the number and quality of medical providers. It was a novel idea that could demonstrate Detroit's commitment to the medical education of Africans.

THE AFRICAN MEDICAL EDUCATION FUND

Charles Wright and his colleagues knew that there were very few medical doctors of African descent being trained in African medical schools. Africans were dispersed among American and European universities, but few were returning home. In the nations themselves, health care was not high on the government agenda. The new leaders were too busy trying to prevent internecine warfare, encourage new investors, establish embassies, and solve immediate economic problems to devote their resources to train more physicians.

Dr. Wright also knew that the medical schools in African universities lacked access to modern medical techniques and research, particularly that which was published in the United States. In America, new techniques were being tested, new drugs created, new medical care equipment being invented. African universities were simply unable to cope with the American advances in medicine and train high quality physicians.

In 1960, Dr. Wright learned of the plight of Mr. Sam Soremekum, a Nigerian enrolled at the University of Toronto, who had run out of money to continue his education. Wright mobilized his colleagues to raise the necessary funds. This was a dramatic case, which made Charles aware of the need for a permanent fund to assist African medical students.

The fund, as Dr. Wright conceptualized it, would assist with tuition cost and other expenses. Having worked his way through medical school, he knew firsthand what not having money was like. Many Detroit physicians had similar stories of working their way through medical school. Wright felt that they would be empathetic with the plight of African students. Since the Africans would be returning to their native countries, they could not be considered potential competitors. So, Dr. Wright began promoting his ideas with colleagues and members of the Detroit Medical Society. The concern about potential competition was reflected in a purpose statement reiterated in the brochure of the new organization.

"The purpose of the organization is to assist in the training of doctors who will practice medicine in Africa. Anyone who has been accepted by an A-Class medical school, and who is in need of financial assistance, is eligible if he agrees to practice on the continent of Africa immediately after his formal training is ended."[5]

There was no strong opposition to the idea and his colleagues were quite willing to allow Wright to take the lead in organizing the effort. His first task was to create a new organization. The second was to draw up guidelines. Dr. Wright crafted a mission statement consistent with the reservation of his colleagues. In 1961, the African Medical Education Fund, with the support of the DMS, was created. The policy statement summarized the purpose of the African Medical Education Fund (AMEF). The following emerged:

The symbolic value of establishing tangible ties lies with our heritage and roots. There is a staggering shortage of opportunities for medical education in Africa. This situation is improving but there are at least 20 African countries without a medical school. Some African recipients of AMEF support will undoubtedly be influential leaders in their countries and will serve as goodwill ambassadors for the U.S. in general and the Black community in particular.

The citizens of Detroit are quite capable of supporting both purposes independently, particularly since our level of support, though deeply meaningful to those that receive it, is a mere token with respect concerning the needs of both groups of students.[6]

The Board of Directors of the Detroit Medical Society thought it necessary to issue this policy statement after being criticized for not supporting Black American medical students. It was only partially successful. Wright met with his critics and took the position that this was not to be seen as a competitive situation, but that he was supporting both groups. He offered to match any contribution any of his colleagues was ready to make toward Black American medical scholarship aid, then and there. He placed his checkbook on the table. There were no takers.

Dr. Wright was elected the first president of the AMEF, and he was left with much of the planning for the new organization. Other physicians served on the board of directors. They were Charles Whitten, Ethelene Crockett, Robyn Arrington, Horace Bradfield, Welford Hill, Clarence Green, and Nimrod Sherman. The other board members were Mrs. Lorraine Aldridge, Mrs. Louise N. Cobb, Mrs. Margaret Dudley, Mrs. Jeanette Hill, Mrs. Norma Hill, Miss Evelyn Sublett, Dr. Juanita Collier, Congressman Charles Diggs, Philip Lenud, Mrs. Lionel Swan, Mrs. Malcolm West, and Louis Morgan. The committee supporting the board consisted of two co-chairmen and more than twenty members. The women in this group consisted mainly of the wives of physicians and other prominent Black professionals. Over the seventeen years of AMEF's existence, it raised nearly $100,000. Thanks to Dr. Charles Whitten's judicious management of funds and applications, the organization supported over 50 students from 15 countries, over its years of existence. These students attended medical schools around the nation and including Canada. (See Appendix for a partial listing of students, their schools and their country of origin.)

The Wright Man

THE AMEF AND BLACK DETROIT PHILANTHROPY

The AMEF put Black Detroit physicians in the spotlight. Their deeds were covered in Black newspapers and were highly regarded by the National Medical Association. AMEF trustees were able to solicit donations across the physician community. The new organization was a perfect vehicle for giving. Although most of the students attended medical school in the United States, African students around the world discovered the name of Detroit. Although the money provided did not cover the total expense of medical school, it added enough so that many were able to remain in school and become physicians.

If Charles Wright had believed Sociologist Prof. E. Franklin Frazier's characterization of the Black middle class in *Black Bourgeoisie,* he would never have attempted to mobilize local Black physicians for this cause. Frazier painted this unflattering picture of Detroit's Black doctors:

As a consequence of the prestige of "society," many Negro professional men and women take more seriously their recreation than their professions. This was an extreme expression of the relative value of professional work and recreation among the Black bourgeoisie. . . .[7]

Dr. Wright did not share Frazier's assessment of professional life in the Black Detroit. He believed that he could persuade professionals to contribute to a good cause. The cause had to be sound and presented in the right way. Charles knew that the stories of financially troubled African medical students would move his colleagues.

Charles also was acquainted with the type of Detroit physician Frazier lampooned, as having installed a "Hammond organ on his luxurious yacht." Charles' task was to reach the physician with the yacht, as well as the one with the social consciousness. Designing a strategy for reaching these individuals was difficult. He had to steer around those who claimed that such an organization should help Black American students first. There were also those who claimed that Dr. Wright was simply making a name for himself. Wright also had to deal with those who were reluctant to take on a new charity.

Although Charles Wright was one of the few board certified Black physicians in the city, he was not at the apex of the social structure for Black Detroit physicians. He and his wife, Louise, were not among the movers and shakers in Detroit "society." Social pyramiding was an art form. Dr. Wright made this discovery at Meharry and at Harlem Hospital. Social status and background were used to determine who got residency training in surgery and other consequent privileges. Students with a physician parent fared better than those from more humble backgrounds. Some of these distinctions continued into establishing practice.

In Detroit, physicians made good and considerable disposal income. They had little competition in the social structure from other Black professional workers. Of course, Black ministers were better known, but they couldn't match the physician's income. The lawyers and teachers, also, were never rivals in social standing. Ironically, the fact that Charles posed no threat to those who were at the top of the Black social pyramid facilitated his fundraising efforts. If Charles' efforts had been as a young physician in search of prestige within the complex social structure, he may have met with more resistance. Yet a gimmick was needed to persuade physicians to give to a cause they had agreed was a worthy one.

With the assistance of the Cotillion Club, the principal organization of Detroit's socialites and professional class, and through his network of practicing physicians, Charles was able to forge a campaign to raise funds for the AMEF. One of his big fund-raisers was an annual banquet in which contributors would be honored.

This tactic was a time-honored method of fund-raising in the Black community. These banquets, held on Thanksgiving Eve, were gala events that featured the leading physicians and other professionals in formal attire. Mrs. Margaret Dudley was chairwoman of the "show." The "show" was the centerpiece of the affair. Featured were well-known Black professionals acting as guest entertainers, as well as fashion models. The draw was to see a prominent person such as a doctor or judge "doing something you didn't know he or she could do." Doctors and lawyers would tap dance and tell jokes.

One show was called "Here Come de Judge" after the famous scene with Sammy Davis Jr. as "de Judge," on the television's "Laugh-In" program. Michael Ward was the Judge and Lionel Swain was the bailiff. Prominent Blacks such as Dr. Charles Vincent and Rev. Nicholas Hood, a minister and City Councilman, served as masters of ceremony for these events. Nicholas Jr's. "Jazz band," the Seven Sounds also performed at these "shows." Besides, Chairwoman Mrs. Dudley played a critical role in the organization and performance of these shows. Physicians' wives organized a chorus line. They would kick up their heels; it was a fun time. The city knew the event quite well. It was always a sellout. AMEF received national publicity from these galas. Reported as a humanitarian effort on the part of city physicians, it also demonstrated the success of these individuals. The initial success of AMEF gave its supporters national visibility. The rise and fall of AMEF reflected the Black bourgeoisie's strengths and weaknesses.

Three factors lead to the demise of the AMEF. African students who came to United States liked it and stayed. This gave support to those in DMS who wanted the money to go to American Blacks. Secondly, the organization lost its leading fundraisers. Third, AMEF could not raise enough money to continue supporting students. Charles Wright had sought to help Africans, but was receiving a first-hand education in the art of fund-raising. From these efforts he established a list of donors and moved freely within the various overlapping social circles of the Black professional class. Members of those circles in turn got to know Charles and Louise better. But Charles never intended to become invested in the social circles of the city. He was always trying to come up with a new project. He had, in fact, raised some money by writing a play.

In the 1960s, Charles wrote a musical drama entitled, *Were You There?* based on the Negro spiritual. The cast included a choir, a dance company and seven actors. The drama was produced on the stage of Detroit Institute of Art's (DIA) main auditorium on Easter in 1964 to a full house. The proceeds were used to support the African Medical Education Fund. In 1966, it was performed again. Twice more in 1966, the drama was performed at MacKenzie High School and at Grosse Pointe Memorial High School's Fries Auditorium. The AMEF, however, quietly ended.

A VISIT TO THE LAND OF HIS ANCESTRY

In January 1964, a Dr. Ray Primus called Charles and introduced himself as a dentist from Pittsburgh. Dr. Primus had heard about the African Medical Education Fund and was impressed with the efforts of the Detroit group of doctors. He asked if Charles would like to visit and work with him in Africa. Dr. Primus wanted Wright to help him set up health clinics in the "bush" as a part of the United States Aid for International Development (U.S.A.I.D.) program for Africa. The plan called for securing the State Department's support for travel to make a survey of Nigeria, Liberia and Sierra Leone. Dr. Wright was intrigued by the idea. The proposal contained all the drama, the adventure, and seriousness of purpose that drove Wright's career.

Pan-Africanism for intellectuals like Dr. Wright was now possible. Yet, they wanted to visit Africa, not live in Africa. The fruits of the first Pan-Africanist conferences dated back to the early part of the 20th century, involving Black Americans and anti-colonist African leaders, and were now ready for harvesting. Wright could visualize the new adventure as he listened to Dr. Primus. He discussed the idea with Louise and his medical partner, Dr. William Bentley. He wasn't asking their permission, but needed to be convinced by them that it was the right thing to do. He saw nothing odd about a physician leaving his practice to do volunteer work in an African clinic.

The Primus group proposal was sent to the State Department at a time when the nation was in the middle of a Cold War. The State Department and the Johnson Administration were eager to be seen as friends of Africa. The proposal was funded and all the travel permissions were granted. Wright met Dr. Primus for the first time in the Kennedy International Airport in New York for his first trip to Africa. The group consisting of Wright, Primus and other health care workers, boarded an airplane en route to Africa. They were scheduled to work in Nigeria, Liberia, and Sierra Leone.

These three nations were very different than Charles had imagined. Liberia, considered by many as an American colony, had been ruled for decades by the descendants of freed American slaves. Established in 1822 by the American Colonization Society as a social experiment, the nation became an independent republic in 1847. However, the social experiment failed, as few slave owners cooperated with the project. The few who arrived were repatriated but were never integrated with the indigenous ethnic groups, the Mandigo, Vai, Gola, Kwepsi, Kru and Greboes peoples. They remained Americo-Liberians, proud of their American roots and their social status. Liberia became an American protectorate in 1909. During this time the Firestone Company, was granted a 99 year lease of 1 million acres of land on which to grow rubber plants. The company became the largest employer, with 35,000 workers.

William Tubman, an Americo-Liberian and leader of the True Whig Party, became president in 1944. When Charles arrived, it was a nation of 2,500,000 people. Monrovia was a city of 41,391 people with the bulk of the population residing in the country's rural villages. The nation had a total of 23 small hospitals, 106 clinics and 1,200 beds. There were only 82 doctors for over two million people. In the villages, traditional medicine was still being practiced. Leprosy, a disfiguring disease, was prevalent. There were 8 Leprosaria in the nation.

Although Firestone made huge profits from the rubber plantations, Liberia was one of the poorest in Sub Sahara Africa. When Charles Wright and Ray Primus landed at the James Sriggs Payne Airfield, they were attached to the Peace Corps. The two Americans were confronted by the economic contradictions of this former American colony. The nation's association with the U.S. had given them no special advantages over their African counterparts who had been colonized by British and French. Christian missionaries had worked to make Liberia a Christian nation, but the indigenous population, half of whom were Animist, remained unconvinced.

Nigeria, a former British colony and the largest of the west coast African nations, was granted independence in 1960. This country underwent a different, more interesting history. The English version of the social experiment was to institute "indirect rule" through the country's traditional leaders. In other words, the English attempted to train and use tribal chiefs as government administrators. This social experiment also failed, as the land of the Yoruba (9,500,000), Ibo (600,000) and Hausa (9,500,000) formally became the nation of Nigeria.[8] Although most of the nation's inhabitants were now Christian, the North was still governed by traditional Muslim religious leaders called Emirs. While still under British rule, Dr. Benjamin Nnamdi Azikiwe, an Ibo, was appointed the first Black Governor General. Like Ghana's Nkrumah, he was educated in America and had also attended Lincoln University. A journalist and publisher of the *West African Pilot,* he entered

The Wright Man

politics as the leader of Nigeria's National Council and as a legislator. When Nigeria became a Republic in 1963, Azikiwe was elected president.

Nigeria, a nation divided into three major regions with a population of 35,105,800, was a relatively affluent nation compared to other West African nations. It produced most of the world's peanuts or ground nuts, something Dr. Wright could relate to as a son of Dothan. The country also produced palm kernels and cocoa. The nation had 188 hospitals and 13,000 beds. The country had 819 physicians and 479 maternity centers. Drs. Wright and Primus worked in one of the six rural health centers. They formed a team with workers from U.S.A.I.D. The two men then divided the territory, with Primus going north to survey the Housas in Kaduna, while Wright went east to Enugu to survey the Ibos.

Sierra Leone, independent since 1961, was a nation with 210 miles of coastline. Its economy was based on mining. Extracted from its rich earth were diamonds, iron, chrome, ore and platinum. Cocoa was also a major export product. Rice was grown for subsistence purposes. When Dr. Wright arrived at Freetown, a city of 88,000 people, the nation was governed by prime minister and president, Sir Milton Morgai, the leader of the Sierra Leone Peoples Party. The other major political party, the Peoples National Party was led by Albert Margai. The two major ethnic groups were the Mende and the Temnes. Dr. Wright discovered that the major health problems of the nation were malaria, venereal disease, ascariasis, dysentery, colitis, sleeping sickness and smallpox. To treat these diseases were 23 government hospitals (1,336 beds), 6 mission hospitals and 2 military hospitals.[9] The number of physicians was woefully inadequate.

In Sierra Leone, Wright and Primus worked with Operations Crossroads Africa and the U.S. Department of Public Health. They were assigned the responsibility of mobilizing a new dental and medical clinic that the U.S. had purchased a month previous. The equipment was in storage in Freetown. "When I asked why the clinic was activated at that time, I learned that the Red Chinese had recently replaced the Taiwanese and opened their own embassy in Freetown. Officers in the U.S. State Department decided to take the clinic out of mothballs and put it on the street to upstage the Communists. I had assumed that my role was to serve the best interest of the indigenous people of Africa, not as a pawn in the cold war."[10]

Wright arrived at a relatively tranquil time for all three governments. However, the seeds of discontent had been planted. The rivalry among leaders became more apparent in the post-colonial period. Tribalism surfaced once the British lost political control. Small military units, trained by Europeans, emerged later as a real force in African politics. Of the nations where Wright worked, only the Liberian government would survive the decade of the sixties. Wright may have been curious about local politics, but his trip was only designed to provide medical services.

There was so much history in these nations, and so little time to learn about them. Wright and his colleagues would arrive at the capitals, pack their Land Rover with canned goods and staples, and drive into the "bush" to organize a medical and dental clinic. The African bush was nothing like Wright had imagined or had seen in the movies. The climate was hot and biting insects were everywhere. Wild plants, birds and animals added the right exotic touch to the setting, but the terrain was very rough with few roads. The "deeply rutted" roads reminded him of his childhood, but somehow the sun seemed much hotter than it ever was in Dothan.

On several occasions the clinic staff would have to go to work by a small airplane. The landings and takeoffs were events in themselves. Wright recalled one landing on a "postage stamp" sized field in Liberia. It was obvious that the pilot struggled to land the small single-engine plane. The passenger, Dr. Wright, had the feeling a crash was eminent. They usually

The Wright Man

landed safely but the worst part was yet to come. Once on the ground again they had somehow to take off. Charles Wright acquired a new respect for these courageous, bush pilots who loved the challenge of flying under adverse conditions. Every landing seemed to be the last.

The townspeople welcomed the doctors. Dr. Wright could see in their faces kinship with Blacks in Dothan. It dawned upon him that Africa was the home of his ancestors but it was another country. These were Third World nations with living conditions below those of rural Black Americans.

At these clinic sites, Wright and his colleagues found all types of ailments and health problems that would require an abundant supply of medicine and good surgical techniques. They had to treat them with simple medicine and techniques. At 46, Wright was used to hard work, but not under such primitive conditions. Some patients had diseases that Wright had only read about in books on tropical medicine. Many of them had ailments that had progressed far.

VILLAGE MUSEUMS

As they traveled, Wright put on his amateur anthropologist hat. He wanted to see artifacts, listen to stories, and record their histories with his tape recorder. The Europeans had changed the landscape and introduced new ways, but the culture of the people and their folkways resisted the lure of modernization. In several of the small towns, residents had created small folk museums. Their collections were often meager but were very precious to them. The artifacts in the museums told their history and culture. These objects connected the villagers to their past and were there as a heritage for their children to view.

Their purpose for the village museum was to preserve the culture and to refute the notion that they had accomplished nothing before the British came. On several occasions, the people would summon the Griot (village historian) to tell the story of their nation's accomplishments. Wright noticed that despite the poverty, illiteracy, and in many instances poor health, they did not appear to feel inferior to any culture. In a 1962 article describing the meaning of traditional culture and its relationship to the new political society, Joseph Ki-Zerbo stated it well:

> To be sure, a civilization is not a museum; it is a living organism—like a tree, which harbors positive and negative elements, young shoots and dead branches, blossoms and fruit. It is the role of the political and cultural leaders to make this new tree of African culture, of African personality, to grow straight, by pruning the deadwood and the new shoots also.[11]

Wright was learning a very important lesson, which would shape his life for the next twenty-five years: African people must preserve their own history and narratives, otherwise they will be forgotten and undervalued or worse, distorted, to their disadvantage. African people retained an ancient history and culture, dating back to long before being colonized by Europeans. There are important lessons to be learned from the past, which can guide the thinking for the present. A man can be rich in spirit if he retains the cultural treasuries of the contributions of his kinfolk and neighbors. Charles Wright left the village with a new respect for Africans of all classes. He had come to help them, see and touch them, but he left with a different impression of himself.[12]

Dr. Wright realized that people of African descent in Dothan, Montgomery, Nashville, Harlem, Cleveland and Detroit were not preserving their history or their culture. Many were busy denying their history. The stories of Blacks in these cities had yet to be written. He realized that it is not the job of white intellectuals to record this history, but it is for Blacks themselves to record it. He felt he had to become a historian.

The Wright Man

THE FIRST TRIP TO EUROPE

As Charles Wright left Africa, he thought about the people in the village clinics he visited and how each village housed its own little museum. En route to the United States, Wright stopped to visit friends in Paris. This was his first trip to Europe. The Left Bank of Paris had been the home of many Black American ex-patriots. Black artists, political activists, and playwrights went to Paris to escape the racism of America. Paris was a truly international city and very capable of living up to his tourist image. Wright felt welcome. . . Wright compared Paris to New York, two different cities. The French were more open. Even in their African colonies they had sought to build cosmopolitan relationships. All Black Americans had been told of Paris, heard of Josephine Baker, and had read about the good treatment by French of Black soldiers. This Paris was good place to visit after working hard in the African bush.

Dr. Primus suggested that they visit his friend in Denmark, Dr. Eigle Moerk, a Danish dentist. Primus thought that Moerk had some international connections that could be useful in recruiting physicians and dentists for the African clinics. Moerk had worked in the Danish Underground during the War, and had fought against the Germans. When they arrived in Denmark, Dr. Moerk suggested that they go back to Copenhagen, so his mother could show them the Freedom Museum. The museum was dedicated to the role of the Underground in the War. It contained documents, testimonies and artifacts of W.W.II.

The founders of the museum had mounted a national campaign in Denmark and had collected memorabilia and artifacts related to the underground struggle against the Nazis' attempt to destroy Jewish citizens. At the end of the war, the Danes launched both a national campaign to gather evidence of their heroic efforts, and a corresponding national fund-raising campaign. A large number of Danes were involved and they were eager to contribute. They gathered printing presses, tattered and bloodied clothes, documents about the captures and killing of the Jews, photographs, etc. The exhibits were arranged chronologically so that a visitor could walk through the museum and relive the "chilling terror of the time."[13] Mrs. Moerk provided them with a written account of the events that led to the creation of the museum.

The museum commemorated the role of the Danes in the War. They sought to help the Jews by protecting them against the Nazis. Everything the Jews were ordered to do, the ordinary Danes would do as well. When the Jews were told to wear yellow armbands, the Danes did also. The first person to initiate this action had been the King of Denmark. Consequently, the Germans experienced great difficulty in separating and identifying the Jews. The Nazis were outwitted and many Jewish families were saved. The museum was a testimony to the heroism of the Danish people. Wright and Primus were overwhelmed with this powerful representation of the Danish people. Wright stopped thinking of museums as large warehouses glorifying the golden age of European civilization. A museum could be used for a variety of purposes, including socializing, he found.

Theodore Low commented on the idea of a museum as a social instrument as early as 1942:

> No one can deny that museums have powers which are of the utmost importance in any war of ideologies. They have the power to make people see the truth, the power to make people recognize the importance of the individual as a member of society, and, of equal importance in combating subversive inroads, the power to keep minds happy and healthy. They have, in short, propaganda powers which should be far more effective in their truth and eternal character than those of the Axis which are based on falsehoods and half-truths.[13]

Wright could see the power of the museum. The German six-year occupation of Denmark represented only a short time in the life of the Danes, but the facility had made Danish

The Wright Man

history stand still. The role of the Danes in the great war would not go unnoticed. It was their history as told in their arrangement of events, artifacts and captions.

Wright thought about the potential of more than 200 years of occupation of Blacks in America, a racist society. The information the first generation of ex-slaves wanted to forget, the third and fourth generations should remember and organize in a coherent fashion. Young Blacks must never forget why they were brought to America and why they have been discriminated against. The task was to teach the new generation about their heritage. A museum could also correct misinformation about the origins of Blacks and their role in the making of America.

The following year(1965), Charles returned to Africa for another State Department sponsored survey. This time he visited Dahomey, now renamed Benin. It was in Dahomey that Wright encountered African royalty. The chiefs wore flowing robes and were followed by an entourage, one member of which had the job of holding a small umbrella over their heads. Dr. Wright thought that the "homage paid by the people was genuine." In Dahomey, he also visited a village museum. Each time he saw a museum, the more impressed he was, and the more convinced that "this was the way to go."

As we have seen, becoming a patron to African medical students served to get Dr. Wright's thoughts away from his practice and the city of Detroit. It also provided training in fundraising that he would use later in his other projects. His efforts also brought him his first national publicity. He enjoyed the exhilaration of success but was still restless.

Although his trip to Africa had served a political purpose, Wright ignored most of the internal politics of the nations visited. He saw beauty in the common people. The idea for a Detroit museum was planted by the small villages. Europe museums also provided him with ideas for organizing exhibits.

He was forty-six years old before the idea of a museum for Detroit occurred to him.

Meanwhile, the nation was at the dawn of a profound change in the legal basis of separation of the races. The turmoil of the old South took Charles Wright back home again. Young civil rights revolutionaries challenged white leadership throughout the region and captured the minds of the nation. And Charles Wright, a fellow Southerner, would play a role in the revolution.

Physician founders of Dunbar Hospital, 1922
(From left; first row) Drs. Joseph Wills, James Ames, James Young, Parker Gamble, George Bundy, and Albert Cleage
(center row) Drs. Lloyd Bailer, Edward Carter, Robert I. Greenidge
(top row) Drs. John Miller, Charles Greene, Leo Welker, Frank Raiford, Emmett Morton, Herbert Sims

The Wright Man

Charles Wright once remarked that "I never forgot the blatant racism of my Alabama origins nor was I lulled into complacency with its more subtle manifestations in the North. Thus, the Civil Rights Movement, even before it had the name, was always Civil Rights." The nascent civil rights movement in the South stirred negative memories in Charles' mind. Throughout his life he experienced indignities and disrespect from whites. He had been forced to attend segregated schools and to practice medicine outside the mainstream.

The fight to desegregate Detroit hospitals for Black doctors had mobilized Wright and his Detroit Medical Society (DMS) colleagues, but no one expected physicians to fight discrimination for the rest of Detroit. This task was primarily the job of the clergy, Black labor leaders, and the local NAACP. The latter was one of the largest and strongest of the nation's local chapters, and was an important fund-raising unit of the national office.

During the sixties, Dr. James McClendon was president of the Detroit Chapter of the NAACP. Under his leadership, physicians were very active in local affairs, and the civil rights organization, along with the Cotillion Club, had worked with the DMS to put pressure on hospitals to end discrimination. Charles had given the annual obligatory $100 contribution long before the famous Detroit NAACP Freedom Fund Dinner was launched in 1956. But, he never served on the board or played a role beyond that of a contributing member. He, like most of his professional friends, regularly attended the popular annual dinner.

119

The NAACP annual dinner provided some of the money needed to cover the legal expenses of jailed civil rights fighters who violated segregation laws in the South. They went to jail to test the constitutionality of the laws. This tactic was called the legalistic approach to ending Jim Crow. As the movement progressed, the NAACP strategy was replaced by a grassroots participatory and confrontational method. The so-called civil rights fighters, with their more dangerous and in your face style, transformed the civil rights struggle in the South to a more activist, confrontation struggle.

For some, the success of the Montgomery Bus Boycott was a turning point in the movement because it demonstrated the saliency of the new approach. The struggles in Birmingham, Alabama and Albany, Georgia also followed the new confrontational approach, which was part religious and part secular. People were asked to bear witness by marching in a non-violent manner throughout the South. Dr. King, the leader of the Montgomery Bus Boycott had been arrested several times. Leaders in other cities followed his example of aggressive leadership.

Wright followed these changes daily by reading the papers, consulting friends, and interviewing returning civil rights fighters—he kept himself reasonably well informed about the events in the South. As a Southerner, he appreciated the work of President Johnson, who had lobbied Congress and had signed the 1964 Civil Rights Bill into law. Now, Charles Wright could theoretically drive to Selma and stay in a hotel, eat in a public restaurant and use the restrooms along the route. Yet, Wright and others knew that this was not enough. Political rights, such as voting and holding elective office were still denied to southern Blacks. But, even Wright could not have predicted that this fight would come so close to his hometown of Dothan, and to Montgomery, where he was educated. It never occurred to him that he would "bear witness" to the injustices of a segregated society in Selma, Alabama.

Selma was a small town much like Dothan. But it differed greatly from Dothan in terms of its history. Selma had a rather interesting antebellum tradition. Located on the Alabama River, Selma was once a major port for the Confederate Navy during the Civil War and for years harbored large plantations. As the center of Dallas County, fifty miles from Montgomery, Selma never had a chance to develop because of its reactionary leadership. The most impressive structure in the town was the Edmund Pettus Bridge, which spanned the Alabama River.

Charles Wright had known students from Selma at Alabama State. They were small town boys and girls on their way out of Selma. A few had attended Selma University before enrolling at Alabama State. Selma University was a teacher's college and divinity school for Blacks. Established in 1878, by the Alabama Baptist Colored Convention, it trained many Black rural ministers and schoolteachers for Alabama's dual school system. Like Wright, many students who left did not return to their rural hometowns after college.

Selma had a reputation as a racist city, but was no different from many other rural towns in Alabama and Mississippi. Whites saw it as a thriving riverboat town. One could go all the way, on a boat, to the Gulf of Mexico from downtown Selma. People fished, picked pecans and farmed for a living. The other source of income was Craig Air Force Base, a training base for pilots. Blacks had lived in the town for generations, but were not allowed to share political power. Most were denied the right to vote. Voter registration procedures were designed to keep Blacks off the voting rolls, but racial violence was the chief method of preventing Blacks from becoming politically involved in their town. Like Dothan, the town exported its sons and daughters primarily to Chicago, Cleveland and Detroit.

No one would have imagined that this little hamlet, a river town known as the last gas stop on the U.S. 80, before Mississippi, would become a landmark in civil rights history.

Selma had become a metaphor for all southern towns. A sleepy rural town with a 28,385 population, a small town white elite and a large working class of Blacks and whites had become a focus point of the civil rights movement. Townspeople of both races must have been puzzled as to why their little town was selected. Many whites had always had cordial relations with the "coloreds," but many also confessed that they were confused by the civil rights movement and did not know what the "coloreds" wanted.

SELMA ON MIDDLE CLASS BLACKS' MINDS

In Detroit's Black community one could knock on any door in the block and find someone who had relatives or knew someone from Selma. All southern states had their Selma. Nestled in these little villages were the original genealogies of Black Detroit. Selma is a metaphor for the Delta Diaspora for many Black Detroiters. The old folks remembered its humid summers, cotton picking and the perils of sharecropping. Southern folkways were not distant memories in the minds of the old folk. They could tell you how much cotton they could pick before noon and how many buckets of pecans they could gather. Now, they rejoiced at being up North. The ubiquitous refrain was, "I will go visit my people but I can't live there." Their children were fascinated by stories of the "crazy white folks" and segregated cemeteries.

Charles Wright's sojourn was part of the second wave of Wrights to migrate to the North. His Uncle Louis had long ago moved to New Jersey. First generation Blacks in northern cities knew things that second and third generation Blacks, who were born in Detroit and Chicago, didn't. They knew "the man." "The man" was the southern white man who wouldn't hesitate to use violence to maintain racial segregation and Black subordination. Sometimes "the man" wore a policeman's uniform, other times he wore a white sheet. It didn't matter what he was wearing; the South gave him the license to kill "uppity niggers." Chales Wright knew that Selma could be a watershed in the movement and time would run out on "the man." He also knew that marching to Montgomery would be tough and dangerous because "the man" could regard such a step as the Blacks' last stand.

Many successful northern middle class Blacks had long ago washed their hands of the old South. They were prepared to fight the so-called "real man" only if he appeared in Detroit or in their city. But Dr. Martin Luther King made a practice of inviting his northern brethren to come back and march with him. His forays into Black churches in the North as well as participating in marching for their causes, were designed to enlist his northern brethren into his southern crusade. On July 23, 1963, Dr. King came to Detroit to lead a massive march of over 100,000 people from the New Center District to Cobo Hall. It was a peaceful march with the Mayor Cavanagh, Governor Romney, and labor leader Walter Reuther marching abreast with Dr. King. King's speech sounded like the old-time religion, but his message was, "Help me win freedom in the South." He also asked them to join him in Washington, D.C. for a march on Washington. Dr. King was just as persuasive with the middle class as he was with working class Blacks. King knew he could gain their money and their participation in the civil rights movement in the South. Detroit boasted the reputation of a labor-activist dominated city with a large NAACP branch. Black Detroit labor leaders were considered both leftist and militant. Nevertheless, Detroit was a difficult recruitment city for Dr. King because Blacks were preoccupied with being incorporated into the liberal Cavanagh Administration (see Rich, 1989).

Dr. King cajoled Black professionals to lend their skills to the movement. Black preachers were the first to answer the call. Black public school teachers went south once the school year ended. Wright was among the group of physicians who felt a need to witness the change in the South. Some felt that forcing this rural hamlet in the South to recognize its Black citizen's rights would galvanize the movement. More than a few were uncomfortable with the anticipated violence in Selma.

WAS SELMA READY FOR CENTER STAGE?

The politics of Selma were conflictual. Mayor Joe Smitherman had been elected by whites, for whites. He felt no responsibility to the Black people of Selma. George Wallace, the segregationist governor had pledged "segregation in the present and segregation in the future." The mayor was determined not to be a bystander in the events unfolding in Selma. He was also a rural son of the South and may have thought the northern civil right folks were attempting to embarrass the South and "stir up the coloreds." Yet, Charles F. Fager, chronicler of the events, concluded that Selma was not the solid wall of segregation that the North thought it was. Fager states:

> Looked at more closely, then, what to northern eyes was a solid wall of segregation in Selma was actually more like a high picket fence, with not a few sags and gaps along its length. The white families loved and cherished, in their own way, the Black maids they paid ten dollars and some old clothes for a long weeks' work, and the gnarled laborers bent in their fields with rarely a quarter to call their own. And some Blacks, the ones who stayed, continued to use the deceptive carriage and vocabulary which could confirm their supremicist images even while it mocked and exploited them for the Blacks' own purposes.[1]

If Selma was atypical, why did the Student Non-Violent Coordinating Committee (SNCC) want to make this a test town? Perhaps, because it had all the flaws of the rural South, a more historic past and, it was closer to Montgomery. What did they know about Sheriff James G. Clark, Jr. and the probable reactions at the sight of "militant Negroes" in town, that the rest of the nation didn't? Was Jim Clark trying to prove himself to the old families of Selma as Fager and others suggested? What about the Sheriff's rivalry with Public Safety

Director Wilson Baker? The more SNCC probed this small town, the more they were convinced that this was the town in which to make voting rights a reality.

The whites also had their questions. Who were John Lewis, James Bevel and James Forman? What were they trying to do to Selma? To white Selmans, they were troublemakers trying to stir up their coloreds. SNCC had been conducting voting registration during the entire summer of 1963-1964. Young Blacks and whites were teaching civics to Blacks who had never before voted in their lives. The deputies had roughed up people, and many had been threatened by local townspeople. During the summer of 1964, law enforcement officials began arresting Blacks who were trying to register to vote. Going to jail for violating segregation law was a tactic used by SNCC and CORE. Civil rights workers knew that if Blacks could register to vote, they could elect their own people to public office. And, they could thereby change the behavior of white elected officials. Sheriff Clark felt this effort had to be stopped.

Although the town had a large Black population, few Blacks dared to vote. Most were literate and were able to read and answer the voting registration form. Even if they could read the form and answer the questions about the meaning of the U.S. Constitution, voting was a courageous act, indeed. To vote meant risking your farm, credit rating and your life. Although many Blacks received civil rights workers in their homes, they were not interested in open warfare with their white neighbors. Whites, on the other hand, elected whites who promised to keep Blacks in their place. The elected officers ran the little town without much regard for their Black citizens.

The civil rights movement frequently ran up against Southern backwardness and indifference. Outsiders knew Selma was a tough city to crack, but that made it all the more challenging. Civil rights marchers were feared and hated by white Southerners. Elected officials pledged to keep them out of their town. For white law enforcement officers, the coming of civil rights marchers or Freedom Riders meant violence. Local white hoodlums were encouraged to attack Black demonstrators.

The Ku Klux Klan and White Citizens Council became the main opposition groups to demonstrators. So-called decent white folk acquiesced to this rise of lawlessness because they thought it would discourage Black demonstrators, but it didn't. In fact, the Black church opened its doors to the marchers and Black families opened their homes. Black males, who in the past would tip their hats at the sight of the so-called white gentry, were seen in the forefront of the marches. But many Blacks feared for their lives and jobs.

After the assassination of President John F. Kennedy, the civil rights movement inherited a strong supporter in Lyndon B. Johnson. President Johnson, the Senate majority leader during the Eisenhower period was instrumental in securing the first post-Reconstruction Civil Rights Law in 1957. However, this law did not afford protection for Blacks attempting to register and vote in the South. After Johnson assumed the presidency, he pushed through the 1964 Civil Rights Act, which outlawed discrimination in public accommodations. Blacks could ride anywhere in public transit and eat at local diners and restaurants. Charles Wright had spent his early years being denied these basic rights, and he remembered segregation signs everywhere in the South. When he got off the train to go to Alabama State and later to attend Meharry, he had to go to the "colored" section of the station. The 1964 Civil Rights Act changed all that, and Blacks rejoiced in being able to use public facilities.

For the first time in history, Blacks were almost treated like human beings in towns where they had spent their lives working and paying taxes. Yet, George Wallace was still governor and promised to hold the line as long as possible. And, he did not have to worry about Black voters voting him out of office. The 1964 Civil Rights Acts did not go far enough because the federal government would not protect their right to vote. It was 1965, and people who had grown up with Wright could not vote in their own country. The Fifteenth Amendment to the U.S. Constitution gave Blacks the right to vote, but the states determined who was qualified to vote. In addition to the literacy test, Negro applicants had to interpret the Constitution and had to fill out complicated and confusing application forms. Most Blacks routinely failed to qualify to vote, which was the point.

President Johnson understood this and consulted continually with Dr. King about strategies for passing a voting rights act. A march from Selma to Montgomery was a natural catalyst for change. Focusing national attention on the issue would give lawmakers the courage they needed to pass a voting rights bill. Selma was perfect because of its reputation as a microcosm of the old South, and because its white leadership was so intransigent. But, as historians have pointed out, the white leadership was not opposed to trying to shape a compromise before King's visit. Wilson Baker, Selma's public safety director tried to solicit the assistance of Assistant Attorney General Burke Marshall in dissuading the King effort. Baker's efforts failed.

Everyone familiar with this city knew that Dr. King and his people were asking for trouble by marching to Selma. Dr. King arrived on January 2, 1965. He warned of a new massive demonstration, if Blacks were not allowed to register to vote. This declaration was delivered at Brown's Chapel AME Church. Dr. King knew the risks involved. First, his Southern Christian Leadership Conference (SCLC) did not want to overshadow the work of the SNCC. Second, he knew that his involvement would pull in the national media. Third, he knew that the FBI would not stop the violence once it started. He acknowledged these difficulties after students were harassed while attempting to register prospective voters. Yet, Selma had to be broken. America had to see racism's ugly face up close. After his speech, Dr. King returned to Atlanta and traveled to other parts of the country.

On January 14, Dr. King returned to Selma and announced a courthouse demonstration for January 18th, a Monday. There was no trouble when Selma restaurants were tested, but no one was allowed to be registered. Tuesday morning was different. Clark told his deputies to arrest marchers and take them to jail. Black marchers confronted Clark, again, the next day. Marchers were arrested. National newspapers published photographs of marchers, some women and schoolchildren, being clubbed by burly deputies. Dr. King was attacked when he attempted to register as a guest at a formerly all-white hotel. On February 1st, he was arrested while attempting to register Blacks to vote. The tension continued to build as attempt after attempt to register people failed.

The federal government monitored the situation in Selma, but did not immediately intervene. King left the city periodically to make appearances in other cities, but he always returned to Selma. After several smaller demonstrations, sit-ins, confrontations, and maneuvering in Washington and Selma, the Big March was planned.

There were many people besides Charles Wright, an Alabamian, who feared that there might be trouble at the Big March. Dr. Wright feared that angry whites would hurt people. Earlier in February, in Marion, Alabama, a state trooper shot Jimmie Lee Jackson, a civil rights activist, while he was demonstrating for the right to vote. He later died in a Selma hospital. A white Michigan housewife, Mrs. Viola Gregg Liuzzo, had been killed while transporting marchers from Selma to Montgomery. Beating and gassing were routine. Dr. King preached at Jackson's funeral, and Rev. Bevel, one of King's trusted lieutenants, announced a march on Montgomery. "We're going to have to put this movement in second gear. We've got to go to Montgomery to see Governor Wallace!" The gauntlet had been thrown down and Wallace, who had stated in his inaugural address, "Segregation now, segregation in the future and segregation forever," had become the symbol of white resistance. Whites saw Wallace as their hero, fighting to keep the races separate. Gov. Wallace authorized state troopers to assist Clark. The march had to be stopped.

On March 7th, 600 marchers, without Dr. King, headed toward the now famous Edmund Pettus Bridge. They were met by 50 helmeted Alabama State Troopers and Sheriff Clark's deputies on horseback. This scene became one of the most memorable scenes in civil rights history. The state troopers began attacking the marchers in full view of photographers, townspeople and FBI agents. Mounted state troopers, county sheriff deputies and Selma police, armed with clubs, cattle prods and tear gas drove Blacks across the bridge. Blacks of all ages and gender fled the scene and retreated back across the Pettus Bridge. Charles recalled, "The mounted horseman invaded the churches and followed in hot pursuit through the pulpit and choir loft to strike the hapless victims with clubs or administer electric shock with the cattle prods." The more seriously injured were hospitalized, including SNCC's John Lewis, who suffered a blow to his head by a policeman and was later one of Dr. Wright's patients.[2] Many whites saw the incident as Black come-uppance.

The encounter backfired on Selma's white leadership. The nation watched on television, as a group of Blacks were marching peacefully and then suddenly being attacked by whites. Many Americans were outraged. Dr. King appealed for help on national television. He asked churchmen across the country to join him in a new march on Tuesday, March 9. There was massive response to King's call. Whites and Blacks, particularly Black professionals, headed for Selma. Selma had become the watershed of the movement.

White marchers from the North saw rural communities like Selma as the source of American racism. They were there to witness a historic change and to make statements about their country and constitution. Black Northerners came because they knew Black Southerners did not have the resources to bring about the needed changes. Besides, Dr. King had put the march into spiritual and patriotic terms. By calling for a national turnout, Dr. King challenged the Black student and professional community to come to Selma. This march turned out to be a massive effort. Civil rights leaders had never conducted a national march in a southern town before. Selma had a whole set of logistical problems. There was little hotel space and few living accommodations. There were no large restaurants. The thousands of whites who came for the second march were housed and fed by the Black citizens of Selma.

No one knew what would happen. The direction of the protest seemed ad hoc at times. Blacks expected the worst, based on history. Southern Blacks expected the Ku Klux Klan to show up and cause havoc. Many northern whites refused to believe southern whites would try something with so many of the nation watching. In order to make the march effective, local organizers needed better organization, more people and living facilities. They needed physicians to treat the expected injuries.

WHY CHARLES H. WRIGHT WENT TO SELMA?

Why did Charles heed Dr. King's call? Was it because he felt his niece was in danger? Was it an accumulation of guilt associated with safety in Detroit? Charles returned to Alabama as a Freedom Fighter because the import of the Civil Rights Movement was closing in on him. Consider the following chain of events.

The year 1955, his year of triumph because he was board certified, was marred by the death of Emmett Till, a Chicago boy killed in Mississippi. To Black professionals in the North,

The Wright Man

the murder reminded them of the fortuity of their escape from the South. Till could have been one of their own teenagers visiting their grandparents. On November 13, 1956, the U.S. Supreme Court upheld the lower court decision, outlawing segregation on buses in Montgomery, Alabama. Blacks had walked the same streets Charles Wright walked as a student at Alabama State. Some of Wright's professors were still teaching at his alma mater.

On February 25, 1960, Black students at Alabama State did something Charles' classmates would have thought suicidal. They had a sit-in demonstration at the County Courthouse. It was the first of its kind in this Cradle of the Confederacy. For two days, student demonstrators were attacked in Nashville. On March 1, Bama State students marched on the Old Confederacy Capitol Building. President Trenholm expelled nine students.

On April 19, Charles was touched by another memory. Z. Alexander Looby, the man he worked to elect to the Nashville City Council and his teacher in medical jurisprudence, had his home demolished by a powerful bomb. The bomb was so powerful that it blew out the windows of Meharry Medical College. Several medical students were injured by shards of flying glass. Yet, students kept the pressure on Nashville by marching again.

Charles Wright, like most Black Americans, viewed James Meredith's attempt to enroll in University of Mississippi, on September 30, 1962, as the ultimate act of courage. No one thought it would happen in Mississippi. Governor Ross Barnett pledged he would not allow it. Yet, it did. President Kennedy went on television and stated that his duty under the Constitution was to maintain domestic peace. He federalized the National Guard and sent in federal troops to escort Meredith to school.

On June 12, 1963, Medgar Evers, an NAACP official, was assassinated after returning home following an evening meeting to mobilize voters in Mississippi. That single cowardly murder reminded Black males all over America of the dangers of standing up for their rights. In July, Dr. Martin Luther King brought his caravan and hope to Detroit. This event was a dress rehearsal for the March on Washington, planned for August 28. At that triumphal march, Dr. King gave his famous "I Have a Dream" speech. Yet, no one could have expected the dangers that lay ahead.

Exactly eighteen days later, September 15, and five days before Charles' forty-fifth birthday, another cowardly act was committed. Four girls, Cynthia Wesley, Carol Robertson, Addle May Collins and Denise McNair were killed in the 16th Street Baptist Church bombing in Birmingham. These murders stirred the consciousness of the nation. Addle Collins, the oldest child, was fourteen. She was the same age as Charles' daughter, Stephanie. On January 30, 1963, Dr. King's house in Montgomery was bombed. No one was hurt, but the act demonstrated the extent of white rage in the South. On February 3, Authurine Lucy was admitted to the University of Alabama. But campus violence led to her suspension four days later. If there had been no Jim Crow laws in Alabama, Charles could have attended medical school there. On September 20, the world stopped as Dr./Rev. Martin Luther King was stabbed by a crazed Black woman in Harlem. He was taken to Harlem Hospital and cared for by the same doctors who were on staff when Charles was an intern. King survived to lead more marches.

The civil rights struggle seemed to be getting more violent. Indeed, the entire nation seemed to be turning more brutish. On November 22, 1963, President John P. Kennedy was assassinated. The nation was in a crisis. The new President Lyndon B. Johnson, married to an Alabama woman and talking with a Southern twang, initially made Blacks apprehensive, but the new president proved to be a blessing in disguise. Johnson engineered the first meaningful civil rights bill in the nation's history. It outlawed discrimination in public accommodations. The freedom riders and sit-in participants had the nation's attention turned to this critical moment in Southern history. Now, Charles could drive to Dothan and expect to be served when stopping at a motel. Southern Negroes could now be served like any other human being. The freedom that Northern Blacks took for granted, Southern Blacks were tasting for the first time.

The fire of the revolution was moving North. Harlem, Charles Wright's home during World War II, witnessed another riot during the summer of 1964. A Black teenager was shot, and tension again swept Harlem as it had when Dr. Wright was an intern in 1943. The civil rights movement never let go of Charles. Living in Detroit constantly reminded him of the South. The people who were being injured were kindred souls. People he knew, streets he recognized on television, cities in which he lived were in the midst of this epic. Charles Wright felt he had no choice but to go to Selma, but in many ways Charles and other former Black Alabamians had never left Selma.

Growing up in Dothan left him with memories, unfinished business, and unspoken declarations. Now that he was relatively successful economically, he could afford to speak out. He was a board certified OB-GYN, respected by his colleagues. He was the father of two girls. Life had been good to Charles. He did not have to go Selma, but he felt he owed something to those less fortunate and those who couldn't afford to go to Selma.

It was time for Charles Wright to prepare himself for the inevitable question down the line, "Granddaddy, what did you do in the "civil rights movement?" It was his sense of history and obligation that generated the urgency in Charles Wright. The young man who left quietly to attend medical school in another state had again, to confront the "system of segregation" and concomitant violence in his home state. Although he had left Alabama almost 30 years ago, Charles, now 47 years old, would find that towns like Selma had not changed.

Dr. Wright's niece, Nadine Battle, was in Selma as a nurse for the Civil Rights Movement.. She had gone to Harlem Hospital for nursing school and had become involved in the Medical Committee for Human Rights, New York Chapter. Nadine had made a previous trip to Hattiesburg, Mississippi to provide medical care for civil rights workers and to report on compliance with non-discrimination provision of the Hill-Burton Act. Dr. King asked the Committee to send medical personnel to Selma, and Nadine responded. Nadine called her uncle Charles and said that things were getting rough in Selma. Charles felt compelled to go to Selma. Several hundred other Americans heeded Dr. King's call for a showdown in Selma. On March 8, Dr. Wright gathered up bandages, splints, medical equipment, etc. He had Dr. Bentley cover his patients during his absence, and called Louise to tell her he was going to Selma.

Boarding the airplane to Montgomery, Charles felt comfortable with his decision. Martin Luther King was in Atlanta at the time, and actually boarded the plane with Dr. Wright. Charles remembered him as being calm and carrying no luggage; only a newspaper. Charles still had to go to Selma, fifty miles down that uncertain road through the no-man's land of Lowndes County. He spotted Jackie Vaughn, a fellow Detroiter and state senator from Michigan in the airport. They needed a ride to Selma. In the Montgomery Airport was Allan Blanchard, a reporter from the *Detroit News,* so they hitched a ride to Selma with him. The group also picked up a white minister who was headed for Selma for his first trip to the South. The group warned the minister that if the car was stopped during the nighttime journey, Mr. Blanchard, the reporter should do the talking. The minister would not hear of it. He was white and was not use to others infringing on his civil rights. The others had to quiet him down. "When we were stopped en route by Klansmen, who held spotlights close to

The Wright Man

your eyes while interrogating you, the preacher started grumbling about his civil rights. I stomped on his foot to shut him up."[3] When they arrived Nadine was nevertheless surprised to see her uncle walk through the door at Brown's Chapel. "I remember I cried. I was so glad to see him."[4]

THE MARCH

Finally, the moment came for the big march. Reporters and observers from around the world came to participate or record the encounter in Selma. After March 7, when protesters routed by billy clubs, tear gas, and cattle prods attempted to march across the Edmond Pettus Bridge, the media was ready for the second encounter. King returned to Selma and vowed to march again. Charles was present for the second march on March 9 1965.

Charles' first aid station, in Selma, was ready for dog bites, police brutality, broken bones or any other kind of injury. Before the march began, the leaders had to close down Brown Chapel, Selma's regular church headquarters for civil rights organizations. The only lines connecting the marchers with the outside world were Charles' first aid station and a local church. Calls were routed there from all over the country asking about the march. Had it started yet? Where is Dr. King? What was happening? Charles had come to be a physician, but was pressed into duty as a press attaché. A Black woman rushed into Charles' station and told him breathlessly that he had to try and get word to Dr. King that when he gets to the Edmond Pettus Bridge he must stop before the tail end of the line of marchers reached the bridge. The woman had overheard that the whites had planned to seal everyone on the bridge "and make a real mess of things."

Charles sent a runner to find Dr. King. Charles had a small radio in his station and heard the broadcast from the site. Everyone was waiting to hear if the line would stop. The tail end of the line was in sight. The march had started. Charles Fager described the day:

> The afternoon was cool but not very clear, with bright sunlight making everything—the turgid river, the steel bridge girders, the people's faces—look especially vivid. The contrast in the atmosphere with that of the first march was marked; Sunday had been overcast, gray, gloomy and cold, befitting the occasion. Now as the front ranks reached the crest of the bridge, they could see the troopers' blue plastic helmets gleaming in the sun; the veterans noticed with relief that there were gas masks dangling from their belts. Dogs were straining at their leashes. Still the line fell silent again at the sight of the well over hundred men standing two deep under the heedless changing traffic signals, their clubs once more at the ready, all across the highway and along both sides for a hundred feet, forming a long ominous cul-de-sac for the first dozen rank. Major John Cloud was again in command, and he let King get with fifty feet before speaking through his bullhorn: "You are ordered to stop and stand where you are. This march will not continue."[5]

They did stop. King and the other leaders of the march started to negotiate with the white officials. Dr. King asked and was granted permission to pray. After the prayer, the group left the bridge and the march was called off. Charles never knew if Dr. King got his message. The curiosity was too much for Charles. When he returned to Detroit, he called Dr. King and asked if he had received the message. Dr. King didn't remember receiving it, but he told Charles that "it had been quite a day."

Charles was not at the Edmond Pettus Bridge that day, and ironically it was the film "Eyes on the Prize" that gave him a full view of what actually occurred at the bridge. He stated, "It was 20 years later that I saw what happened."[6]

Charles later discovered that there had occurred several mini-dramas that day in Selma. One of his friends from medical school, a dentist named John Williams, breathed a sigh

The Wright Man

of relief when it was over. Dr. Williams explained: "Things were not, today, as they had been on Sunday." Charles replied, "Yes, no one got hurt but Rev. Reeb. I hear he was hit over the head with an axe handle." Williams stated, "That did not happen during the march. We were ready for them this time." Charles asked, "What do you mean?" Williams replied, "Every Black Selma male in that line today had a weapon. We decided: Never again! Never again!" Charles responded, "What?!!" Charles recalled, "My expression of horror, and disbelief gave way to mortal fear when Williams pulled from his belt a loaded revolver. He had only prepared for cattle prods and that type of injury. He was not prepared for gunshot wounds. If there had been any action on the part of the police today, there would have been the worse massacre in the history of this country." Wright remembered, "I got scared. King hadn't known! Women had carried razor blades and men had carried guns."[8]

The next morning, Charles hitched a ride back to Montgomery, and boarded a plane to Detroit. It was March 10, 1965, and he couldn't forget the Williams conversation. Charles asked a woman on the plane for paper and envelope and wrote a letter to Hobart Taylor, a lawyer he knew in Detroit, now an assistant to the President. The letter read, "You've to do something because yesterday could have been the biggest mess in this country. Those people in Selma do not think that President Johnson is in their favor. They think the federal government [Johnson Administration] is just dilly dallying around."[8] Charles recalled, "I tried to convey to him some idea of the desperation of the voteless masses and their potential for violent retaliation if something was not done to assist them to gain the ballot. A few days later, [Taylor] replied, thanking me for the alert. He said he had shown the right people my letter. He hoped that President Johnson's recent We Shall Overcome speech would provide assurance.[9]"

On March 15, President Johnson asked a joint session of Congress to enact a new voting rights law. Two days later a federal judge issued an injunction against interfering with the March to Montgomery. Between March 21 and March 25, thousands of marchers walked the fifty miles to Montgomery under the protection of federal troops. Nevertheless, Mrs. Liuzzo was killed on March 25, while transporting marchers who were the vanguard for the main group. The main group of marchers did make it to Montgomery, and became participants in one of the most memorable moments in civil rights history. The civil rights movement had won the hearts on the nation.

In May, the 1965 Voting Rights Law was passed, and Blacks for the first time since Reconstruction were guaranteed the right to vote in the South. The new law enabled the nation to enforce the ninety-five year old 15th Amendment of 1870. The federal government was now authorized to protect this right. This Act would permanently change southern politics.

Charles Wright continued his interest in the struggle and joined a newly formed Medical Committee for Human Rights. This group was expected to be dispatched anywhere in the South in cases of likely confrontations and violence with white law enforcement officers. Dr. William Bentley, Charles' partner, was also a member. and had spent time in Montgomery, Tuskegee, and other small towns in Alabama. When Bentley returned, Wright took his turn.

In the summer of 1965, Wright volunteered again for medical duties in the South. He flew to Baton Rouge, Louisiana, but was met at the airport. He was told that emergency physicians were needed in Bogalusa, about 92-miles away. This time it was to help civil rights fighters who were attempting to integrate the paper mill in Bogalusa, a tiny hamlet with almost as many racists as it had mosquitoes.

When Wright arrived, he was met by a nervous young white female civil rights worker. She had not expected to meet a Black man. She explained her dilemma and admitted that she was very apprehensive about driving to Bogalusa. The problem

The Wright Man

was that it would be dark before she would arrive. "The white men who were watching us were members of the Ku Klux Klan. As I got into her car, they reported us via their car's short wave radio to their headquarters." Wright was ready to go, but she kept insisting that the place was infected with the Klan and was unsafe. This trip occurred a few weeks after the Viola Luizzo murder. The young woman was frightened. After a brief discussion, she suggested that Wright wait behind a nearby building. She decided to call Bogalusa for advice on what to do. She went to a pay phone, and when she returned, she said she was told to take him halfway. They were to be met by a detachment of the Deacons for Defense and Justice in Covington, halfway to Bogalusa.

As they entered the car, the woman pointed to a car across the street. She told Wright that they were all members of the Ku Klux Klan.

KLAN AND THE WHITE CITIZENS COUNCIL

The two took off for Covington but when they arrived at Covington, the Deacons were nowhere to be seen. The woman again asked Charles to go behind a building and wait until she could obtain more information. She called again and learned that they were at the wrong bus station. They hurried over to the other bus station and were met by two Black males.

Wright's bag was tossed into the trunk and he got into the back seat. The youngest escort put a pistol on the seat between them and started off. "When I questioned the necessity for such precaution, he told me that the Klan sometimes uses the highway to Bogalusa for target practice.[10] Therefore, they had to be ready," he said. They drove very fast to Bogalusa. There had been a march that day and the marchers had been pelted with frozen fruit. On the way to the first aid station they passed a boy talking to two white men. They stopped the car to ask what was going on. The boy said that the two men were questioning him. The driver challenged the white men and they pulled out their FBI badges. Dr. Wright's driver said, "Well, when you are finished, little boy, get on back home."

Charles was surprised. Black males who are not afraid of white folks were what Southerners called "bad cats." Calling themselves, Deacons for Defense and Justice, they were armed Black men who provided security and protection for civil rights fighters. Dr. Wright was made an honorary deacon, but he didn't get a gun. They drove Wright to the first-aid station and started treating the injured. He worked in Louisiana for 10 days.

THE 1967 DETROIT RIOT

Charles Wright's 1965 words about dilly dallying were prophetic, as the hot Detroit summer of 1967 became a watershed in the city's history. The Cavanagh administration, thought to be one of the nation's most progressive municipal administrations, was completely unprepared for the disturbances that grew out of a police raid of a blind pig (illegal gambling establishment). Black leaders were continually consulted in racial matters. Cavanagh had carefully incorporated Blacks in city government, but had done very little for the bottom tier of the Black community. The antagonism between the police and the working class Black community grew worse.

Throughout the Cavanagh period there were charges of police brutality. Detroit's poor felt alienated from their leaders and their elected officials. B.J. Widick, a historian, attributes this alienation to poor schools, youth unemployment, and poverty. He observed that "no significant attention was paid to the new mood of dissatisfaction among Black youth. No organization had attracted them in real numbers. No program really involved them as full participants."[11] When the disturbances occurred, vandalism became the norm. Many felt

The Wright Man

they had nothing to lose. Others were caught up in the crowd. Still others just saw opportunities and seized them. A few engaged in mindless vandalism.

For several days, the residents of the Black community burned and looted their neighborhoods. Forty-three individuals lost their lives. Hundreds were injured. Many of Charles' patients lived in those neighborhoods. Charles' niece, Anita Kitson, was a student at Wayne State at the time of the riot and had been involved in a sit-in at the student union. She remembered the tanks, sirens and curfews.[12]

Although Charles and his family were working aboard the S. S. Hope in Cartegena, Columbia during those infamous days, the Wrights felt the impact of the rebellion. It was their city being burned.

The Kerner Commission was a study group created by President Johnson to study the riots. The Commission members found that the riots were a reflection of the alienation of northern Blacks over the lack of jobs, education, and protection from police. It concluded that America was moving toward two nations, one white and one Black. The impact of the riots was still unfolding as the report was being written. White flight, which had started in the late fifties, accelerated. Detroit was slowly becoming a predominantly Black city. In 1969, labor leaders, particularly UAW president Walter Reuther, tried unsuccessfully to elect Richard Austin, a Black accountant, as mayor. Austin lost by 5,000 votes. Roman Griggs was elected. His administration turned out to be a transition government. Four years later, Coleman Young was elected as Detroit's first Black mayor.

The sixties had been a decade of turmoil and change. Charles Wright's all-Black world was turning upside down. The civil rights movement was a catalyst for the reemergence of the militant Charles Wright. Seeing those kids challenge the system awakened him to the possibility of confrontation as way of changing things in America.

Dr. Wright's niece, Nadine Battle

Wright and other physicians in the turbulent South in the 1960s — Members of the Medical Committee for Human Rights

The Wright Man

This Museum Was Once A Dream

This Museum
was once a dream
inscribed inside
the walls of
slave quarters
the gates were guarded
by ghosts in colored bottles
of glass swinging from string
between bleeding trees.
they held secrets
of millions severed
from their stories.
brick by brick
memories rebuilt
the amber flare
of ancient Abyssinian
splendor.
the ancestors insisted like the swelling
of the mighty Mississippi
like escaping fugitives
tracing moss from
limb to limb,
from Alabama
through Tennessee,
from Africa through
Tuskegee
swollen fingers molded
like mortar along
the angles of pyramids
following long rivers
and vanishing borders
recollecting cotton blossoms
strewn beside a
narrow stream
of blue light

splitting the distance.
the entrance
to this museum
was hidden within
memories rediscovered.
the dream restored
on the frozen path
of freedom
was the imprint of
God's great reach
and the immortal
human story.

Dr. Melba Joyce Boyd

The Wright Man

The Melba Boyd poem seems amazingly appropriate for this part of our story. The dream of Charles H. Wright, M.D. appeared and began to take root in the early 1960s. About that time, Dr. Wright began to think seriously about the future of the babies he was bringing into the world. Sure, their minds and bodies appeared sound, but as they grew and as he looked around, he saw that many children displayed a lack of self-confidence, lack of vision, and a lackluster attitude toward learning. This bothered Dr. Wright greatly.

In spite of the fact that Wright's plate was full, his thoughts remained focused on ways to help the city's youth. In 1964 and 1965, in what seemed a distraction, but proved to be part of God's plan for his life, Wright agreed to join medical survey trips to Africa, as was described in Chapter Six.

Returning home from Africa more inspired than ever, Wright expressed his wish to organize a museum-a museum that would exemplify the accomplishments of African Americans and provide positive images for children. As he talked, his friends, who suggested he turn his ideas into action, increasingly challenged him.

Wright set the date of March 10, 1965 for a museum organizational meeting. Invited were thirty-two persons representing a true cross section of the Detroit community.

Myrtle Adams

James Babcock

Gloria Bigham

James Boyce

Dr. Henry Brown

L.Ann Conley

John M. Dorsey, M.D.

Murray A. Douglas

Dean Katherine Faville

Mildred Gottdank

Sister Marie Dolores Keller (SSJ)

Golda Krolik

Josephine Martin

Philip Mason, Ph.D.

Jessie Metcalf

Dr. Bernice Morton

Leonard W. Moss, Ph.D.

Dorothy Mottley

Catherine E. Obeng

Arnold R. Pilling, Ph.D.

Victor A. Rapport, Ph.D.

Esther Road

S. Carolyn Reese

Jane Ronan

Ida J. Searles

Audrey Smedley, Ph.D.

Dean Martin Stearns

Christina Taylor

Oretta Todd

Henry Watts, Ph.D.

Willis Wood

William Woodward

Charles Wright, M.D.

The date of the organizational meeting for the museum arrived with no word from Wright. The group began to assemble in the office of Dean Katherine Faville, at Wayne State University School of Nursing. As the last guests arrived, Wright dashed into the meeting. Because the Detroit News had reported that Wright was in Selma, many were surprised to see him.

Dr. Wright's problem with this planning group's discussion started at the first meeting. Members wanted to know, why build a separate institution? Why not make the Detroit Institute of Arts (DIA) and the Detroit Historical Museum (DHM) more relevant to the Black community? Where would the funding for this new venture be found? If Blacks do not attend DIA and DHM in large numbers, why would they be interested in a Black museum? What type of exhibits would the new institution feature?

The chemistry of the group was interesting. Some members had agendas. Mr. Babcock, for example, the director of the Burton Collection at the Public Library, acknowledged

The Wright Man

the need for more archival data on Blacks. The proposed museum posed no threat to Burton since that collection concentrated on written archival materials. Mr. Wood, of the Detroit Institute of Arts, could envision the proposed museum as a competitor, despite its understated objectives. Other members were more encouraging in their comments.

During the meeting, a motion was made and passed to support the concept of a museum that was "dedicated to the task of correcting the distortions and filling in the deletions of the recorded Black experience, insofar as our resources would permit." In other words, it would be an educational institution dedicated to revising the historical record of Blacks. At first glance, this seemed to be the stage for extending Black History Month beyond its traditional month of February.

Many of the participants in the first meeting became board members of the proposed museum, but none of them had any idea of how dedicated Dr. Wright was to the idea. Once he decided to do something, he would work tirelessly for the cause. To some of them, Dr. Wright was just another Black physician with a dream and no experience as a museum organizer or benefactor.

At the second meeting, there was a notable drop off in attendance. Many of the first attendees did not show for the second meeting. Some of the Wayne State deans and professors only came to the first planning meeting because Dean Faville invited them. Dean Faville had encouraged Willis Wood, of the Detroit Institute of Arts, and Henry Brown, of the Detroit Historical Museum to come to the second meeting. At this meeting, the group further discussed the role of the proposed museum and the possible sources of support.

The third meeting witnessed dramatic changes in the sociology of the group. The white members began to assert themselves in the discussions. They disagreed with their Black colleagues about the direction of the proposed museum. Dr. Wright, supported by Dr. Audrey Smedley, announced that this time, Blacks were going to run the show. "If whites want to come along, fine. If not, we will get along without you." Dr. Wright's comments were greeted as impertinent, ungrateful and anti-white. Some white members quickly disassociated themselves from the project. Only Dr. Wright's good friends, Dean Faville, Golda Krolik, and Sister Marie Dolores stayed with the group. They came to succeeding meetings that were held at the Omega House, churches and private homes.

Henry Brown of the Detroit Historical Museum did not attend any additional planning meetings, but offered valuable assistance to the new museum. Since he was in the museum business, he often made equipment and technicians available to the new group. Each meeting was a combination of teaching, brainstorming and winnowing out.

The group decided that they first needed to have an exhibit to establish their presence as a cultural player. They took advantage of the DHM offer of expertise and personnel to hold their first exhibit of the new museum, at the Detroit Historical Museum.

Cooperation with the DIA was a different matter. Willis Wood, the director, was openly hostile to the idea of a new museum. Wood was accustomed to dealing with the movers and shakers of the corporate and political world. The meeting of this museum group did not include the regular museum supporters, who belonged to the DIA Founders Society. Wood decided not to attend any further meetings. Wood's absence at the next meeting not only denied Dr. Wright and his planning group some expertise in museum management, but it robbed them of the DIA's prestige that the new upstart institution needed.

Mr. Wood, three years into his DIA directorship, taught Dr. Wright a lesson in big-league museum politics. Wood knew that Wright's museum would not present any real competition

The Wright Man

for the DIA, but could attract a potential Black museum crowd. Wood was smart enough to know that Wright could also make a case for his museum as the only institution that catered to the needs of the Black community. Such an argument might be an appealing case for support from foundations and museum donors. Wood may have thought that he could prevent these problems by not becoming identified with this fledgling new group. Or, he might have thought that his involvement with Wright's project would jeopardize relations with Mr. Arthur Coar, who was marshaling support for an African art gallery at the DIA.

In 1962, the members of the Detroit Chapter of the Association for the Study of Negro Life and History (ASNLH), chaired by Mr. Coar, proposed to the DIA a joint sponsorship for a special gallery of African Art. This project was the work of the African Art Gallery Committee of ASNLH. Organized as the committee to work with the Founders Society, Mr. Coar and Mr. Wood were responsible for the planning of the new gallery.

In its first meeting at Mr. Wood's home, the group, which included Marc Crawford, agreed to raise $50,000 to acquire African art for a new museum wing. The work of this committee was an important linkage between white upper class suburban interests and Detroit's black bourgeoisie. Dr. Alfred Thomas, Dr. Haley Bell and Charles C. Diggs, Sr. were among the first contributors to the fund. The Press Attaché of Ghana and the Cultural Attaché of the Liberian Embassy presented works of art at the group's first fundraiser.

Charles Wright was not involved with, nor aware of this planning effort. The planning for his museum started three years after Coar's committee met. In June 1966, the African Art Gallery was opened in the South Wing of the DIA. The opening was organized as a joint venture between the ASNLH and the DIA. The Coar group entered into an agreement with G. Mennen Williams, former Governor of Michigan and

Undersecretary of State for African Affairs, that his extensive African art collection would be donated to the new gallery, recognizing the role of ASNLH. Eleanor and Edsel Ford gave monetary support to the new wing. The plan was to have joint DIA and ASNLH sponsorship of the African, Oceanic, and New World Cultures Gallery opening.

The opening of the gallery took place on June 25, 1966. Williams' donation was transferred to the DIA well in advance of the opening of the new gallery, but was not displayed at the opening. The members of the ASNLH, already angered by the DIA's refusal to allow them to hold a fund-raiser on the premises, expressed great disappointment that recognition of the ASNLH major contribution to the event was nowhere in sight. They were further displeased that Mr. Coar was not included in the opening program, nor was he allowed to address the gathering. At the reception, only white women were allowed to pour tea and distribute cookies. In other words, there was no ASNLH participation, whatsoever.

Dr. Wright, then a member of the ASNLH's board of directors, decided to take direct action regarding the omission of ASNLH's presence at the gallery opening, *without consulting* Mr. Coar or the others.

On the day following the opening, he called David Rambeau, a Black host of a television talk show, "For My People," to discuss a course of action. They decided to protest at the DIA.

Rambeau recalled that several artists and activists had attended the organizing meeting for the protest. "Black artists were attracted to and alienated from the DIA. They got very little play in the DIA." Dr. Wright had little trouble soliciting them to picket the DIA the next day. The protest group was unaware that DIA's Board of Trustees was scheduled to meet at the same time.

A press release was prepared that detailed all of the aforementioned grievances. It implied that Wood's failure to display Williams' collection was politically motivated. The Museum did not want to irritate Mayor Jerome P. Cavanagh who was running against G. Mennen Williams for a U.S. Senate seat. The press release suggested that Wood's allegiance to his boss, the Mayor, could possibly have been a factor in keeping Williams' collection in storage.

Picket signs were prepared and strategies were reviewed. The press was notified, and the group synchronized their watches for the rendezvous at 9 a.m. the following morning at the DIA. The press came, as did a curious crowd, who wondered: What in the world is going on at the DIA? The crowd was handed copies of the press release.

Director Wood, taken by complete surprise, had a larger problem than Wright and his group realized. A trustees meeting was scheduled within the hour. In a desperate move to clear his sidewalk, Wood sent an emissary to invite Dr. Wright in to negotiate a settlement.

Unaware of the enormity of Wood's dilemma, Wright told the emissary that there was more space to negotiate outside than inside the DIA. The press did go in, and asked Wood if the absence of the Williams collection was related in any way to Cavanagh's campaign for the Senate. Wood scoffed at the "very idea" of such a proposal, and explained that the collection had arrived too late to be cataloged before the opening of the African Art Gallery. Mayor Cavanagh also issued a disclaimer.

The trustees were temporarily stymied by the pickets. The *Detroit Free Press* carried a photograph of Dr. Wright with a picket sign. An article in the June 29, 1966 edition states:

> Dr. Wright was the spokesman for the five pickets, claiming that the ASNLH was left out of planning for the DIA's dedication ceremony for the African Art Gallery. Dr. Wright demanded that the ASNLH be allowed to

participate fully in future planning and implementation of such plans. Arthur Coar, president of ASNLH, said the Association did not, in any way, authorize this (Dr. Wright's) disgraceful action.

If the cultural world didn't know Dr. Wright before this confrontation, they knew him now (see Appendix).

This confrontation was a big story for the Detroit cultural community, and an even larger one in the so-called genteel museum community. While some people were disturbed by the picket line around the hallowed wings of the DIA, Dr. Wright's bold bid for recognition as a member of that community could not be ignored. The whites who ignored Wright realized that the new Black museum could be used as an instrument for social action.

Dr. Wright remembers being told, "*You should not have forced the Fords and the Whitneys to make the unpleasant choice to cross your picket line.*" The Fords and the Whitneys represented the zenith of Detroit's "white society." Also in the trustee group, were Lawrence A. Fleischman and William M. Day, presidents of the Arts Commission of the City of Detroit and the Founders Society of the Detroit Institute of Arts, respectively.

Wright was surprised at the vehemence of the rebuke he received from his "side." He had assumed that he was expressing a common dissatisfaction of his group. It came as no surprise then, when his name was dropped from the ASNLH list of trustee board members. Wright never attended another meeting.

The International Afro-American Museum (IAM) was incorporated in February 1966, and granted a tax-exempt status in December 1966. Annual membership fees, at the time, ranged from $.50 for youths under eighteen to $2.00 and up for adults. Dr. Wright's thought was that "the establishment of a museum would enable us to seize the authority of researching, interpreting and publishing our history from those who had done so to our disadvantage." The museum would work (a) to increase one of the rarest commodities on the American market, racial pride, among Black people and (b) to help fill the information gap about Black people for all Americans.

The International Afro-American Museum survived its first years primarily with the sale of memberships. The founders, board members, auxiliary members and friends of the Museum worked tirelessly. The funds were supplemented by the auctioning of paintings at "artists of the month" receptions. The participating artists enjoyed displaying their creativity and providing assistance to the Museum.

Also, during the formative years, Dr. Wright not only contributed love, time and work, but approximately $1,000.00 per month from his personal funds. He continued to say "we are dedicated to one of the most important tasks of our times, to ensure that generations of Negroes to come, will be aware of, and take pride in the history of their forebears and their remarkable struggle for freedom."

The Museum was housed in the basement of 1549 West Grand Boulevard, the building that served as Dr. Wright's home and office. Before long he moved his living quarters and then his office to 50 Westminster on Detroit's north end. Soon after, his Meharry Medical College classmate, James H. Robinson, M.D. moved from the adjoining building, 1553 which he donated to the Museum. This allowed for expansion into that building as well.

During the early days of the Museum, tenants lived in the upper floors. When they decided to move out, Dr Wright had the site remodeled. He removed the sink and redecorated the living room. The larger space allowed for more visitors which, in turn, meant more publicity and donors. The donations enabled Dr. Wright to hire a part-time staff person. He donated a typewriter from his medical office and the Museum took on an official look. Soon, more than 300 exhibits, seminars, book exhibits and radio programs emerged from the Grand Blvd location. By 1966, the Boulevard site had become a "bee-hive of activity, as though we knew what we were doing." A radio program about Black history was recorded by Obie Newman. Dr. Wright dutifully kept a written record of these exhibits and a diary of the early days of the Museum activities.

Dr. Wright became the curator, manager, promoter, and historian. He had never taken a course in museum organization or history. He had to teach himself the business and profession of museum-keeping. Having never talked to the great curators and museum-builders of his time, he did not hold a clear idea of the features that made a popular museum. The great international collectors did not covet his personal collection of African artifacts. His ideas about how to start such a museum and how to sell it to the Black community were limited. His daughter recalled, "He wanted it for educational purposes and for the kids. He did not want it to be a hands-off experience, a stuffy approach." He needed people, capital, space, and volunteers. Most of all, he needed feedback from visitors.

What Dr. Wright lacked in museum knowledge, he made up for in enthusiasm. He was a master at getting people to volunteer their time to the new museum. Robert Shannon, an Alabama State College classmate, was a dedicated supporter of the Museum, and served as president of the Board, from 1972 to 1984. Shannon described himself as Wright's confidant. He further described Charles Wright as a "no nonsense taskmaster." Shannon worked for the Detroit Board of Education and was responsible for the Neighborhood Youth Corp. The name of the program later changed, but essentially it was a program to help find jobs for the city's young people.

Margaret Dudley, a schoolteacher and alumnae of the African Medical Education Fund, was a key player in the development and success of the Museum. She once served as

The Wright Man

director, and worked on fundraisers. Norman Dillard, an employee at UNSYS, was described as rendering "exemplary service" to the Museum. He was responsible for many of the in-kind donations necessary to operate such a facility. Margaret (Boone Jones) Zarif, a writer of children's books and Margaret Ashworth were also fundraisers and dedicated workers for the Museum.

Physician's wives, schoolteachers, and friends were tireless workers for the Museum. At the 1979 annual Museum banquet, Ms. Dudley and Ms. Ashworth were honored for their efforts on behalf of the Museum. But it was Wright, who had the vision and enthusiasm to carry the Museum forth. He had to rally the troops, decide on the theme of the exhibits, and cajole the owners of the art, photographs and other items, for permission to use their property in exhibitions. Yet, they were still not getting the working class, the so-called grass roots persons, to the Museum. Wright needed a gimmick to get this group involved, so he decided to take the Museum to them rather than have them come to the Museum.

THE MOBILE MUSEUM

By 1967, a mobile museum was considered the ideal way to lure more visitors and create more supporters. The mobile home, towed by truck, would take an exhibit to the people, into their neighborhoods and onto their turf. At first, Wright tried to get the Michigan Council of the Arts to pay for the trailer, but the Council did not like the idea. The Council staff recommended that the Museum produce films to promote exhibits, but was not willing to fund them. Charles Wright was learning his third lesson in the cultural war, new ideas are not met with enthusiasm by granting agencies. They would rather do business with established institutions.

The response of the Council was conveyed to the Black Legislative Caucus, in Lansing. The Caucus convened an emergency meeting with the Council, with nothing else on the agenda. A few day after the joint meeting, the Museum was notified that the Council had changed its mind about the need for a mobile museum, and a check was forthcoming.

The 10' by 30' trailer was purchased for $3,500. Several persons including Dorothy Mottley and Jonathan Rucker worked on the renovation of the trailer. Henry Brown, of the Detroit Historical Museum, still supportive, made the facilities at Fort Wayne available for the renovation of the new trailer. Dr. Audrey Smedley and her friends also volunteered to repair and decorate the vehicle.

Mr. Don Petty, a carpenter, built the exhibits for the mobile museum, assisted by Dr. Earnest Singleton. Both rolled up their sleeves, volunteering time, energy, and skills. Others, whose voluntary assistance made the exhibits possible: Robert Johnson, Hugh Barrington (electrician), Douglas Gaillard, Hubert Craig (sign painter), Charles Rhodes, Bob Wright and other members of the laboratory of the Detroit Historical Museum. Also assisting were Miss Maudestine Bell, Mrs. Yvonne Catchings, Byron Reid, Mrs. Violet Jones, Charles Davis, Marvin Brown and many others. The Madison Electric Co. on Woodward Ave. donated electrical supplies. The project was under the direction of the Research Committee of IAM.

James Lewis prepared the artwork for the exhibits. All involved with the mobile museum were volunteers except Ms. Roslyn Walker, a graduate student who was hired from the Art Department of the University of Indiana. She remained with the project long enough to make sure that it was properly launched.

This mobile museum allowed exhibits to reach an audience that could never be reached in a stationary building. People might come to a mobile unit, whereas dressing up for a visit to the Museum's Grand Blvd location would be out of the question. Once the mobile unit was equipped, it lured a new constituency for the Museum. It was opened at the 1967

The Wright Man

State Fair, and was viewed by 10,000 visitors. Donations of $1,000 were received after visits to the exhibit: "The History of Africa."

In reality, just getting the mobile museum off square one was not easy. Wright selected the corner of 12th and Virginia Park as the ideal site to introduce it to the neighborhoods. The Museum board questioned his sanity—as that was the site of the core of the activity of the rebellion—the eye of the storm, so to speak. Wright argued that the "eye" would be safe. Many expressed fears that the children in the area would totally wreck the "vehicle museum" The rector of the Grace Episcopal Church on 12th Street was contacted by Wright and he agreed to allow the mobile museum to be parked in the church lot. The rest is history; not a single act of vandalism occurred during the two weeks in the "burned out" area.

The neighborhood children were so very excited about the museum that it "played" to a full house every day. A few of the youngsters, who came repeatedly, were put to work as guides. The children proudly announced this to all who "boarded" the museum.

The mobile museum traveled first to Sampson Elementary School. The principal of the school was Eugene Gilmer, a member of the Museum board. Joanne Sanneh, the curator of the museum on wheels, took the unit to schools upon request. Of the ten exhibits, the most popular was the history of Black inventors. Most children did not know that a Black man named Garrett Morgan invented the traffic light and the gas mask.

Other popular displays were the various African exhibits which children loved, but were surprised to see photographs showing modern buildings in some African cities. Many did not know that in Africa there were cities with skyscrapers and accused the volunteers of showing pictures of New York. The Museum secured an agreement with the board that principals would keep the trailer in the school yard for a week and the school would pay a rental fee which helped with the upkeep and to pay for some of the costs. Teachers were encouraged to visit the museum before the children, in order to prepare themselves as guides. Some teachers saw this orientation process as an added chore, but others incorporated the museum into their curriculum as a learning experience.

The Museum board's decision to include churches was yet another attempt to reach the various social and class tiers of the Black community. In addition, the mobile unit was displayed at Northland, Eastland, and other shopping malls and was also taken to Lansing and Jackson, Michigan. An attempt was usually made to locate the unit in a high volume traffic area, an innovative method in reaching out to the community.

The emergence of the mobile museum came at a time when Black nationalism was at its peak. Increasingly, people wanted to know about their heritage. After the 1967 riot, the city provided some funding for school cultural enrichment programs. These funds were also used to pay for the weekly visits of the mobile museum to every public high school in the city. It housed over fifty exhibits during its 20-year run, covered 50,000 miles, and was viewed by at least 100,000 visitors.

The year 1967 was an extraordinarily busy time for Dr. Wright. Early that summer, as mentioned in Chapter 7, Wright had an opportunity to serve as staff obstetrician-gynecologist on the S.S. Hope to Columbia, South America. A rich byproduct of the trip was the recruitment of two members to a newly formed International Board of Directors of IAM, which Wright decided would be helpful. One was His Excellency, Mr. Radol Fawkes, Minister of Commerce and Labor in the Bahamian Government. The other was Manuel Zapata Olivella, M.D., one of Colombia's first men of letters. Other members of the International Board were Carleton B. Goodlet, Ph.D., M.D. of San Francisco, California; Eigle Moerck, D.D.S. of Aahus, Denmark; George Shannu Taylor, Sierra Leone, West Africa;

The Wright Man

Roy Sieber, Ph.D. Indiana University, Bloomington, Indiana; and Audrey Smedley, Ph.D., Wayne State University, Detroit. Each of these board members had distinguished her/himself in many ways, especially in the fight for freedom.

Aboard ship, Dr. Wright found himself the only physician who could speak Spanish. Even the patients thought he was a native. A patient asserted, "We came to the ship to be treated by North American doctors." One of Wright's colleagues replied, "But, Dr. Wright is a North American doctor." The patient responded "Oh no! He can't be! His Spanish is too good!" They thought that Dr. Wright was a Cuban physician. Wright's Spanish proficiency was one of his private joys. This incident stuck in Wright's mind and became one of his favorite stories.

Spanish was a way for Wright to reach beyond his narrow education as a physician. It allowed him to converse with people of other lands with different backgrounds. He equated bilingualism with cosmopolitanism. The more Wright traveled, the more he realized his need to know more about his world.

Louise and their daughters joined Wright on the ship for two weeks. Louise helped to organize the ship's library and to catalog the system. Being abroad, the entire family missed one of the worst rebellions in the nation's history, the Detroit riots of 1967.

In the meantime, activity at the Museum steadily accelerated. The IAM Research Committee published, early on, a newsletter called the *IAM Newsletter*. The staff consisted of Nathaniel Leach, editor; Ada Cyrus, news editor; Agnes Miller, copy editor; and Robert Shannon, circulation manager. Persons such as Margaret Dudley, Mildred Pitts, Margaret (Boone Jones) Zarif and Dorothy Mottley, spent endless hours helping with the newsletter and to promote the Museum.

By the end of 1967, membership had doubled over 1966 and the income exceeded $14,000. Major support now came through memberships from grass-roots people who were aware that they were participating in a project to spread racial pride among Black people. Some of the larger donors were the Rose Bud Club; Gamma Phi Delta Sorority; Omega Psi Phi Fraternity; Alabama State Alumni Association; The Association; The Jolly Workers Club; Church of God-Young Adults; The Detroit Medical Society; The Michigan Chronicle; and anonymous donors.

In the meantime, the main buildings on West Grand Boulevard began sponsoring a variety of programs designed to educate and inform the general public. Among the many programs was a special class in African history, taught by Dr. Wiley of Michigan State University, whom Wright had met in Africa in 1964 when he was in the Peace Corps. Twenty-six people were awarded certificates for having attended the sessions at the Great Lakes Mutual Life Insurance Company building on Woodward Avenue from January 9, 1967 to May 1, 1967.

The fall issue of the IAM newsletter, interestingly, contained an extensive article on Joseph Cinque, and how he was put aboard the Amistad, a slave ship. (In 1997, when the movie, *Amistad,* was released, it was said that little had been known or written about the ship). The Museum was right on target for those who embraced its programs and dissemination of important information.

And, all the while that Wright was busy with his medical practice and his other projects, he and numerous volunteers (who also had busy lives) worked day and night to "nurture" and "raise" the Museum. Robert Shannon, one of Wright's earliest supporters was an Omega Psi Phi fraternity brother, and their ties are long and strong. This includes his wife, Eloise, and their sons and daughters. Shannon was physically and spiritually connected to the Museum from the beginning, and Dr. Wright often turned to him for guidance. During this time, John Williams and Owsley Spiller, and Leonard Douglas, fraternity brothers, also were "at his side."

When Wright began to attend meetings with local museum directors, he picked up ideas about fund-raising and museum management. He often attempted to incorporate the best of these into the small museum. Margaret Dudley, a former executive director, described an occasion when the Museum closed for lack of money. She stated, "All the lights went off. The gas was turned off. I called Dr. Wright and he ran over with the money." The Museum had no endowment. The contributions, exhibits and shows provided the sole income. Groups sponsored bake sales and fish fries, and small parties were also used as fundraisers. Nevertheless, the Museum was in a perpetual fiscal crisis. Mr. Gilmer states that most of the money came from Black people. Wright knew how to inveigle potential small contributors and make them feel a part of his dream.

The money raised through these sources covered some expenses but it was inadequate to cover a paid museum staff. Some of the museum staffing problems were alleviated when it qualified for Comprehensive Education and Training Act (CETA) funds in 1973. The Museum also used staff assistants from the Detroit Board of Education. Aside from the off-duty assistance of Mr. Shannon, Eugene Gilmer and Mrs. Catherine Blackwell, Bill Cody served as acting director of the Museum for six months while on loan from the school system. Dr. Jefferson, general superintendent of Detroit's Public Schools, explained the staff loans and school's relationship with the Museum.

> I, as superintendent, give my blessing to those activities. I admire Dr. Wright very much. He is very committed to developing a vehicle for our people. He wants them to understand themselves and where they came from. I also admire his focus on young people. There was a natural bonding between the school and the Museum.

Meanwhile, Dr. Wright's work with the struggling museum had attracted the interests of many Detroiters. Other organizations were impressed with his energy and commitment to non-profit causes. Somehow, he devoted time to the board of trustees for WTVS Channel 56 (PBS in Detroit) 1967-1977; University of Detroit (1971-1976); Hutzel Hospital (1979-81); and the Dunbar Medical Project, Inc. (1979-1981). Dr. Wright's positions in these organizations helped the Museum message to reach beyond the Black community and build new friends elsewhere. However, Dr. Wright never compromised his principles when serving on the boards of WTVS and University of Detroit. He never hesitated to raise questions about the organization's race relations. He finally resigned both boards because of disputes over policy.

Meanwhile, the Museum grew in popularity. As the years went by, the physical limitations of the Grand Blvd location became increasingly apparent. Certainly, all of the space in the terrace buildings had been occupied by 1983; there was no room for expansion. Eugene Gilmer recalled "you could get 50 people [in the Museum] but it was an overflowing crowd. We ought to be able to do better than three row houses. At the age of 18, the Museum had matured and was forced to seek larger quarters, preferably, a new building designed for museum needs. The question of financing such a structure became the main topic at board meetings.

The second annual lecture series, sponsored by IAM, consisted of ten weekly Monday lectures, beginning on March 4, 1968, in the auditorium of the Wright Mutual Insurance Company on East Grand Boulevard. For this series, the Museum sought out members of the community who had outstanding knowledge of and interest in the history of African people in the Americas. Each was highly acquainted with a special field, and spoke on topics that were of vital interest to all that were present. The lectures presented a rare opportunity for IAM members, and the general public to get important information.

The lecturers and their topics:

March 4—Dr. Audrey Smedley—"Modern Anthropology and the Meaning of Race."

March 11—Dr. Charles Whitten—"What is a Negro?"

March 18—Hon. Otis Smith—"The Afro-American in Politics and Government."

March 25—Dr. James Jay—"The Negro in the Sciences."

April 1—Dr. Reginald Wilson—"Economic Aspects of Neo-Colonialism."

April 8—Mr. Harold Lawrence—"The History of the Afro-American in the Field of Technology."

April 15—Mr. Charles Cotman—"The Negro and Education"

April 22—Dr. Alvin Loving—"An American Negro Takes a New Look at Africa."

April 29—Mr. Thaddeus Gailliard—"The Future of the Afro-American in Business."

May 6—Mr. George Norman—"Slavery."

Although busy with the many museum programs and activities, Wright was a dedicated member of the Detroit Medical Society (DMS). He saw the DMS as another source of information dissemination and opportunity for the community; he knew the Society took its educational functions seriously. It particularly wanted to make Blacks more aware of the variety of available medical careers and professions. In 1968, Charles came up with the idea of making a film about a subject dear to his heart—the education of a physician. After he researched the cost and the art of making recruitment films, he prepared a small production budget for the Detroit Medical Society. In order to make the film, *You Can Be a Doctor,* members of the DMS were asked to contribute $10 to $15 per member. The DMS agreed to fund the documentary.

An unexpected critic of the project was Dr. Lionel Swan, a member the National Medical Association board and a

Detroit physician with considerable influence with the Black medical establishment. He was not enthusiastic about Wright's film project. Apparently, Dr. Swan convinced Dr. Montague Cobb, perhaps the most famous Black medical historian in the country, that Wright's project was a bad idea. In a speech to the DMS, Cobb reminded the DMS that a movie was expensive thing to make. He stated that he made them all the time. He also implied that the money spent on that movie would not be well spent. This speech had the effect of undermining Wright's lobbying efforts with DMS members. Indeed, Wright's final budget for the movie had increased to about $40 per member. Some members of the DMS balked at his final figures. In characteristic manner, Dr. Wright decided that he would go ahead with the project. He paid the initial costs of production out of his pocket. A few physician friends also helped with the final costs. As it became clear that Dr. Wright was determined to make this film, the DMS contributed some additional funds. The total cost of the film came to $6,000.

The filmscript was a straightforward story of a boy wondering about what it is like to become a doctor, what do physicians do, how do health clinics work and how one becomes a doctor. The film takes the boy through all the steps of a medical education. The filmed location was Kirwood Hospital on Davison Street in Detroit. Completed during the summer of 1968, Dr. Wright wanted to have the film shown at the annual fall meeting of the National Medical Association. He left the responsibility for making the arrangements with Dr. Lionel Swan, then president of the NMA.

Meanwhile Wright continued to give speeches on medical as well as cultural issues. He was invited to speak at the annual meeting of the National Association of Planned Parenthood in St. Thomas, Virgin Island. After a side trip to Tampico, Mexico, Charles went to Houston for the 1968 NMA conference. To his dismay, Dr. Swan had not made arrangements for the showing of his movie. Charles found himself trying to make last minute arrangements to show the film between

The Wright Man

meetings. This failed, so Wright set up the film in the lobby of the hotel. He tried to buttonhole conference participants to watch the film, but few were interested. He was so angry and disappointed that he left the conference before the end of the scheduled meetings.

When Dr. Swan returned to Detroit, he told people that he had prevented Wright from showing the film at the formal meeting, but that Dr. Wright had tried to show it in the lobby. To Swan, the showing of the film was a self-promotion ploy by Wright. The film became a controversial topic for the DMS and it divided the group into factions. Dr. Wright was finally allowed to show the film at a Detroit Medical Society meeting. One physician remarked, "That damn Wright changed the film. He is not even in this one."[3] The showing helped erase the impression that the film was a self-promotional effort on Wright's part.

The following year Wright visited New York and saw a sign soliciting professional films at the McGraw Hill Book Company. He went in and asked to talk to someone about his film. A Black employee listened to Dr. Wright's description of the recruitment production, and encouraged him to send it to the company's film division. The company liked the film and entered into a contract with the Museum for national distribution. The film sold well for many years, and the commissions from the film were donated to the Museum.

Frank Seymour, a prominent Detroit public relations person, liked the film projects and suggested that a similar one be made for banking. A proposal was written, and Mr. Seymour presented a it to the National Bank of Detroit (NBD) for funding. Aubrey Lee, a vice president and a rising star at the bank, was chosen for the lead role in the movie. The film was shot at several bank locations. The script included a small boy entering a bank and asking questions about its operations.

The Corporate NBD liked the movie, and scheduled a lunch-hour preview at the bank. Community people were invited to see the film. The NBD was so pleased with the final production that they sent an executive officer to New York's Chase Manhattan Bank to show the film. It cost the NBD $14,000 to make, and they subsequently sold the film nationally. The Museum received a gratuity from the sale. The film was submitted to the Ohio Film Festival where it won the second-place award.

Dr. Wright's playwriting skills soared to even greater heights after he heard The Wings Over Jordan rendition of the song, *Were You There?* It seemed to him that he personally was being asked the question and he was spiritually directed to write the play. It opened to a standing room only crowd at the Detroit Institute of Arts.

One major force in the early and progressive development of the Museum was the Support Group. This was a group of volunteer men and women of diverse backgrounds...molded together by a single purpose...to forge a permanent place in the minds of Detroit citizenry for the lasting appreciation for the African American experience and heritage. For much of the early years of the Museum's existence, the foremost promoter and leader of the Support Group was the late Margaret (Boone Jones) Zarif, who was an untiring devotee of the Museum, dedicated to the concept that people must know and understand their past in order to build a positive future.

Initially, this auxiliary, founded in 1969, was comprised of some of the thirty-two original museum founders and a collection of their friends and associates. They shared their desire to learn more about 'our past' as the key for providing a better understanding of the present world we live in, while promoting an enlightened future generation.

As one of the original founders, Dorothy Mottley recalls that in the early days, they performed a variety of tasks which are conducted by employed staff members today, including typing, mailing, filing, telephone operations, housekeeping, tour guide services, as hosts for various functions, preparing

The Wright Man

exhibits, recruiting, procurement, etc. Others among that early auxiliary were Bedia Thomas, Bernice Morton, Oretta Todd, Mildred Pitts, Jacquelin Washington, Gloria Rucker and Pauline Sims, to name a few. One of the most successful fundraisers of this pioneer group was an art auction jointly sponsored with the Junior League of Birmingham. Known as "Artistry In Black," it not only provided high visibility for the museum, but also provided a socially satisfying and cultural interchange between the Museum representatives and the community. Mildred Pitts chaired the program.

Later in its development, the group became known as the I.A.M. "Society." Among those joining the group during this period were Willia Billingsley Miller, Ida Drewery, Marguerite Farmer, Kris Stodghill, Erma Davis and many others who served diligently. When the museum's name was changed to the Afro-American Museum, the group became known as the Support Group of the Afro-American Museum. With the addition of paid staff, the Support Group devoted its efforts primarily to raising funds for non-budgetary items and occasional emergencies, recruitment of new members and supporting various events. Members of the Support Group served in key roles in all of the major programs, projects and building fund drives.

THE 1970S

The 1970s proved to be equally as exciting and productive as the 1960s. The Museum held its first dinner, honoring Detroit "Firsts," at the Book Cadillac Hotel on Washington Boulevard. Among these were the first Black superintendent of schools, the first Black television anchor, and the first Black television station owner. "We are proud of these pioneers," stated Wright, "they all overcame great obstacles to reach their goals and so have we."

Volunteers, full and part time staff, and museum friends continued to work tirelessly. The popularity of the Museum continued to rise and the Museum, not many years into its life, had increased membership to nearly 1,500. Names of many of the volunteers are in the Appendix. Unfortunately, it is not possible to list the many employees who sacrificed so much through the years. Without their hard work and diligence, the Museum would not have grown as it did. However, two long time employees should be highlighted: Billie Van Leer and Kevin Davidson.

Van Leer, through the years, was sort of an ombudsman, working as registrar, secretary and in several departments. She joined the Museum in 1978, and has many memories. She recalls frozen and bursting water pipes, which damaged museum materials, as well as the repeated break-ins and thefts at the buildings. But, primarily she remembers the good times and the good people who came to volunteer or to visit. (She left the Museum in 1998.) Davidson, a master artist in the broadest sense of the word, is the Museum's senior designer. He, too, has weathered the ups and downs of the Museum, but has been of immeasurable value throughout the years.

Beginning in the early 1970s, the Museum had a productive, creative, relationship with artist, Leroy Foster. Joint ventures with and between the Museum, Foster and others, yielded several outstanding works of historic art. In 1972, the Museum initiated a cooperative venture with the Detroit Public Library. Wright had visited the Frederick Douglass branch library at 3636 Grand River and was surprised to see a large portrait of Walter Reuther on the wall, recognizing, however, that it was a tribute and that Reuther had recently died. He contacted Mrs. Clara Jones, then director of the Detroit Library System and they agreed to talk with artist Leroy Foster. Foster concurred that a portrait of Frederick Douglass would be most appropriate for the library that bore Douglass' name. Foster's painting, a beautiful mural, was entitled, "The Life and Times of Frederick Douglass," and was unveiled at a public reception at the library with a distant relative of Frederick Douglass in attendance.

Dr. Wright's play, Were You There?" continued to be presented on into the 1970s. In 1972, the drama was adapted for an in-house, hour long, Easter presentation for Detroit Public Television station, WTVS. The $5,000 production cost was raised by public subscription. The production was televised over several Midwest public television stations (see Appendix). It was also seen on Chicago and Newark public television stations.

During the initial stage presentations of Wright's drama, a Black teen-age group of boys, the Krakow Gang, was recruited to serve as ushers at the DIA. Their presence at the performance created moments of apprehension among the audience, but all was well since it ended well. Wright wrote a second play The *Krakow Gang,* which was never produced. In addition, he wrote a history of the NMA entitled, *The National Medical Association's Turbulent Third Quarter 1945-1970.* For Wright, this was once again the same journalist (in him) that surfaced in the "Bama Brief," and again at Harlem Hospital. It was also his way of crediting Blacks for their contributions to this country. He felt that this history must be written. Charles was never a man who waited for others to do what he could do himself.

Another effort to raise money for the Museum was a golf outing. The Museum was still closely allied with Frank Seymour, who talked to Wright about a plan to create a Black golf tournament. Seymour and Wright worked together and decided on a Frank Lett Golf Outing. It was named in honor of the late Frank Lett, who worked in the public relations department at the National Bank of Detroit. Lett was a Black golfer who had fought against the discrimination of Black golfers. Blacks could not join the Professional Golfers Association and were not welcomed on some golf courses.

More than 100 duffers played in the Museum's first Frank Lett Golf Outing at the Rochester Golf Course on July 7, 1974. Through the persistence of Robert Shannon and a host of golf loving supporters, these outings served as an annual source of financial assistance. (The series was discontinued in 1983).

Dr. Wright's friendship and admiration for Leroy Foster's work continued. In 1976, the medical staff of the soon-to-be closed Boulevard General Hospital was planning a large "bash" in honor of the closing and the merger with Southwest General Hospital. Boulevard General had a specially accumulated fund, which was to finance the celebration party. Wright, hearing of these plans, called together the major players at Boulevard General and *boldly* suggested that a mural in the new building might be better than a party. He was successful in getting them to finance a "mighty mural" called Kaleidoscope, for the lobby wall. The huge painting was completed in Foster's studio on a canvas that had to be transported by truck to the hospital.

Leroy Foster, continuing his relationship with the Museum and the community, joined with UAW workers to do a series of paintings of Paul Robeson in 1978 for his 80th birthday salute, showing his many careers. They were placed in several public buildings around the city. In addition, Foster, a graduate of Cass Technical High School, had presented a painting to the school as a gift. Some months later, someone splashed paint on the drawing, causing serious damage. The vandalism was reported in a long and descriptive article in the Detroit Free Press. Wright, Leno Jaxon and others read the article and set about to raise funds to have the work restored. The public responded eagerly and Foster was greatly pleased. He restored the painting and was the center of attention at the "completion reception." Wright contacted the same Free Press reporter and asked that this positive event be "covered." It was.

Once again, Wright's attention was directed to the needs of the Detroit Medical Society. Charles Wright's writing ability was recognized by his colleagues when he was asked to play a key role in the Dunbar Project. In 1977, Dr. Wright, on behalf of the Detroit Medical Society, was asked to make a presentation to the Medical Center Citizens' District Council. He asked for permission to purchase the building, which housed the old Dunbar Hospital, founded in 1918. Dunbar, named after the poet, Paul Laurence Dunbar, along with Mercy Hospital, had been one of the few places Black doctors could send patients in the twenties. It also served as a place to train nurses and interns. The Frederick Street building, later, had been sold to the Diggs family, and used as a funeral home. In disrepair, in later years it was saved from demolition by Hilanius H. Phillips, a city planner. The Detroit Medical Society wanted to restore the building and make it their organizational headquarters. The site, at 580 Frederick, was designated an historical site by the State of Michigan. (It was a sad time in 1992 when thieves stole the dedication plaque from the building's yard.) The committee to restore the building was dubbed the Dunbar Medical Project and Wright served on the Project Committee Board. This project was consistent with Dr. Wright's interest in setting the historical record straight.

By 1979 it became apparent that the Museum was rapidly outgrowing the limited quarters at 1549-53 West Grand Boulevard; additional space was badly needed. The Museum's collection and activities had grown steadily over the years. The location on West Grand Boulevard was inadequate to properly house the present and future exhibits and library, to store art and artifacts in a properly controlled environment or to provide space for growing staff.

In June 1979, the Afro-American Museum of Detroit Building Fund was officially formed, the sole mandate was to raise the necessary funds. Frank Seymour had complained about the Museum's name, especially the "International" and it was dropped.

The Building Fund, like the Museum itself, was community based. Community organizations, clubs, businesses, churches, the Detroit and suburban public schools, and concerned individuals all played an active role in the campaign.

THE BUY-A-BRICK CAMPAIGN

Building a new facility from the ground up would cost an enormous amount of money. Wright and the board believed that they could build a new facility much like Black churches, one brick at a time. The Buy-A-Brick Campaign, with John Copeland, of the YMCA as chair, had a goal to build a new facility by 1980. This was a bad time to start a fundraising campaign. The country had elected a Republican conservative to the Presidency and it would not be a good decade for Blacks. Ronald Reagan and his tax-cutting proposals fascinated the nation. Mayor Coleman Young was gearing up for one of his toughest reelection campaigns in the midst of rumors of a major fiscal crisis. The 1980 census revealed that Detroit was now 73% Black, up from 44%. The following year the nation was in a mild recession, with slow growth and rampant inflation. The automobile companies were not holding their own with their market share, against the Japanese and the Europeans.

If the Museum had an enthusiastic constituency, it was the students in Detroit Public Schools. Wright and his board had done an excellent job of selling the concept of museum visiting to the school system. They had opened their mobile museum there and had produced several exhibits at various schools. Wright recalled, "The idea of allowing students to raise the seed capital for their museum caught on among the teachers and spread to the students like a brush fire. When the proposal for a Buy-A-Brick Campaign was presented, Dr. Arthur Jefferson, general superintendent of Detroit's Public Schools, was hopeful that his "struggling school system" could make a representative showing in such a public campaign. The students and teachers were enthusiastic about the idea.

The Wright Man

Dr. Jefferson and the Detroit Board of Education authorized the promotion of the project in the schools and the eight-week drive was on. Every child in a Detroit Public School had an opportunity to buy a brick for the Museum. There was no fixed price and all donations were accepted. The idea was that children could come to the Museum and have a sense of ownership since they had bought a brick to build it. Wright recalled, "the students knew the product and seized the opportunity to buy into it. Among other things, they sold candy, sponsored discos, ran errands, delivered papers and begged their parents for 'quiet, folding money.'" "Children were proud to say, 'I bought a brick for the Museum.'" Administrators, teachers, and students were mobilized for the campaign. There was competition among schools for the greatest per capita collection. Reporting on the result of the Board of Education's Buy-A-Brick campaign, Wright was delighted to announce that $86,000 had been contributed to the Building Fund. Even with Detroit's slumping real estates prices, it was not enough. These funds were also used to start a fund-raising office needed for the new facility.

TAKING STOCK OF PROGRESS

In 1981, Robert Shannon's presidential report announced that the future of the Museum was "definitely up-beat." He reported that the Buy-A-Brick program had raised $86,000. The Paul Robeson Award and Frank Lett Memorial Golf Tournament were going well. The Museum had also received grants and donations from WDIV, the Phillip L. Graham Fund, the Webber Foundation, the Detroit Council of the Arts and the National Endowment for the Arts (NEA). The NEA gave $30,000 for architectural services. Mr. Shannon reported that many clubs and organizations had also pledged to help the Museum. The Cotillion Club pledged and gave $10,000. By church building standards, this was a lot of money. However, a museum building would cost millions.

Meanwhile, the current museum facility had operating cost problems. In 1981, the Museum lost its CETA funds, its paid staff, and was forced to rely very heavily on its volunteers. The Wright family invested more and more time and energy into the Museum.

The 1981 Anniversary Dinner, chaired by Owsley G. Spiller and Dr. Janice G. Frazier, celebrated sixteen years for the Museum. Margaret Dudley, executive director; James A. Lewis, curator; and Robert Shannon, board president welcomed the dinner guests. Distinguished Service Awards were presented to Snow F. Grigsby, retired U.S. Postal worker and Community Leader; Reginald B. Henderson, Quality Laboratory owner; Donald S. Vest, Ford Motor Company, Personnel; and Johnetta Cross Brazzell, Oakland University, Urban Affairs. The Hon. Ronald V. Dellums, U.S. Representative for the 8th Congressional District, California, was keynote speaker.

Dr. Wright's sister, Pearl Battle, moved to Detroit in 1982 and later became director of volunteers at the Museum. A great deal of publicity was generated when she bought a $1,000 lifetime membership for her granddaughter, Danielle Kitson, who was then six months old.

No one knew at the time, but the solution to their fiscal crisis would be found at the 18th Anniversary Banquet. In 1983, many of the founding members, new supporters and contributors met to celebrate the Museum's "coming of age" and "to pass the baton for the next lap of the journey for a new museum building. Delta Sigma Theta Sorority had made annual contributions to the project, as had Reginald Henderson's Quality Clinical Laboratories. Prior to the banquet, Dr. Wright proposed to the trustees that the adult's campaign would be called the Million Dollar Club (MDC). The plan was to solicit a $1,000 building fund pledge from each banquet attendee. Assuming they could get one thousand $1,000 pledges, they would have a million dollars. Despite the fact that the contributions were tax deductible, the trustees were lukewarm about the proposal.

The Wright Man

Some trustees questioned charging people $50.00 to attend the banquet and then asking to pledge another $1,000. After a heated discussion, the group decided to approach the idea at the banquet as a trial balloon. Dr. Wright's daughter, Stephanie, mobilized her staff to solicit commitments from potential MDC members. They wanted to have several pledges before the 18th Anniversary Banquet. Mrs. Mary Bell, owner of radio station WJZZ, was the first person to pay the entire $1,000 before the banquet. Besides her contribution, Comerica Bank pledged $20,000.

The highlight of the banquet was the speech by Mayor Coleman Young. Young had been mayor for nearly ten years. A speech to museum supporters was a treat for those who had worked tirelessly to interest the city in the Museum's plight. Securing the mayor's participation at an event would always increase the attendance and attract media attention. During the meal, Dr. Wright told the mayor about the MDC effort. The mayor was surprised to hear that Comerica bank had promised to make a $20,000 contribution toward a new museum facility. He was also impressed with the money that had been collected already in cash and pledges. Wright recalled:

"When told about the Million Dollar Club, the Mayor smiled, wryly, and used a few well chosen oaths that suggested that I was devious and was not to be trusted. In good humor, he added: "I knew there was a catch to it. I guess I can afford a thousand dollars."

Wright: "Sorry, Mr. Mayor, but a thousand is not enough for you."

Mayor: "But you just said."

Wright: "Yes, I know, But the thousand is for the ordinary citizen. Detroit's first citizen must pledge $5,000. We must give the others something to aim at."

"The Mayor's explosive declamation confirmed my untrustworthiness. Realizing that he had been had, Mayor Young smiled, and agreed to make his pledge when called upon."

After the address, Dr. Wright introduced the Million Dollar Club to the crowd. He explained its purpose, and on cue the Mayor responded with a $5,000 pledge, followed by the Comerica pledge, and then Mrs. Mary Bell's pledge. People began making pledges. The brief campaign netted $85,000 in cash and pledges. The mayor was impressed. Before leaving, he turn to Dr. Wright and said, "Charlie, I think you've got something going here. I'll call you in a few days, and we'll talk about it."

And talk they did. The news was that the Mayor, for the first time, saw the potential for the Museum and decided the city should become involved. Before long, the City of Detroit agreed to lease property at Frederick and John R streets to the Museum at a nominal cost, for the site of the new facility. The Mayor also offered to share the cost of the construction. The architectual firm of Sims-Varner & Associates developed the plans. The projected costs of the facility was $5,000,000 with an initial phase construction cost of approximately $2,000,000.

No one would have anticipated that the Detroit Board of Education and its staff would emerge as the strongest and most consistent supporters of the Museum. By pitching the Museum to children and stressing its educational benefits, Dr. Wright was able to mine the considerable goodwill of the public school establishment. Without its assistance, it is doubtful the Museum could have sponsored the mobile museum, the Robeson Scholarship and the Buy-A-Brick Campaign.

Charles Wright had also proven that he could confront the art patron establishment and survive. He had gotten support from people who never supported museums in their lives. His appeal across the class lines in the Black community worked. It was a difficult struggle keeping the doors open, but Wright was committed.

The Museum grew, and with its growth came the continued realization that it needed a better facility in a better location. The fundraising continued at a steady pace. The prospect of the City's involvement kept their spirits high.

In 1983, the Museum's board members were searching for more ways to raise money for operating expenses and programs. A street race was decided upon as one fundraiser, because of the popularity of running. Don Vest became the Street Race Director and the race was named after Jim Ramsey. Ramsey, a Detroit resident, was known throughout the state for his running abilities-races of 6 miles, 10 miles, 15 miles and even marathons. Vest described him as a "beacon and mentor, as a physical activist and a role model for both young and old because of the kind of life he leads." The 1983 race was an economic and social success (as were those that followed).

Just prior to 1983's summer session, Detroit's Department of Recreation eagerly met with museum officials regarding the Ethnic Festivals at Hart Plaza in downtown Detroit. The city representatives expressed a wish to include each year, a Black festival that contained a strong African component. After some discussion the museum representatives agreed to sponsor an "African World Festival," the first in 1983. It had as its theme, "The African World Is One." The museum's festivals have proven to be the most successful of all of the city's summer programs.

The Million Dollar Club continued to grow, adding special membership perks. One was that all who contribute $1,000.00 or more would have their names engraved on a scroll of honor in the new building. In the next few years, the Million Dollar Club raised more than $400,000. When persons complained about the $1,000.00, Wright would remind them that it would cost only $1.00 per day for 3 years.

With this kind of salesmanship, a large percentage of Detroit's population became Million Dollar Club members.

Among the numerous exciting programs at the Museum was the role played by the City's artists. In the spring of 1983, the Afro-American Museum's Support Group sponsored a program called "The Artists' Showcase" with an excellently crafted program book. Wright stated, "We of the Afro-American Museum of Detroit, have had a rich and rewarding relationship with the artists in the community; it began in the late 1960s, soon after the Museum was started." Dr. Wright also pointed out that when the first newsletter needed a drawing to attract the public to the front page, Yvonne Catchings came forth with the work that launched the Museum's literary career. When the Museum needed a site to try a hand at auctioneering, Henri Umbaji King offered ideas, objects and a site on East Adams. Artists who were highlighted during the Showcase program are listed in the Appendix.

Besides the listed artists, were others who made significant contributions and are named in their program booklet. This colorful event, an expression of appreciation from The Support Group for the long-time assistance from the artists, was captured on videotape by Project BAIT (Black Awareness in Television), under the guidance of teacher, writer David Rambeau.

On June 20, 1983, Dr. Wright spoke on the great educator and historian, Dr. Carter G. Woodson. Dr. Woodson founded the Association for the Study of Afro-American Life and History and wrote "The Mis-education of the Negro," which criticized the educated Black elite who failed to aid fellow Blacks.

A subsequent lecture discussed the controversial and continual debate between Booker T. Washington and W.E.B. DuBois. Dr. DeWitt Dykes of Oakland University gave an in-depth analysis of the viewpoints of both of these great Black

The Wright Man

leaders. The evening and series ended with a documentary film produced by Ben Frazier, aired on WTVS-56, entitled, "Two Paths to Freedom." The well-known actor, John W. Hardy, read poems about the life and times of both Washington and DuBois.

THE 19TH ANNIVERSARY

The Museum's "19th Anniversary Celebration" was innovative and historic. The March 30, 1984 Celebration had a new format which began with a champagne reception, cultural exhibits and concluded with some of Detroit's finest performing artists, rocking the usually staid Rackham Auditorium. Dr. Phyllis E. Robinson chaired the celebration and Kathryn A. Bryant and Dorothy H. Moore were co-chairs. Robert Shannon, board president, voiced his pride in the many projects and programs and thanked the staff, volunteers, and friends for their support, encouragement, and dedication. He stated that a particular source of pride was the fact that the groundbreaking ceremonies for the new home in the Cultural Center would occur in the very near future. Thanks were also extended to the following people for donating their time and talent to the Anniversary Celebration: John W. Hardy, producer of the show; The B Ballade String Quartet - Phyllis M. Fleming; The Afro-Musicology Workshop Ensemble - Dr. Morris J. Lawrence; Rod (Nimrod) Lumpkin; Kim Weston; and Ben Frazier and Dayna Eubanks, who were the program's host and hostess. The New Breed Bebop Society Instrumental Quartet, Teddy Harris, Kim Weston, Afro-American Studio Theatre - Dr. Von Washington; Orthea Barnes; Earl D.A. Smith; James Tatum Trio; Miche Braden, Carol Morisseau; Marcus Belgrave - Ron Jackson; The Sultans, and Lloyd Storey all donated time and talent.

Billie VanLeer was the recipient of the 1984 Outstanding Museum Service Award, in recognition of her never-ending, valued support, and long-time staff service. Other awardees were Aretha Watkins and Mary Bell, for outstanding corporate service; and Hon. Erma Henderson, for outstanding community service.

During this time of activity and planning the Museum board agreed that the word "Afro" was not appropriate for the name. Dr. Margaret Burroughs, on one of her visits to Detroit, from Chicago, heard of the discussion and stated that the name should be Museum of African American History. She indicated finality and no one contested her "suggestion."

THE CULTURAL CENTER

The dream of the new building was now much more than a dream. Everyone was elated about its future location.

The site, at the corner of Frederick Street and Brush was ideal. The lot extended to John R on the west; across John R Street is the Detroit Institute of Arts. Adjacent to the lot is the Center for Creative Studies, with programs in several other buildings in the area.

The ground breaking on May 21, 1985, was a special occasion for the many museum followers and for the City. Students from nearby Golightly Education Center were invited and joined in the momentous occasion. One student who attended, Deidre Proctor, will appear in our story on two other occasions.

From 1985 to the grand opening, on May 7, 1987, there was ceaseless work in every conceivable direction. On February 2, 1985 the newspaper carried an "Advertisement for Bids" for the construction of the Museum of African American History for the City of Detroit Community and Economic Development Department. The Museum contract was awarded to Joe Gough of Gough Construction Company.

Needless to say, 1985 was a busy time. However, the plans began to take shape more firmly in 1986. Initially Betty

The Wright Man

Allen was given leave from her job at the Detroit Historical Museum and was asked to oversee the transition to the new site and its construction. It was an awesome task but no one doubted Allen's ability to succeed.

Pearl Wright Battle, sister of Dr. Wright, was selected in 1986, as chief of volunteers. The volunteer roster shows a listing of some of the most dedicated persons imaginable. They served as docents, having full knowledge of the museum and an acquaintance with the plans for the new construction.

PREPARATION & ACTIVITIES

Amidst the boxes and preparation for the move in 1986, a few activities continued without interruption. In accordance with the by-laws of the Museum of African American History, the annual meeting was held on September 20 at Plymouth United Church of Christ, led by Martha Vincent and Clarence Stone. Dr. Charles Adams of Hartford Church gave a stirring address. The meeting agenda included a financial statement, reports from the various departments and a progress report on the new Museum site.

A church committee was organized under the chairmanship of trustee, Dr. Elizabeth Hood to help with fundraising for the Museum. Members included Robbie McCoy, Bishop P.A. Brooks, Rev. Earl Calloway, Rev. James A. Caver, Annette Clardy, Keller L. Coleman, John Copeland, Dr. Austin Curtis, Frances Curtis, Rev. Robert Dulin, Eugene Gilmer, Rev. Havious Green, Ann Haney, Sarah Haygood, Rev. Matthew Jones, Rev. Joseph Jordan, Rev. James Lewis, Barbara Turner Mays, Franklin Mills, Latrell Powers, Dr. Mary O. Ross, Nellis Saunders, Robert Shannon, board president; Louvert Weldon and Lauretta Whitsett.

This committee's first project, "The Great Hours of Caring," was launched on October 12th. Each congregation was asked to make a special, tax-deductible, financial contribution to the support of the Museum. This was the beginning of an annual event that was of great help to the Museum, in 1986 and in future years.

Needless to say, one person did not turn the wheels of this organization. It was a massive effort by many who shared the dream and shared the commitment of Dr. Wright. Although the Museum had been operating out of cramped quarters and with limited resources for 21 years, it still managed to host over 500,000 visitors, make hundreds of presentations in Detroit area classrooms, mount more than 400 exhibits, and house the beginning of an important collection of African art, artifacts and historical papers.

During the period from 1965 to 1986, many individuals took over the helm of the Museum at crucial moments to steer the course through stormy as well as calm seas. Each, in his or her own way, contributed to the Museum's survival and growth.

Presidents/executive directors from 1965 to 1990, are as follows:

Betty Allen	Henderson Hendricks
Nancy Allen	Charles Howell
Leonard Andrews	James Jemison
Margaret Ashworth	Leno Art Jaxon
Marvin L. Brown	Dr. Marion Moore
Dr. Edward Cody	Edward Morris
Robert Shannon	K. Audley Smith
Margaret Dudley	Barbara Ward
Jane Ulmer Ford	Elrie Crite*
Edward Gee	

* First Executive Director

The vision of the new building occupied everyone's thoughts. Howard Sims designed it to complement the

The Wright Man

landscape of the Cultural Center. The design was a modern structure, with a large exhibit area, offices, storage space, a multi-purpose room, and parking areas in front of the building. Each stage of the building was captured on video, courtesy of David Rambeau. Rambeau also taped interviews with the builders at the building site. The $3.5 million building was completed in the spring of 1987.

Dr. Wright was fully engaged in the planning for the new Museum. He even proposed that there be no admission charges. He reasoned that the public had paid with taxes included in the Block Grant money. He envisioned museum space to be available to visitors at a minimum cost. He also wanted to utilize the staff for public programs. Dr. Wright foresaw the management of the Museum as a joint venture with the City. He even suggested that the development committee agree to raise sufficient funds to cover 40% of the operating expenses. In these twenty-two years, Wright had proven that museums can be created by "the people."

The birthplace — 1549 W. Grand Blvd
Opened March 1965

The Mobile Museum — Opened summer 1967

Opening May 1987 — 301 Frederick Douglass

Opening April 1997 — 315 E. Warren Avenue

The Wright Man

Mobile Museum — Parked on 12th Street

Dr. Wright and Volunteers on W. Grand Blvd

A Wall Street Journal reporter interviewing Executive Director Audley Smith and Wright

Groundbreaking ceremony, 1985
Dr. Elizabeth Hood at podium
Ron Hewitt, Hon. Erma Henderson, Mayor Coleman Young, Wright, Louise Wright, Rosa Parks

The Wright Man

Margaret Zarif, museum board member

Groundbreaking 1985
From left — Museum friend, Councilman Clyde Cleveland, Dr. Leonard Douglas, Leon Atcheson,
Catherine Blackwell, Dr. Arthur Jefferson, Lonnie Bates, Rev. Jesse Jackson, Wright, Norman Dilliard, Robert Shannon

Construction in progress
301 Frederick Douglass
Wright and Executive Director Betty Allen

Wright's sister, W. Pearl Wright Battle, Director of Volunteers

The Wright Man

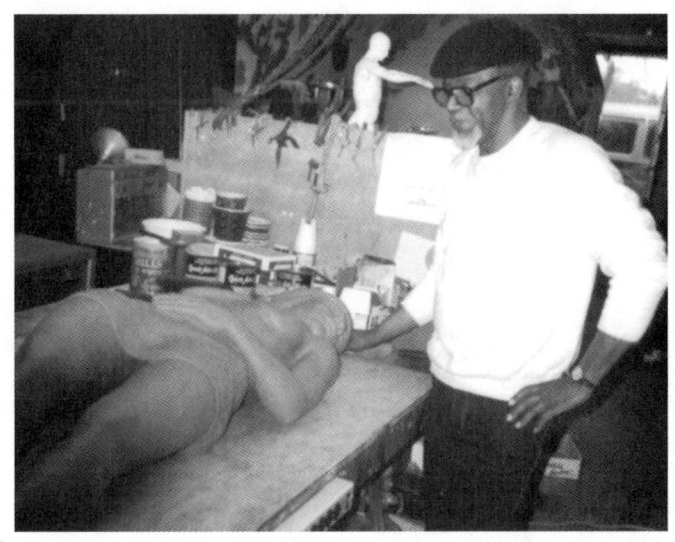

Sculpturer, Oscar Graves, at work on museum exhibit

Slave ship designed by Oscar Graves for museum's permanent exhibit — 1987-1997

The Wright Man

A NEW PHASE

At the January 25, 1987 board of directors meeting, Dr. Wright stated "We are gathered here to re-format for the next phase of the Museum's development." The Museum would be 22 years old on March 10. Wright expressed thanks to the people of Detroit. He was always aware of their love, concern, interest and involvement. Wherever he went, people stopped him to congratulate him on "his Museum." His immediate response would be that "this is not my Museum, this is our Museum."

> Lying, thinking
> last night
> How to find my soul a home
> Where water is not thirsty
> And bread loaf is not stone
> I came up with one thing
> And I don't believe I'm wrong
> That nobody
> But nobody
> Can make it out here alone.

Maya Angelou

Dr. Wright also expressed thanks to the personnel of the Detroit Historical Museum for their assistance and, of course, for Betty Allen. Fred Martin, Mayor Young's assistant, attended the meeting and attempted to explain the relationship with the city of Detroit. He agreed that the existing board would constitute the first board. This pleased Dr. Wright.

The contract would soon be finalized; but, the level of the City's support would be somewhere between $800,000 and $1,200,000. Committees were appointed as the transition proceeded including a transition committee. At this meeting Betty Allen was appointed to fill the position as the executive director.

Dr. Wright, not missing an opportunity, had given thought to the street sign, "Frederick," and decided it should be changed to "Frederick Douglass." The petition was sent to City Council and Council granted the request on May 1, 1987. The name change was a media event—cameras, reporters, and spectators lined the street. It was further requested that all future structures to be built on Frederick Douglass, between John R and St. Antoine, be limited to those related to African American history.

In place of the open field and cottonwood trees, now stood the almost completed trapezoid shaped structure. By spring, the stunning, 22,000 square foot facility was completed. The facility housed exhibition space, two multi-purpose rooms, a gift shop and administration area, which included offices, storage, a fabrication shop and a library. The main entrance from the parking lot opened into a glass enclosed lobby which led past the Million Dollar Club "Scroll of Honor", listing names of individuals who had contributed at least $1,000.00 and organizations that had contributed at least $5,000.00 to the Building Fund.

UNDERGROUND RAILROAD AND SLAVE SHIP

It was Dr. Wright's suggestion that the inaugural exhibition would relate to the Underground Railroad. Larry Thomas, who worked for the Smithsonian Institute in Washington, D.C., was recommended to design the exhibition. Thomas agreed to accept the challenge and visited Detroit regularly. He met with several fabrication houses in Detroit and

The Wright Man

made the selections of all the individuals that would be involved in putting it together. Sadly, Mr. Thomas suffered a heart attack and died before he could perform the final steps. The Smithsonian sent Kenneth Young to complete the project. The work was titled "An Epic of Heroism: The Underground Railroad in Michigan 1837-1870."

Oscar Graves designed the slave ship, a focal point in the Museum's display area. It was the subject of discussion by all who visited; the crowded ship was a reminder of the horror of the middle passage. The story is often repeated about Wright's reaction when he saw that one of the bronze figures (a ship "passenger") was smiling. The sculptor was given a stern reprimand and ordered to remove the smile post-haste and before delivering it to the Museum.

Cooperation was the key word during 1987. The Detroit Institute of Arts assisted with lighting installations, prior to the opening. The Detroit Historical Museum helped with the exhibit design. Oscar Graves, the sculptor, continued his work as did mural painter, Kevasi Asante. Historic Wayne helped solve some of the storage problems and Burroughs/Unisys, thanks to Norman Dillard, donated an entire computer system.

Other companies that came forward to provide major assistance were Hudsons, MichCon, Kresge/K-Mart, and the Michigan Sesquicentennial Commission on which Wright served. George Johnson and Company, auditors, worked diligently; and board members and staff rolled up their sleeves and got the job done. The Sims-Varner company's architectural drawings and vision, combined to produce a spectacular structure. The bright red "hut motif" symbolizing African villages, gracing the museum roof, brought positive comments from the visitors. The wooden doors leading into the main exhibit area were carved with Adinkra symbols by the Daris' Design Group of Detroit, and were called the "Portals of Sankofa."

May 7, 1987, heralded the beginning of the five-day Inaugural Ceremony of the new site of the African American Museum of History. The decision to extend the opening over five days was suggested by Wright. The five days would allow all persons associated with the Museum to be honored and accomodate the entire community as well.

The week of activities included a luncheon, a parade, an elegant evening party and a brunch. Mayor Coleman Young spoke at the luncheon at the University of Michigan, Rackham Graduate School on Farnsworth Street. After the luncheon program, the Mayor, Dr. Wright, and 9-year-old Deidre Proctor, led the short walk to the Museum. Dr. Wright selected Deidre because she had been present with the Golightly school classmates at the groundbreaking and also at a photo session sponsored by Hutzel Hospital. (Hutzel wanted to showcase Wright in their next publication and had scheduled his appearance at the construction site. Wright agreed, only if some students could join him in the picture.)

The ribbon cutting and release of hundreds of balloons produced a spectacular scene as the crowd gathered around for more speeches and celebration.

Charles Wright reflected over the entire history of the Museum that day, from its inception. It had been 24 years, 2 months and five days since the founding on March 10, 1965. The opening festivities continued throughout the week with the scheduled special events, involving schools and churches.

The last day of the opening ceremonies was entitled Church Day. Charles Wright knew that the backbone of the Black community was the church. It was the single most stable institution and a major source of funding. The churches involved were Metropolitan Baptist, Pilgrim Missionary Baptist, Antioch Church of God in Christ, First Baptist Institutional Church, Metropolitan Church of God, Fellowship

The Wright Man

Chapel, Bethel AME Church and Sacred Heart Catholic Church of Detroit. Local high school bands provided music, as did the churches.

The Scroll of Honor, located on the lobby wall, carried the names of the Million Dollar Club members. They came to see their names and to have others see their names emblazoned on the bronze-plated scroll. Wright basked in the praise and the recognition, but he also thought about what was behind the facade; a beautiful building would attract some visitors but would it deter others? Would people be intimidated by the slick, modern architecture? Would it lose its folk artness? Were its financial worry days really over? These thoughts quickly disappeared from his mind as he savored the moment.

U.S. CONSTITUTION: 200TH YEAR

After the excitement of the opening days lessened, Wright set about to the business of continuing to fulfill the museum's mission. Aware that the United States Constitution was ratified in 1787, he decided the Museum's role was to feature some of the major, significant historical happenings for the 200th anniversary.

Three programs were planned for 1987 and one for 1988. Each was preceded by many weeks of planning and with the assistance of some truly dedicated presenters and sponsors. The first, on June 19, 1987, entitled, "The U.S. Constitution and Its Impact on African Americans" drew a large group to the Rackham Building auditorium. The distinguished presenters were the Honorable Avern Cohn, U.S. District Court Judge; the Honorable George Crockett, U.S. Congressman; the Honorable Wade H. McCree, Professor of Law, University of Michigan and former Solicitor General of the United States; and Professor Harold Norris of the Detroit College of Law. McCree came, although ill, and Wright was at a loss to know how to fully convey his deep and sincere appreciation. The supporting sponsors for the program were the National Conference of Black Lawyers; Wolverine Bar Association; Michigan Association of Black Judges and Wayne State University.

The second program was entitled, "U.S. Constitution and Slavery," and was held at the Museum on October 25, 1987. Professor Paul Finkelman, the lecturer, was a constitutional historian at the State University of New York at Binghampton. Co-sponsors of this interesting and provocative program were University of Michigan - Dearborn; the Phylon Society of Wayne State University; and the Black Legal Alliance of the Wayne State University Law School. The Hon. Avern Cohn was responsible for helping Dr. Wright secure the presence of Professor Finkleman.

Derrick A. Bell, Jr. was the guest speaker for the November program, sponsored by the Museum and the University of Michigan-Dearborn and held at the Rackham Building. Bell, professor of law, Harvard University, drew a large crowd to hear his talk, "Were the Framers of the U.S. Constitution Righteous Racists or Programmatic Politicians?" It was a discussion examining the Constitution and its impact on African Americans. The guest panel of responders were the Honorable Anna Diggs-Taylor, Federal District Court Judge; Heath Meriwether, Executive Editor, Detroit Free Press; and Harold Cruse, Professor Emeritus, History and African American Studies, University of Michigan. The post program reception was held at the Museum and Professor Bell autographed copies of his book, "And We are Not Saved: The Elusive Search for Racial Justice." Co-sponsors of the program were the Phylon Society, Wayne State University, Black Legal Alliance, Wayne State University Law School. Joseph Wright, Esq., then an administrator at U of Michigan-Dearborn, worked closely with Dr. Wright in the planning of all of the programs.

The Wright Man

In August, just before the African World Festival, a *Detroit Free Press* article told the wonderful story of Dr. Wright's friend, Ann Flanders:

Ann Flanders' contributions to the Museum of African American History are made with the hope that she, in her own way, will be able to give black youngsters an introduction to their often-ignored ancestry.

"I really think they feel sort of lost from our culture," she said. "All you have to do is walk down the street. . . and they avoid your eyes. . . When I walk along the streets. . . I speak to them so they know I see them."

That's why Flanders, 70, of Battle Creek, a retired nurse who worked in hospitals when the wards were segregated and remembers hearing stories of Black patients being abused by white staff members, cried when she heard that the newly opened Museum, located in the Cultural Center, had been scarred by swastikas and racist graffiti.

"It shows that racism is still alive," said Flanders, who responded to the incident with a $5,000 donation check." I just couldn't visualize it. . . vandalizing it. Even now, it still makes me want to cry." Ms Flanders' check was accepted with much gratitude. However, Dr. Wright responded quickly to each and every person who called expressing disgust at the vandalism and to persons who mailed in donations, no matter how small, to help toward the cleaning.

Since Flanders first visited the Museum during a February 1985 business trip to Detroit, Museum officials say she has donated a significant amount of money.

"She has adopted the Museum as her museum," said Dr. Charles Wright, the Museum's chairman. "We certainly appreciate her involvement."

An earlier gift to the Museum was a 1959 Karmann Ghia car that was raffled off at the African World Festival, Aug. 21-23 in Hart Plaza. Proceeds from the raffle were used toward the cost of the African World Festival.

"I had tried over the years to give it (money) someplace that will help.... Otherwise, from a spiritual standpoint, the money is ruining your life," she said. "It has to do some good; it can't just be money to buy you things and things and things."

It is this message that she said she appreciates the most:

"The children, the Black children really do have to have a focus that is going to help them make themselves know that they are persons, just like everybody else and just as good as everybody else," she said.

Flanders discovered the Museum almost by accident during a business trip to Detroit. She read about the facility, then located on W. Grand Boulevard, in a booklet in her hotel room, and summoned a taxi to take her there.

Ms. Flanders, who now lives in Kalamazoo, Michigan, continues her support and love for the Museum.

Besides the raffle, the staff and Dr. Wright's family assisted with the exhibit for the Hart Plaza Gallery. Highlighted were the contributions of Nellie Watts, Dr. William Banks, Attorney Harold Bledsoe, Dr. Robert Greenidge; Marcus Garvey; the Walls Family of Windsor, Ontario, Canada; Dr. Haley Bell; Mary O. Ross; and the families of Dr. William Ferguson and William Webb.

In September, the Louise Lovett Wright Research Library was dedicated. Mrs. Wright, the late wife of Dr. Wright, who was a renowned librarian, had expended effort toward the establishment of the library at the new site. Unfortunately, she did not live to see the library, but her family planned a very special program in her honor. The ceremony opened with a welcome by former director, Mrs. Margaret Dudley. Mrs. Margaret Ward, librarian and archivist, told of the plans for the Research Center. The Hon. Richard Austin joined Stephanie Griggs and Dr. Carla Wright in the unveiling of the Carl Owens painting of their mother. Among the many donations made to the library was $500.00 for the establishment of a Book Award from Lillian Dunn Thomas of Nashville, Tennessee, who was a Million Dollar Club member and a close family friend.

PROGRAMS & FUNDING

On October 10, 1987 the Black United Fund of Michigan through Director, Brenda Rayford and Lawrence C. Patrick, Jr. presented a check of $100,000 to the Museum. Black United Fund had been a supporter of the Museum through the years and Dr. Wright, as chairman, and the entire board of trustees were elated over this generous and much needed donation.

EMANCIPATION PROCLAMATION CELEBRATION

As an introduction to 1988, Dr. Wright planned a January party at the Museum in honor of the 125th anniversary of the reading of the Proclamation of Emancipation. The community room was decorated with baskets, straw and farm "instruments;" and, guests were asked to dress as "field Negroes." Wayne State University professor, Tyrone Tillery, led a lively discussion and the party was interesting and fun, thanks to the efforts of Catherine Blackwell, Norman Dillard, Billie Van Leer and others. Prizes were given to those whose "attire" best suited the aura of 1863.

The Emancipation party was followed by recognition of one of America's most admired freedom fighters. A national 75th birthday tribute was held for Rosa L. Parks. Mrs. Parks was always a favorite of the Museum and, of course, to the large crowd that gathered to salute her. The program consisted of musical selections by the Rosa Parks Middle School Choir and the Martin Luther King Educational Center Suzuki Violinists. Mayor Young and Hon. John Conyers spoke and introduced Carl Owens who unveiled a portrait of Mrs. Parks.

Hon. Damon Keith and Dr. Wright rounded out the program with additional tributes.

THE JAPANESE & THE CONSTITUTION

In February 1988, the fourth of the programs relating to the U.S. Constitution and in honor of the Bicentennial also dealt with the failure of the Constitution to provide equal protection to all citizens. This session was directed to the problems of the Japanese, with the leader being Judge William M. Marutani of Philadelphia, Pennsylvania. The Honorable Maryann Mahaffey, City of Detroit Councilperson, was instrumental in bringing the illustrious judge to the Museum. He had served in the U.S. Military Intelligence as a 2nd Lieutenant and was a member of the Commission on Wartime Relocation and Internment of Civilians. The Japanese community joined with representatives from Detroit's International Institute and the Museum of African American History to commemorate the 46th Anniversary of the activation of Executive Order 9066, by President Franklin D. Roosevelt. With the implementation of this Order, the constitutional rights of 120,000 Japanese Americans, mostly citizens, were imprisoned without charge, for up to three and one half years. The informative lecture, by Marutani, was followed by a reception featuring Japanese cuisine and an exhibit at the Museum of African American History.

These are the kinds of programs Dr. Wright sees as being important and meaningful because they are about history. All four programs attracted sizeable audiences.

1988: A BUSY YEAR

This was the first year that Black History Month had been celebrated in the new building. With the observance of Dr. Martin Luther King's birthday coming two weeks earlier, the entire celebration encompassed six weeks.

It began with an exhibit that commemorated the 25th Anniversary of Dr. King's Walk To Freedom down Woodward Avenue. This engagement was followed by a month-long exhibition in the Museum and three weeks in the Blue Cross Blue Shield Building, in downtown Detroit.

On February 14, Essie Robinson's Quilt Exhibit "A Woman and Her Handwork", opened to an enthusiastic crowd in the lobby of the Comerica Building for a six week run. The colorful, artistic designs, tastefully displayed, drew not only crowds but also buyers during the period of the exhibit. The 19 quilts, on display, represented only a small sample of the more than sixty years of creativity of Mrs. Robinson. It was an unforgettable experience "to abide among these quilts."

On February 28, members of the American Jewish Committee visited the Museum for a tour of the exhibits and a discussion with staff members to explore the possibility of joint ventures that will improve the communication between Blacks and Jews. Considerable progress was made to develop an agenda of mutual concerns, one of which was to arrange visits, tours of the Holocaust Museum and the African American Museum, by young people of each community.

Betty Allen resigned as executive director, due to illness, and the Mayor selected Nancy Allen to help with the transition and serve as acting director. Nancy Allen, in her March 1988 Annual Report, summarized some of the activities that had taken place since the move to Frederick Douglass. In addition to listing the programs, she complimented the staff and volunteers.

"These activities are the result of hard work and dedication from the staff, and I must include the hard work and commitment of our volunteers who have given over 7000 hours of service, in administrative affairs, with the Museum Store, and serving the public. Our volunteer tour guides have helped several thousands of visitors to better understand and appreciate the historical and cultural heritage of the African American."

"I would like to say to all of our staff and volunteers thank you for a job well done. While we have not always had a very smooth transition from one program to another, we have survived this hectic period with an impressive record. Let us now begin to plan for year two in our new facility as we work toward consolidation of our gains, correcting our mistakes, and continue to build a strong and sound foundation for the future. Thank you and keep up the good work for your Museum and community."

In January 1988, Dr. Wright received the prestigious annual reward from the Detroit News as one of the "Michiganians of the Year." A special newspaper supplement highlighted the lives of the honorees. This was followed by an awards ceremony and an elegant dinner party.

On Saturday, April 9, 1988, Dr. Wright helped to sponsor at the Rackham Auditorium, a program that featured such greats as Edward Pierson singing some of Robeson's songs, a prominent Detroit actor and narrator, Von Washington as Paul Robeson and the Hartford choir from Hartford Memorial Baptist Church under the direction of Jimmie Abbington. The program celebrated Robeson's 90th anniversary and was co-sponsored by the U.S. Peace Council. The event also featured a visual presentation from the Robeson family archives.

AN EPIC OF HEROISM: STUDIED

Because of the popularity of the Museum's primary exhibit, staff and resource assistants produced a well-written, informative *Study Guide and Resource Booklet* for the inaugural exhibit, "An Epic of Heroism: The Underground Railroad in Michigan 1837-1870." The Study Guide explained that the exhibit chronicled the events, activities, and people of the United States as they struggled with the issues of African slavery, and the efforts of many people of goodwill as they provided the leadership, strength of character, and will to aid in the struggle for freedom for the African Americans held in bondage.

The exhibit provided a panoramic view of the historical episodes of the struggle for freedom in America, and also a perspective on the development of world civilization on the African continent prior to the African slave trade. The known and unknown heroes of the era were presented from the beginning of resistance on the African continent, to captivity aboard slave ships on the sea and to the evolution of the secret organization known as the Underground Railroad.

Since the territory of Michigan entered the Union as the 26th state in 1837, the exhibit focused upon the role of the people of Michigan in the struggle for freedom. Michigan, originally a part of the Northwest Territory where slavery was prohibited by Congress in 1787 under the Northwest Ordinance, was presented from the frontier days under the control of the French to the time of the Underground Railroad, when Michigan would become an intrinsic part of the network of people and locations for anti-slavery activity. Detroit would emerge as a center of the Underground Railroad, as many of its residents would take on leadership roles in helping fugitive slaves escape to freedom. The exhibit ended with a display on men and women of Detroit who would lay a foundation of African American presence and leadership in Detroit.

The Study Guide was compiled by Dr. Benjamin Wilson, Western Michigan University; Katrina Boston, curator of exhibits; Rochelle Lipsey, activities coordinator; Marvin Chatman, curatorial assistant; Marilyn Parker, curatorial clerk; Kevin Davidson, exhibit preparer; Rosemary Powell, accountant; Dr. Marilynn Bell, U of Mich; Nancy Allen, Museum acting director and Reginald Witherspoon, curator of education.

NELSON MANDELA

In the eighties, Dr. Wright's attention turned again to the problems of Africa. He had spoken and written much about the plight of Nelson Mandela. Also, in 1985, Winnie Mandela was invited to the Museum to accept an award after her clinic in Brantford, South Africa was firebombed. Their daughter, Zenani, who was then living in the United States, accepted the award on behalf of her mother.

On July 18, 1988, Nelson Mandela celebrated his seventieth birthday while in Poolsmoor Prison, near Capetown, South Africa and the world celebrated with him. It was an occasion where all those supporting human dignity, justice and peace stood up to be counted.

Pope John Paul expressed his admiration for Mandela. The West German Chancellor, Helmut Kohl, challenged South Africa, urging the government to speak with Mandela and other previously outlawed forces. Greetings came also from Jaruzelski of Poland and Mitterand, the French President. Mitterand praised Mandela for devoting his life to the ideals of justice, dignity and liberty.

The Scandinavian countries sent word hoping Mandela would be able to celebrate his birthday in freedom in liberated South Africa. The European Community, through the foreign ministers, sent messages calling for the unconditional and immediate release of Mandela and other political prisoners.

The World Council of Churches sent word that Mandela's continued imprisonment was proof of the policy of repression of the South African government. Mike Tyson, the world heavyweight champion, sent Mandela his world title winning boxing gloves. The New Nation, on July 27,1988, reported that from Holland alone, came 170,000 letters and birthday cards. London held a big birthday concert and paved the way for concerts all over the world.

The Wright Man

In Detroit, the local papers took note of the occasion, but by far, the most meaningful and significant event took place at Bethel A.M.E. church on Warren Avenue. The Reverend Norman Osborne, pastor of the church, gave Wright access to the church's community room. The celebration had been planned well in advance. Although others younger and older could "crash" the party, it was primarily for those born in 1918. These 70-year-olds were charged $25.00, a dollar for each year of Mandela's imprisonment.

Wright and Margaret Dudley were the principal planners. They asked David Smedley, who was completing a work assignment at the Museum before heading to the University of Pennsylvania in Philadelphia to pursue a masters degree in Fine Arts, to design and construct an appropriate greeting card. The result was a beautiful 3½' by 5' birthday card. Party attendees were asked to sign it, hoping that some day Mandela night be able to see it and know of the thoughts and prayers of his Detroit area friends. (The card was later taken to the African World Festival at Hart Plaza in August 1988 so others could sign it.) Appropriately, African style food for the party was prepared by Arthur White, a native of Liberia.

ZARIF

On January 8, 1989, a Salute to Margaret (Boone Jones) Zarif was held at the Museum. Zarif was killed in 1983, along with 268 others, on Korean plane, Flight 007 that was shot down over Russian territory, after the efforts by a Soviet military plane to warn that it had invaded Russian air space. Zarif had been one of the Museum's hardest working volunteers in its infancy. She asked everyone she met to join the Museum; she believed strongly in its value and purpose. Zarif spent much of her life studying, teaching and writing in the field of elementary and religious education. Born in Detroit, Zarif had great love for the City and for people, in general.

Zarif left a considerable sum of money to the Museum which, thanks to the timely intervention of David Lawrence, then publisher of the *Detroit Free Press* - the Knight Ridder Foundation, a matching grant was made to the Zarif fund. The money was designated for the establishment of an audio-visual department at the Museum. (In 1998, a museum classroom was named in her honor.)

MUSEUM FRIENDS

On Sunday, March 12, 1989 a group of museum supporters, who called themselves "Friends of the Museum of African American History," sponsored a reception in celebration of the 24th Anniversary. Museum supporters, concerned citizens and interested individuals from the greater metropolitan area were invited. Special invitees to this commemorative affair were museum founders, some of whom came from as far away as New York, Florida and Wisconsin.

One of the highlights of the evening was the unveiling of a founders' scroll that was paid for in part by proceeds from the sixtieth wedding anniversary celebration of Mattie and Ulysses Smedley, parents of founder, Audrey Smedley, and grandparents of Dr. Brian Smedley and David, designer of the founders scroll. Mattie Smedley was an instrumental force in cultivating the Museum. Her living and dining rooms regularly served as gathering places for discussion of matters as staff and volunteers groped for solutions to thorny problems. She also devoted time to work as a museum volunteer.

After the unveiling, each founder was introduced to the audience and welcomed by trustees Eugene Gilmer and Dr. Wright. Each expressed his and her delight at the progress the Museum had shown for the past twenty-four years and pledged full support for all future endeavors.

Proceeds from the reception covered the balance of the $1,925.00 due on the founders' scroll.

The Wright Man

The celebration committee was chaired by Dr. Leonard Douglas and Margaret Dudley, and all of the committee members were congratulated for implementing a most successful and rewarding project. The founders in attendance were James Boyce, Sister Marie Dolores (Keller), Dr. Phillip Mason, Dr. Bernice Morton, Dorothy Mottley, Catherine Obeng, Esther Road, Dr. Audrey Smedley, Dr. Oretta Todd and Dr. Charles Wright.

Guest of Honor at the Museum on April 9, 1989, was the renowned professor, author and historian John Hope Franklin. The Museum, in conjunction with Miller Brewing Company, invited guests to a reception for Dr. Franklin and a viewing of art. This year's theme was "Gallery of Greats: Black Education . . . Building the Foundation" art collection.

During 1989, the Museum Board, selected Dr. Marian J. Moore to replace acting director, Nancy Allen. Dr. Moore came to the Museum from her job as assistant curator at the National Afro-American Museum in Wilberforce, Ohio. Allen was given accolades for a job well done. One of Dr. Moore's first directives was to dismiss Stephanie Griggs, Dr. Wright's daughter as development director. This was confusing to the family because Griggs served without pay and brought in several large contributions. Letters were written to many people and received from many people, but Moore did little to explain her actions.

History, in all its wonderful glory, was depicted in a delightful set of pictures that Dr. Wright obtained for the Museum. In response to a call from a family, living at the tip of the "thumb," Port Austin, Michigan, Wright set out for this little town on the lake. The trip was worthwhile many times over. The paintings, depicting the famous Bert Williams' *Cake Walk*, were precise, colorful and beautiful and attracted much attention while on display.

BLACK NOBEL PRIZE WINNERS

Dr. Wright had a special interest in the Nobel Prize winners and encouraged the Museum to highlight their achievements. The Museum featured the six Black Nobel Prize winners as one of its permanent presentations. This included a very popular poster purchased by many visitors. A handbook was produced so the visitors could be informed of the accomplishments of each. This, as with many other exhibits, was a favorite to discuss with young people.

The Black Nobel Prize Winners and dates of the awards:

Ralph Bunch, 1904-1971—Dr. Bunch received a doctorate in government from Harvard University. He won the Nobel Prize in 1950 for his work in arranging the 1949 Arab-Israeli truce in the Palestine War.

Albert J. Luthuli, 1898-1967—Luthuli led the nonviolent resistance against South African apartheid in the 1940s and 1950s. He received the Nobel Prize for Peace in 1960.

Martin Luther King, Jr., 1929-1968—Dr. King led the Civil Rights Movement of the late 1950s and 1960s preaching that nonviolence was the most effective weapon. Dr. King received the Nobel Prize for Peace in 1964. At age 35, he was the youngest person to ever receive the Peace Prize.

Sir W. Arthur Lewis, 1915—Sir Lewis was deeply concerned about need and poverty in the world. He received the Nobel Prize for Economics in 1979.

Bishop Desmond M. Tutu, 1931—Bishop Tutu worked with South African activists to channel anger into peaceful demonstrations. He raised the most heard Black voice to articulate the churches' opposition to apartheid. Bishop Tutu received the Nobel Prize for Peace in 1984.

The Wright Man

Wole Soyinka, 1934—Soyinka's writings speak compellingly against racism and fascism. He was jailed several times for his efforts for peace in Nigeria. Soyinka received the Nobel Peace Prize for Literature in 1986.

ROBESON

The Museum and the U.S. Peace Council in 1989 again celebrated a landmark date for Paul Robeson. Entitled "Paul Robeson and Peekskill" this exhibit gave a 40-year retrospective of the fateful time in 1949. Speakers for the symposium moderated by Dr. Wright were Louise Patterson of California, Flora Hommel, Kay A. Moshier and Dr. Lamont Yeakey. There was an unveiling of a bust of Paul Robeson, the work of sculptor, Tom Batchelor, M.D. Chris Alston purchased the bust and donated it to the Museum.

The panel discussion centered around the time when Robeson and President Harry S. Truman clashed seriously when Robeson led a citizen's delegation to Truman's office, seeking his support for legislation to outlaw lynching and to legalize voting for African Americans.

The President denied both. After a year of worldwide unrest and with Robeson constantly talking of peace, he met with disfavor in the United States. On August 28,1949, Robeson scheduled for a concert, arrived at Peekskill, New York railway station, alone and unaware that a mob awaited him at the concert site. He was hurried back to New York City before anyone recognized him.

On September 4, 1949, against the advice of friends, Robeson returned to Peekskill, protected by a husky horde of "guards" to sing before a crowd estimated at 25,000. An even larger, angry crowd converged on the concert field to prevent him from singing. Concert-goers were attacked with sticks and stones, sending fifty-four persons to the hospital.

A month later, Robeson embarked on a cross-country crusade for peace. Arriving in Detroit on October 9, 1949, Robeson was greeted by thousands at the Forest Club on Forest Avenue and Hastings.

Looking back, we see that Wright first encountered the Robeson mystique during his internship at Harlem Hospital in 1943. Robeson lived on 139th Street, in what was called Striven Row, a block away from the hospital. In 1943, Robeson's popularity was at its peak. Wright saw him in the play, *Othello*, on Broadway. Robeson had made a famed appearance as the Shakespearean moor at Stratford-on-Avon. In the Broadway production, which ran for several months, Uta Hagan and Jose Ferrer played supporting roles. Like Ferrer, Robeson had a booming and authoritative voice. Wright also saw Robeson at Madison Square Garden, selling War Bonds. For his efforts as a speaker and civil rights advocate, Robeson was awarded the Springarn Medal from the NAACP in 1944.

The accolades for Robeson stopped after the war, and Robeson went on record as opposing the Cold War. He looked upon the Russians as friends, not as enemies. He spoke out at a time when the nation was in the middle of the "Red Scare." Communists were thought to be everywhere. Any statements which supported the Soviet Union were considered subversive. J. Edgar Hoover, director of the FBI, and Senator Joe McCarthy made a career of ferreting out supposed American communists and their supporters/apologists. Even though Robeson denied being a Communist, he quickly became a persona non grata. Even baseball hero, Jackie Robinson, was forced to denounce Robeson. By the time Charles Wright had returned to New York as a resident, Robeson's career was in ruins.

Wright admired Robeson and wrote a book about him entitled, *Robeson: Labor's Forgotten Champion* (1975). This was Wright's first book. It was a reminder that Blacks must write their own histories. In the course of the research for the book, Wright learned that Robeson had helped many union organizing efforts and encouraged Blacks to support the UAW-CIO rather than the rival AFL. Robeson also criticized Henry Ford and his union policies. The research for the book took Wright to Canada, London and France. He also traveled to American cities where Robeson performed and spoke.

Balamp, a Black publishing firm owned by Dr. James Jay, a Black biology professor at Wayne State University, published Wright's book. Jay became a publisher because he felt many Blacks were "under-published." Jay and Dr. Wright met at the Detroit Council for Political Education meeting, a non-partisan group that helped elect Black Detroiter, Richard Austin, as County Auditor. Dr. Jay was an admirer of Dr. Wright and stated, "Wright didn't own any boats or throw lavish parties. He is no social butterfly. He has little patience for nonsense. He is one of the most unique Blacks this City has ever seen." In effect, Wright represented a contrast to many Black physicians in town, and to E. Franklin Frazier's image of Black professionals.

Jay served as the editor for Wright's book and encouraged Dr. Wright to keep his original title. When the work was completed, Dr. Wright traveled to New York with the idea of personally presenting the book to Mr. Robeson. However, since Robeson was ill in Philadelphia, his son, Paul Jr., delivered it to him and reported that his father was pleased with the book.

The book was not well received by some Blacks. They felt that Dr. Wright was supporting and publicizing a man who was an enemy of the Country and a Communist. However, Superintendent of Schools, Dr. Arthur Jefferson helped set up the Paul Robeson Scholarship, and encouraged his principals to participate. Jefferson also served on the selection committee. The scholarship was awarded to a student who is a top scholar and a varsity athlete in the Detroit Public Schools. Winners received $300 to $500 dollars and/or a Savings Bond. The funds for the scholarship initially came from royalties from the book.

As interest heightened, the award program attracted more attention. Jefferson and Shannon persuaded the principals to donate $100, making the award worth $1,500. The name was changed to High School Principals and Coaches Paul Robeson Scholarship Award.

In addition to this close association with the Detroit Public Schools, Dr. Wright regularly attended programs at Wayne State University and at the other Cultural Center sites. From November 20 to December 2, 1989, Wright was an exhibitor at the Detroiters Collect, Fifth Exhibition at the Detroit Public Library. His powerful display of Robeson memorabilia received praise and accolades.

MANDELA REVISITED

On Wednesday, February 14, 1990, the Museum, in conjunction with the City of Detroit, led a march of 2,500 people from the Museum site to a rally at Ford Auditorium in celebration of the release of South African leader, Nelson Mandela after 27 years in prison. Among the marchers were hundreds of youngsters who shared the excitement. At Ford Auditorium dignitaries saluted Mandela, called on the South African government to lift the state of emergency and release all political prisoners, and urged U.S. President George Bush not to lift sanctions against the white minority government.

Mayor Coleman Young called it an "inspirational day" and gave an emotional speech that caused the audience to leap from their chairs. "When I saw Nelson Mandela in all his dignity walking out of that prison, his head still high, the fire coming out of his eyes", said Young, "I was moved." "If a man can spend 27 years in prison and still come out fighting, we can, too, over here," he said. "Let all who want freedom come together and stop stabbing each other in the back." U.S. Representatives John Conyers and George Crockett also spoke, as did Detroit City Council President, Maryann Mahaffey.

The Wright Man

MANDALA* FOR MANDELA

The brown earth cracks
and shouts.
The wind chants a planetary salute,
Stars turn night to day,
Millions of hearts burst.
The toi-toi trotting of the young warriors
sounds like thunder,
convulsing the hills.
The world's wheels squeal, racing
to the greeting circle.
We hold each other, crowding like
shy, happy children
to behold the WONDER:
YOU BACK AMONG US.
The sky smiles.
Hello, Nelson,
AMANDLA!
Our arms ache to embrace you,
SURVIVOR OF SOLITUDE,
DARK SUN OF CERTITUDE,
FLESH AND BONE of Africans'
deepest longings,
AMANDLA, AMANDLA!
Another son, who is the
Word, is home and
dwelling with us.

Gloria House, Ph.D. (Aneb Kgositsile)
Mandala is an image used as a focus of meditation

THE 25TH ANNIVERSARY

At the time of the 25th Anniversary in March 1990, Dr. Moore had nearly completed her first year as executive director. Unexpectedly, Dr. Wright chose this time to announce his resignation. He told the audience that he had served long enough and it was time to step aside. During the years 1989 and 1990, Wright had been truly out of sync with the board

213

of directors and with the Mayor (see Appendix for newspaper articles).

Aside from the obvious disappointment of the attendees, the dinner was a great success with a first-ever attendance of 1,000 dinner guests. Special guests, Ruby Dee and Ossie Davis, received a standing ovation for their superb performance.

On November 30, 1990, the volunteers of the Museum showed their affection for Dr. Wright with a celebration for him. Dinner and the presentation of a beautifully decorated cake followed the program. Mariel Wardell was chair of the event and the program mistress of ceremonies was Brunetta Vinson. The welcome and invocation were by Ruth Stephens, coordinator of volunteers, and Norman Dillard. Other participants:

SOLO	Miss Virginia Winters
COMMENTS	Mrs. Frances Curtis
COMMENTS	Dr. Hugh G. Blanding
SOLO	Mr. James Ramsey, Jr.
COMMENTS	Dr. Alegro J. Godley
SOLO	Miss Virginia Winters
PRESENTATION	Mrs. Elaine Phillinganes
REMARKS	Dr. Charles H. Wright
CLOSING	Mrs. Mariel Wardell
SOLO	Mr. James Ramsey, Jr.

HOSTESSES & COMMITTEE

Kathy Bradfield	Ethel Owens
Cordelia Betty Brown	Elaine Philliganes
Geraldine Bryant	James Ramsey, Sr.
Hazel Forest	Julia Ramsey
Rozella Miller	Eugenia Rucker
Tinnie Morman	Barbara Stewart
	Barbara Williford

OTHER OFFERINGS

On April 30, 1990 Mayor Coleman Young and friends, and supporters of Carol Anne-Marie Gist, sponsored an official homecoming reception for Gist, the 1990 Miss USA. Before the program, held on the Museum grounds, Dr. Wright and chairman Eugene Gilmer gave Miss Gist a tour of the Museum.

Later in the year, The National Links, Inc. presented a check in the amount of $25,000 to the Museum. National president, Marion S. Sutherland, surrounded by Detroit area Links members, made the presentation to a very pleased museum administration. This was one of many large donations made by The National Links, Inc. to the Museum. Also, the Detroit area Links-the Detroit Chapter, the Oakland County Chapter, the Greater Wayne County Chapter, the Renaissance Chapter, and the Great Lakes Chapter all have been generous in their contributions to the Museum.

The Museum, through its executive director, Dr. Moore, reported that the ongoing struggle of 1990-1991, to economically survive, "continues to be sharply challenged by the present day realities of complex, urban politics, unprecedented budget deficits, and a national recession." However the effort to continue to attract a variety of audiences was successful. The program featuring native Detroiter and nationally renown brain surgeon, author and role model, Dr. Ben Carson, brought out more than 2000 children and adults to hear an inspiring lecture based on his book, *Gifted Hands*.

An exhibition that focused on the political influences of Marcus Garvey touched the lives of some older citizens who remembered the Garvey movement first hand. An exhibition reviewing the life of Malcolm X, and a nationally traveled exhibition featuring seventy-five African American women such as Rosa Parks, who affected changes in the twentieth century, attracted more than 15,000 visitors to the Museum during a six week period. Also, a locally based organization, Espoir, collaborated with the Museum to educate the community about the Haitian Revolution, through the exhibition, "A Battle of Titans."

The Honorable Craig Strong and Dr. Wright were friends for many years. Judge Strong expressed his love for the Museum by sponsoring Annual Membership Drives. For many years prior to the 25th Anniversary and for every year following, Judge Strong brings together friends and associates to assist in planning an annual party. Many donors look forward to the gathering each year because of the music, fun, and casual elegance of the affair.

The year 1991 marked the first year since 1965 that Dr. Wright was not serving as chairman of the Board of Trustees. Eugene Gilmer, who served on the Board for many years, was selected to lead the trustees. Even though Wright continued to remain "out of sync" with a few of the members, he never faltered in his deep commitment to the Museum.

In February 1991, Ollie Harrington, the renowned political cartoonist living in Berlin, Germany contacted Wright about his plans to visit the United States. He had met Wright during his first visit to the U.S. forty years previously. In March, Dr. Walter Evans, a prominent Detroit surgeon who is known nationally and internationally as one of the premier collectors of African art and "first editions," announced that the 79-year-old cartoonist would travel to the U.S. in conjunction with an exhibition of his works at the Museum of African American History.

The exhibition opened to the public on April 17. Harrington was best known for his characters "Bootsie" and "Little Luther," which were syndicated in African American newspapers nationally in the 1930s and 1940s.

The Wright Man

"Doctor Jenkins, before you read us your paper on inter-stellar gravitational tensions in thermo-nuclear propulsion, would you sing us a good old spiritual?"

As Langston Hughes wrote about Harrington's work in 1958, "The trials and tribulations of Bootsie and his friends are typical of the trials and tribulations of the average Negro from Lenox Avenue in Harlem or Hastings Street in Detroit...woman problems, pocketbook problems, landlady problems, and race problems are the same. And fat little Bootsie, with his surprised little eyes, is always staring problems in the face..."

In the summer of 1991, the Drs. Wright traveled to Charleston, South Carolina to do research for Roberta's book, *Lay Down Body: Living History in African American Cemeteries.* While in Charleston, friends spoke of St. Helena Island and Penn Center. Penn Center's museum, in fact the entire island, they were told, would be of great interest. Their friends were right. (See Chapter Ten for the story of Penn Center, St. Helena Island, and of course, the Michigan Support Group which was founded by Dr. Charles Wright.)

The Detroit Association of Black Storytellers, in 1991, performed their special brand of narration at the Museum. They featured their unique talents, which included performing folktales set to music with both ancient and modern instruments. During their performance, the Storytellers explained and demonstrated to the audience the function of the instruments they sometimes use, such as steel drums, gongs and shakers.

On January 15, 1993, the Storytellers became an auxiliary organization to the Museum. They continue with their mission "to seek to promote and perpetuate the art of storytelling by preserving and passing on the folklore, traditions and culture of African Americans and their ancestors." Several of the Storytellers were members of the Penn Center / Michigan Support Group and performed at some of the Group's indoor and outdoor fundraisers.

In 1992, Eugene Gilmer, board chair, announced "long rumored to be in the plans of the City of Detroit, the construction of a new facility, designed to museum standards, will begin in early 1993, if approved by Detroit voters. The five year old, 28,000 square foot current building has limited exhibition space, which inhibits the ability of the Museum to house some major exhibitions, or to have more than one substantial exhibition simultaneously."

He further stated, "the lack of theatre space also impedes our ability to schedule some major events in the building, requiring us to make expenditures for rental of other sites."

Also announced was the closing of the Million Dollar Club as of December 1992. The statement read thusly:

> After nearly 10 years of existence, the Million Dollar Club (MDC), the successful brainchild of Dr. Wright, closed its doors to new membership. Current Million Dollar Club members retain their status and continue with all privileges associated with the prestigious membership category, but no new members will be added to their ranks as of January 1, 1993.

"The Million Dollar Club has been the most powerful and supportive group of individual family donors of the

The Wright Man

MAAH," stated Gilmer, board chair. "The generosity of spirit and financial gifts from the more than 500 members in this organization is unsurpassed in the history of the institution. We extend our greatest thanks for the tangible show of support from this segment of our community." Dr. Wright was not consulted; he had hoped his plan of having 1,000 members would be fulfilled.

From February 2 through April 29, 1992, the Museum was host to the Mexican exhibition of Elizabeth Catlett and Francisco Mora. Titled "A Courtyard Apart," it included the works of sculptor, painter, print-maker Elizabeth Catlett and painter, print-maker Francisco Mora. The title refers to the Cuernavaca, Mexico-based home and studios of the couple. Dr. Wright had met Catlett and Mora years ago, introduced by Hon. George Crockett. Wright always enjoyed speaking Spanish with them and did, in fact, speak to the audience in Spanish at the opening of this exhibit.

A major 1992 fundraiser was in conjunction with the opening of "The Real McCoy," an exhibition that focused on the inventions and innovations of African Americans from 1881 to the mid-twentieth century, highlighting Elijah McCoy (1844-1929). McCoy's inventions were primarily connected with the automatic lubrication of moving machines. Born in Canada, McCoy moved to Ypsilanti, Michigan after the Civil War. His parents had been enslaved in Boone County, Kentucky, but had escaped to Canada in 1837, by means of the Underground Railroad. McCoy studied in Scotland and in Canada, and at age 21 came to the United States. He acquired some fifty-seven patents for devices designed to streamline his automatic lubrication process. McCoy died at age 85 and was buried in Detroit Memorial Park, East.

THE FUTURE

It was just prior to the twenty-fifth anniversary dinner that Mayor Coleman Young and Wright first discussed the plans for a new building. The Mayor felt strongly about the need for a larger facility and to have it in a more visible location. He announced that land was available on Warren Avenue and Brush streets, adjacent to the Science Center. Dr. Wright expressed his thoughts to the Mayor about the high cost of construction and the dearth of personnel trained in museum work. He suggested that an addition could be constructed at the same site.

The Mayor told Wright that it was not something he should be concerned about and that the money to operate a larger facility would be available. (Note: It was not until the spring of 1997 that Wright initiated a meeting with the ailing former Mayor and the two of them came to grips with their differences. Wright commended him for his vision.)

From the time of Wright's resignation, as mentioned, he continued to visit the Museum and to enjoy the exhibits, confer with visitors and quite frequently speak to student groups. (Wright never turns down an opportunity to speak to young people).

In 1993, ground was broken for the third site for the Museum. After the groundbreaking the residents of the City were caught up in the excitement of the construction. The building, designed by Harold Varner of Sims Varner Architects was obviously going to be "world class." One wonders how adequate praise can be bestowed on Mr. Varner for his remarkable design.

The City was authorized by the citizens of Detroit to sell bonds for the design and construction of the new building. The Detroit Building Authority was requested by the city of Detroit to facilitate and manage the design and construction of the new

The Wright Man

120,000 square foot building. Through an open bid process, Jenkins / Turner, a joint venture, was contracted as construction managers. Jenkins Construction, Inc. is a Detroit based, minority business enterprise. Sims-Varner had been awarded the contract also through an open-bid process.

Kimberly Camp began her duties as executive director/ president on January 18, 1994. Dr. Moore resigned in 1993. In the spring of 1995, Eugene Gilmer, who had served for five years as chair of the Board of Trustees, turned the gavel over to Dr. Arthur Jefferson, former Detroit Public Schools General Superintendent. Dr. Jefferson became the Museum's third chairman (see Appendix for Trustee list).

Prior to the time for the closing of the museum and preparation for the move, several programs attracted the attention of Dr. Wright and the public. From December 1, 1995 to March 3, 1996, the exhibit, "A Slave Ship Speaks: The Wreck of the Henrietta Marie," filled the exhibit space. The exhibit highlighted the findings of a slave ship and the historical treasures of material culture that were found as it sat at the bottom of the ocean.

As summer approached, in celebrating the contributions of African Americans to music, the Museum's Department of Education did its part to educate the next generation of talented young artists. By presenting the "Legacy Motown Alumni" each Sunday during the month of June, as part of the National Observance of Black Music Month, the Museum sought to strengthen its already strong support for the "Motown Sound."

On October 31, 1996, the Museum invited families and friends to gather together to enjoy stories of ancestors and families. A text, completed, written, and edited by Michelle Parchment, was a presentation to the public, including an Ancestors Coloring Book and the Family Tree Illustrations. Planned for the evening was a visual interactive play that encompassed African and African American folktales.

Ancestor Night was originally instituted by Ms. Imani Humphrey, director of the African-Centered elementary school, Aisha Shule, to counteract the negative atmosphere created by traditional Halloween practices. The Museum's annual celebration of Ancestors Night offers an enlightening and culturally enriching alternative to the usual and often senseless Halloween activities.

And, at years end, following the traditional Christmas observation, Kwanzaa time arrives. Kwanzaa has been observed at the Museum annually for several years. Kwanzaa is an African American celebration derived from the harvest celebrations in traditional African societies. The seven principles of Kwanzaa are observed all seven days at the Museum, December 26 to January 1. Some years, in the spirit of Kwanzaa, participants are asked to bring canned goods to be donated to the homeless in area shelters.

Kwanzaa, in the Kiswahilli language means, "first fruit of the harvest." It was created in 1966 by Maulana Ron Karenga, chairperson of Black Studies at California State University at Long Beach. The seven principles:

December 26:	UMOJA (Unity)
December 27:	KUJICHAGULIA (Self-Determination)
December 28:	UJIMA (Collective Work and Responsibility)
December 29:	UJAMAA (Co-operative Economics
December 30:	NIA (Purpose)
December 31:	KUUMBA (Creativity)
January 1:	IMANI (Faith)

THE SEVEN SYMBOLS OF KWANZAA

1. The Mkeka (straw mat)—symbolic of our African tradition and history

2. The Kinara (seven lamp candle holder)—symbolizes the parent stalk

3. The Mshumaa (seven candles)—the seven principles of our Black Value System

4. The Muhindi (ears of corn)—our children, most valued treasure of our race

5. The Zawadi (gifts)—rewards of correct actions

6. The Mazao (crops)—fruits of our labor

7. The Kikombe (unity cup)—oneness of purpose

Since the Museum at 301 Frederick Douglass was closed to the public for a few months, there were no more scheduled programs or events. The job of packing and moving seemed a tremendous, almost impossible task to some staff persons. However the excitement and anticipation of the move superceded the fear and anxiety. Hard hat tours to the "building in construction" were scheduled and Roberta Hughes Wright, twice trampled through the mud to get to the entrance. Then, once inside, she ignored the drills and hammers and dust, ducked under or stepped over beams, and enjoyed the unfinished splendor.

The workmen had to put in place a 55-foot high glass dome and tackle a structure with overall dimensions of 120,000 square feet; a 317-seat theatre, with a floating stage; and 6,000 square feet of exhibition space with 33-foot ceilings. The cost was upward of $34 million. The voters of Detroit approved a $20 million bond issue in 1992 and a second bond issue for $10 million in 1996.

During this time, Dr. Wright spent little time at the Museum. The Frederick Douglass site was closed for the move and he refused to take the hard hat tour of the new site. Dr. Wright, and in our opinion, rightly so, was greatly disturbed because he had not been asked his opinions, ideas, suggestions, or whatever on any phase of the construction, design or planned programs. If he came into contact with the Museum's executive director, there was always a polite, "When are you going to call us?" or, "We would like you to take a tour." It was a serious rejection of all that he stood for and all that he had done for the past twenty-nine years.

Dr. Wright did send a messenger asking for assurance that the Louise Lovett Wright Research Library would be moved to the Warren Avenue site. This, too, was ignored, except for messages that a major company had given a large donation to the Museum for the library to be named in its honor. This remained the situation in spite of calls from City Council members and several local VIPs. It was only through the firm action on the part of the Deputy Mayor (with the backing, of course, of the Mayor) and a eyeball to eyeball directive by her, that the name was included on the library wall.

Nevertheless, Wright's many, many friends unanimously insisted that he attend the opening of the new facility. He was pressured by former volunteers, former patients, friends and all who loved him. It was, however, his "Maker" who is credited with the final decision to go.

THE MUSEUM'S NEW SITE

A series of public and private events was planned to celebrate the grand opening of the new site of the Museum of African American History. On Tuesday, April 1, 1997, the staff of MAAH hosted a brown bag lunch for the local taxi and limousine drivers. Drivers could swing by the front curb of the Museum and be served a brown bag lunch which included a map to the Museum, a schedule of the Grand Opening Weekend activities, a complimentary family pass to view the core exhibition and, of course, a delectable deli sandwich, chips, dessert and a soft drink.

On Thursday, April 3, the local, national and international press were invited to a press preview of what the public would see the following week. On Sunday, April 6, the board and staff of MAAH hosted a special Volunteer/ Construction Worker Family Day to thank them for their work on the Museum. Then, on Friday, April 11, the celebration continued with a Black Tie Gala Benefit at the Museum. Dr. Wright and family attended the gala and both before and after addressing the capacity crowd, received great ovations.

On Saturday, April 12, the public was invited to the Ribbon Cutting and Dedication Ceremony, performed by Mayor Dennis Archer, followed by the opening of the doors to the public. Dr. Wright also received a thunderous applause on Saturday. After Saturday's program, the public—"his public"—lined up for autographs. What was he signing? Programs, pieces of paper, whatever. It was a good day for the "tenacious warrior."

The Michigan 1279th Combat Engineers and Michigan's National Air Guard joined in the opening celebration. There followed an around-the-clock marathon open house, free to the public, beginning at ten o'clock a.m. on Saturday, April 12, continuing through the night until the next morning ending at ten o'clock a.m. on Sunday, April 13. Participating in the strolling excitement all day and all night were quilt makers, doll makers, weavers, jewelry makers, storytellers, hambone players and musical performers. Also, there were various children's activities and voter registration.

Book signings and readings by local and nationally renowned African American authors took place on Sunday, April 13. Dr. Wright signed his book, *The National Medical Association Demands Equal Opportunity: Nothing More, Nothing Less* and Roberta Hughes Wright and Wilbur B. Hughes, III signed, *Lay Down Body: Living History in African American Cemeteries*. Following the book signing, the public was invited to attend a Gospel Concert in the Museum's theatre.

THE CORE EXHIBIT

When the Museum opened its doors on Warren Avenue to the world, it reportedly presented the largest exhibition ever created in this Nation on African American people. Contained in the core exhibition gallery, the exhibit covers 16,000 square feet of space.

Borrowing widely from some of the nation's leading archival collections, the core exhibition reflects a 400-year survey of African American legacy and heritage. Specifically, Detroit's history is interwoven in the ongoing story. Some of the artifacts included in the core exhibit are Mae Jemison's NASA flight suit, a replica of Dr. King's Birmingham jailhouse door, a ballot box used by Blacks, Dr. Wright's first medical bag, the gas mask and traffic signal invented by Garrett Morgan and brought to the Museum years ago by Dr. Wright, and many other artifacts which help to tell the story of African Americans in this Nation.

Ralph Applebaum and Associates, a world renown exhibition development company, was contracted in 1993 to design the core exhibition, with content script, artifact identification, and focus steered by the body of consultants.

The core exhibition space is complemented by two changing exhibition galleries devoted to the arts, history and technology. These galleries host exhibitions developed by the Museum as well as traveling exhibitions from other institutions around the world. They serve to continue an ongoing dialogue about our past, our present and the future, for our local, regional, national and international audiences. Historians Dr. Norman McRae and Dr. Robert O. Bland were among the large committee of educators assisting with the exhibits.

Historian, Dr. Norman McRae, contributed information about the local history of Detroit pertaining to African Americans to the core exhibit, "Of the People: The African American Experience" which is featured in the 16,000 square foot gallery of the Museum.

"It was a very exciting process. I had an opportunity to meet and exchange ideas with a group of brilliant and exciting people about the issues of African and African American people," stated Dr. McRae.

The Wright Man

Robert O. Bland, Ph.D., vice president and dean at Lewis College of Business is a renown educator, activist, lecturer and historian. Since childhood, Dr. Bland has collected artifacts, books and historical material about Black culture. He has worked toward the development of a monument to victims of the slave trade, "The Bowels of Hell." The elegant museum doors designed by Richard Bennett and the great masks adorning the building's exterior are a tribute to Bennett's enormous talent and artistry. Also, Hubert Massey's "Ring of Genealogy" spanning the rotunda floor, is a true reflection of his genius.

MUSEUM, CENTER—FRONT

After the opening at the new site, Dr. Wright became increasingly interested in helping in any way possible. His first attempt to present a program in the new building was in December 1997, when he brought together a Paul Robeson 100th Birthday Celebration Committee. Meetings were held monthly in the Museum's Lewis Latimer Café. By April 5 1998, the Committee topped off the several months of work with an "all-out" anniversary dinner celebration chaired by Sam Thomas and Shirley Northcross. Josephine Harreld Love, director of Your Heritage House, a "partner" with the Museum for many years, was active with the Robeson Centennial Committee, as were many of Wright's friends and associates.

The Committee's exhibit in the Coleman A. Young Archives room was visited by hundreds of people during its seven-month stay. Displayed were large paintings by Leroy Foster, owned by the Wrights and by Leno Jaxon; a terracotta bust of Robeson by sculpturer Ruth C. Goens; books, records, and artifacts loaned by Judge Norma Dotson-Sales; numerous albums by museum board member and committee member, Nate Shapiro; a metal sculpture by Susanna Linburg and posters by Willie Smith.

In addition, many programs were held throughout the city. Dr. Charles Adams, pastor of Hartford Baptist Church, preached, "Paul to Paul," on Sunday, March 29 at both services. It was a roaring success, as was Wayne State University's program, sponsored by Dr. Melba Boyd of Africana Studies, featuring former City Council president, Erma Henderson and Dr. Wright. Dr. Robert Perry and Dr. Melvin Peters sponsored a highly successful all-day program on Robeson at Eastern Michigan University in Ypsilanti, Michigan and presented Dr. Wright with a stirring written tribute and a beautiful award (see this book's opening).

Radio and TV appearances and announcements continued throughout February, March and April. Programs led by JoAnn Watson; Tom Pope of Dudley Broadcasting; BBC-TV, taped in Chicago; and Dave Rambeau's television program, "For My People"—all featured Dr. Wright.

The annual Paul Robeson—Detroit High School Principals and Coaches Association Scholarship Award program took place at the Museum on Robeson's birthday, April 9. Mamie Humphrey, Robert Shannon, and Dr. Emeral Crosby chaired the program with enthusiastic encouragement from Wright, as this is one of his favorite programs. Wright had hoped that this would be the year that all former awardees would be present. However, a few could not be located. Some of the 1998 students who were participants because of excellence in academics, sports, and/or music are listed in the Appendix, along with the 1976-1998 Paul Robeson Scholarship Award Recipients. Chrysta E. Sweeney of Martin Luther King Senior High School and the Golightly Career Technical Center was the 1998 awardee.

Highlighting the program was the presence of some of the former scholarship recipients. The recipients present included Wilbert McCormick, 1976; Patricia Ferguson, M.D., 1980; Monique Martin-Johnson, 1981; Tracey Johnson, 1985; George Ahmad Goff, 1987; Lori L. Hall, J.D., 1990; Brie Fort, 1994; and Larry Charleston, Jr., 1996. All of these awardees are doing extremely well and have followed in the footsteps of Paul Robeson in their skill, talent, and achievement.

Dr. Wright was also elated with the Robeson program he had instigated at Southfield Public Library, featuring Dr. Wallace Peace. The large crowd was mesmerized by Dr. Peace's awesome presentation. Wright had heard that Dr. Peace would be discussing Mozart and the Magic Flute at the library and made arrangements to attend. After the program, they went into a huddle and the next thing you knew, Dr. Peace had agreed to do a program on Robeson. His hour-long presentation, with the assistance of Don McGhee and Wright, has been in demand throughout the Metropolitan Detroit area.

As mentioned in Chapter One, the Museum was renamed, in March 1998, in Dr. Wright's honor. The board of trustees then set the date of September 13 for the official renaming.

The Board of Directors and staff worked diligently to plan the dinner gala which was appropriately and affectionately called "The Rites of Passage." More than 300 guests celebrated the changing of the name from the Museum of African American History to the Charles H. Wright Museum of African American History, "after its founder and guiding light." Dr. Wright, in his speech, stated, "I am eternally grateful to everyone, including the original members who started this with me 33 years ago. It's been an exciting journey."

September 20 signals the date of Wright's "first" birthday party at age eight. Now in 1998, there were many parties. Wright had no hesitancy about publically proclaiming his approaching age and reminescing that few in his "line" had lived to see age 80.

Dr. Wright's formal birthday tribute began when he joined Judge Craig Strong and photographer Larry Smith's Virgo celebration. Wright was an honored guest and was photographed doing the "hustle." The next day, at the "Rites of Passage," mentioned above, he was saluted, serenaded and after the dinner received two large delectable cakes, one so large it was on a cart. However, the flames from the eighty candles caused some consternation and need for caution, so it was quickly removed.

The following week, Wright's daughters and son-in-law sponsored a fun-filled surprise birthday party with family and many of his longtime friends in attendance. Then, the following week, the Honorable Brenda M. Scott sponsored a free party for persons who were unable to obtain tickets for the September 13 celebration. Dr. Wright was especially pleased that so many young people from area schools were present and performed so brilliantly.

During the months preceding September, Dr. Wright's health was "excellent," as he described it. But friends and family, noting his tendency toward tarrying and faltering, tried unsuccessfully to contain him. He ignored all suggestions to slow down, and retained his implacable appetite for projects.

Among the exhibits at the Museum that Dr. Wright favored were Detroit's Black Bottom and Paradise Valley; Celebrating Hispanic Heritage; Michigan Quilts; The Buffalo Soldiers: The African American Soldiers in the U.S. Army 1866-1912; and Wade in the Water: African American Sacred Music Traditions.

The Ford Freedom Award ceremony, held on February 11, 1999, at the Museum and on February 12th at the Museum and in the evening at the Detroit Opera House, featured Ambassador Andrew Young, who received the first annual Scholar's Award. The legacy of the late Mayor Coleman A. Young was celebrated by the receipt of the Inaugural Freedom Award, accepted by members of his family and his cousin, Dr. Claud Young. The Museum placed the Coleman A. Young bronze plaque in the "Ring of Genealogy" as a permanent tribute to his accomplishments. This terrazo artwork was designed and created by the renowned Detroit artist, Hubert W. Massey.

OTHER CITIES

Following the excitement of the renaming, requests for help and direction regarding new museums increased twofold. Wright's answers to questions were frequently sent by letter or given by telephone, but occasionally a trip to the site of the new museum was scheduled. Wright routinely starts with this advice:

The organizer must be dedicated and strong willed, determined to proceed in spite of some persons expressing great interest and then reneging on the promise. The original group should be diverse with representatives from every walk of life. Determine and record your mission; involve everyone in this endeavor. If a history museum is planned, don't be tempted to lose sight of that fact. An art museum differs from a history museum.

During the summer of 1998, one visitor to Detroit and to the Museum, was Joseph McGill, Jr. (formerly Penn Center Museum director), who was selected early in 1998 as executive director of the African American Heritage Foundation in Cedar Rapids, Iowa. While awaiting the completion of the building for the African American Museum & Cultural Center of Cedar Rapids, McGill and the organizers established a board of directors, hosted banquets and fundraisers, planned educational programs and even initiated an informative and well-packaged newsletter, *The African American Pride*. Wright "signed on" as a consultant.

In October, Wright received an invitation to join a museum organizing group in Toledo, Ohio, as guest speaker. The very spirited Toledo group, led by June Boyd, plan a 2000 opening of the Museum. The October 10, 1998 reception and fundraiser took place at the site of their new museum, a large, stately home on Glenwood Street. Dr. Wright spoke and then responded to numerous questions about organizing and operating a museum.

Also, in October, Dr. Wright was invited to San Francisco, California to discuss the Detroit Museum, to join in programs on Paul Robeson, and to talk to a group of physicians regarding the National Medical Association and his book.

On October 18, Wright spoke on the importance of Robeson to the labor movement at the African American Museum & Library at the Golden State Library in Oakland, California. ext, Dr. Wright spoke at the Oakland Main Library; the topic was, "What Was the Role of Paul Robeson's Peacemaking?" The Vukani Mawethie Choir was also featured. And later that evening the program was titled, "Teenagers of the 1930s." Dr. Wright's hosts, the David Aroner family and Harriett & Alex Bagwell, had scheduled activities for the entire week, although not certain Wright would be able to maintain the pace. He did; they managed to keep up with him.

During the rest of the week, Wright spoke on Paul Robeson's history with friend and orator, Joe Johnson and marveled at the vocals performed by Harriet and Alex Bagwell. The Center for Labor Research & Education cosponsored the program with the Department of African American Studies, History & Center for Theatre Arts at the University of California-Berkeley. The San Francisco African American Historical and Cultural Society and Archives sponsored another well-attended gathering.

Later in the week, Dr. Wright had an enjoyable evening at the home of Dr. Ben Majors, who hosted a reception for medical doctors from San Francisco, Oakland and Berkeley. Dr. Wright's book, *The NMA Demands Equal Opportunities: Nothing More, Nothing Less,* was the center of attention and discussion. Dr. Wright eturned to Detroit, finally exhausted, but greatly buoyed by the enthusiasm of the many people he met in the Bay Area.

Two new committees at the Museum are operating under Wright's guidance and have as their goal, to support and nurture the growth of the Museum. Dr. Leonard Douglas chairs the Museum Millennium Membership Committee with co-chairs Dr. Mark Smith; Hon. Craig Strong; and Bedia Thomas. David Northcross chairs the second committee, the Museum/Wayne State University, Museum Studies Committee. Dr. Melba Boyd, director of Africana Studies at Wayne State University, administrators and faculty, have joined in with the Museum representatives to plan joint programs, courses, internships and scholarships. The Museum Millennium Membership Committee and the Studies Committee meet regularly and both are well-grounded and well-focused.

If the membership attendance and interest displayed at the Museum's annual meeting in December 1998 could be used as a barometer for success, it appears that the Museum is headed for a great future. The "mantra" often repeated is "not just the largest, but the best."

The executive director/president, Kimberly Camp, resigned and accepted a position in Pennsylvania as of November 1, 1997. Ernest Duncan, formerly vice-president, was selected by the board of trustees as acting president. The year, 1998, saw the filling of several administrative positions that have been unfilled for some time. Among the new "acquisitions" were Harry Harrison, Vice President for Education and Public Programs; Dale Mott, Director of Development; and Patricia Carrolle, Public Relations Director. Other staff persons, as of 1999, are listed in the Appendix.

When Dr. Wright was briefed on the programs and exhibits extending through the year 2000, he was most pleased. The mix, the variety and the projected quality of these exhibits signal a portentous excitement for the public and for the future of the Museum.

Wright renaming Frederick Street

The Wright Man

Robert & Eloise Shannon and Willia Miller

Wright on hard hat tour during construction of third Museum site

235

Joan Maynard, director of Weeksville and Bedford Stuyvescent Society of Brooklyn, New York and Councilwoman Maryann Mahaffey at AAMA meeting

Dresden, Ontario Uncle Toms Cabin

The Wright Man

Dresden, Ontario Uncle Toms Cabin

North American Black Historical Museum and Cultural Center in Amhertsburg, Ontario, Canada

At Carl Owens' unveiling of his portrait of Rosa Parks, Ms. Parks, Hon. John Conyers and Judge Damon Keith approve

Ossie Davis with the Wrights at the Museum's 25th Anniversary

Dr. Marion Moore, executive director; board chair, Eugene Gilmer; and Wright receive check from Marion S. Sutherland, national president of The Links, Inc.

Marymal and Charles Dryden of Atlanta, Georgia enjoy Michigan exhibit

March from luncheon to ribbon-cutting — May 1987
Wright leads the way with student, Deidre Proctor
Mayor Young, family, friends in background

Judy and Architect Howard Sims — Opening Party

The Wright Man

Wright talks to Dr. & Mrs. W. Bentley and Dr. & Mrs. N. Rangarajan

Robert Shannon & Dr. Marjorie Peebles Meyers at Opening

241

Museum Lecture Series on U.S. Constitution
The Hons. Wade McCree, George Crockett, Avern Cohn, Dr. Wright, Professor Harold Norris, and Hon. Dennis Archer

Ann Flanders flanked by the Wrights and the Karmann Ghia she donated to the African World Festival raffle

The Wright Man

Detroit News, 1988 Michiganians of the Year
Wright and other honorees

Volunteers on Museum steps

Wilbur B. Hughes, III with exhibit of inventor, Elijah McCoy

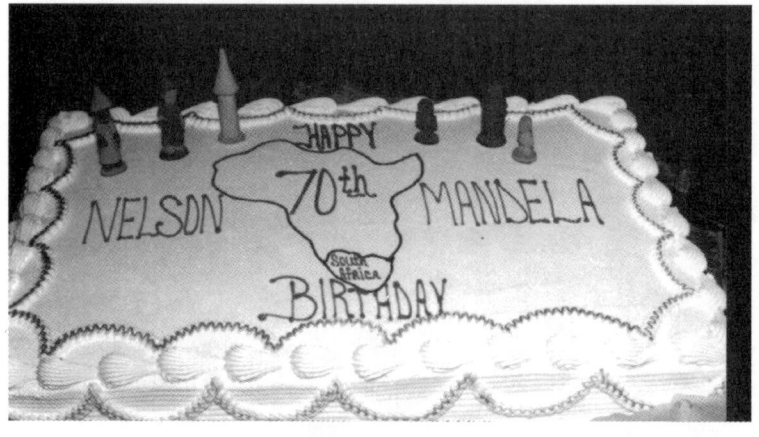

Nelson Mandela's birthday cake

The Wright Man

Bert Williams' famous CAKE WALK

Artist Carl Owens, Wright, and Hon. Damon Keith

Barbara Hughes Smith, Barbara Henson Carter, and Dolores Shreve Harold
"Canadian Cousins"

Wright and Dr. Bryan Walls participating in Dresden's celebration

The Wright Man

Aquadilla, Puerto Rico

Pero, donde estan los Indios ahora?

247

Chef Wright shows off cabbage treat to Great Lakes Link R. Wright at "Gentleman Cooks"

Wright signing books. C. Wright was recepient of the Dr. Robert Greenidge, Ulti-Med Award

The Wright Man

Wright talking to young people

Wright talking to adults

The Wrights at 100th Anniversary of NMA in Atlanta

Detroit Memorial Park board members
From left — Robert Bass, DDS; William Andrews; George Dunbar, Jr.; Allen Rawls;
Hon. Richard Austin; George Dunbar, Sr.; Wilbur B. Hughes, III

The Wright Man

Wright, Barbara Hughes Smith, Wilbur B. Hughes, III and Roberta Wright at booksigning

*The Hon. Avern L. Cohn; Professor Harold Norris; Professor Melvin Peters
at "Pre-Emancipation" party given by MSG for Penn Center*

Dr. Wright greets the Hon. James Blanchard and the Rev. Jesse Jackson

Dr. Verona Morton, Dr. Arthur Johnson, Dr. Rich, and Dr. Wright

The Wright Man

Wright and Omega Psi Phi fraternity brothers

The Wrights
Photo by Monica Morgan

The Wright Man

Dr. Wright, an ardent daily reader of the *New York Times* (and a conscientious article clipper), read a fascinating story in the "Sophisticated Traveler" section about Sgt. White's Diner, located on Highway 21 on the road to Beaufort, South Carolina. The writer stated that she knew the food was good when she drove by and spotted a pickup truck and a sheriff's car among others, parked in front. She went on to describe the food in such a manner that one thinks of giving up all one's possessions for just a plate of "down home collards and a taste of the 'low country boil,'" shrimp, sausage, corn on the cob, green peppers, celery, and hot sauce.

Well, that became a planned side trip from Charleston, S.C. to Hilton Head Island, after completing a visit to Charleston cemeteries. By the way, Wright was getting his "comeuppance." He had married a lady who no longer packed her swim suit (you'll read about the Puerto Rico trip), but wanted to spend the entire ten-day "vacation" walking in and through cemeteries. And they did—in Burton; Beaufort; Hilton Head; Daufuski; St. Helena Island; Charleston; Columbia and Winnsboro, South Carolina; and Savannah, Georgia.

Anyway, when the DeCostas (Herb and Emily) of Charleston, told Dr. Wright about Penn Center (Herb had been on the Penn Center board for many years), they knew this was his "cup of tea." The brief synopsis of the history of Penn Center was mind boggling to Wright. Afer a fabulous two-day visit in Charleston, he was off to the "low country boil" and to see St. Helena Island.

The diner was in a rugged country setting on Highway 21 and the small restaurant was a delight in all ways. However, many others had read the *New York Times* article; and, within five minutes Wright realized that seated in the restaurant were travelers from several different states and from Canada. Wright asked the very outgoing and friendly Sgt. White, where was his guest book. Well, the young brother wasn't sure what Wright meant at first, but soon realized that this man from "up North" was serious.

Sgt. White had no guest book. Wright ran out to his car, tore the used pages out of the little notebook he had been writing in, and dashed back into the restaurant (Wright almost never runs, but this time, he did). Then, Wright passed the notebook around the diner and had everyone sign his or her name and home state. Although spotted with barbecue sauce, it was a mission accomplished.

Wright, of course, reprimanded the former Marine sergeant and told him to keep the notebook in a visible place on the counter for all future visitors. He also reminded Sgt. White that the New York Times story was worth its weight in gold and to be sure and write or call the writer of the article to give thanks and to report the results. Sgt. White is now located on Boundary Street in Beaufort and still serves the same great food.

Penn Center was not far—just a few miles through Burton and Beaufort, over an expansive bridge to Ladys Island, and across a creek to St. Helena Island. It's difficult to describe the feeling—to see this remarkable historical site, tucked away out of view of the world. St. Helena had and has no traffic signals and no "developers." It is just a wondrous island with moss-laden, live oak trees that, if they could speak, would tell the incredulous story of the 1800s in vivid terms.

The reader is urged to purchase some of the books recounting the Gullah culture, in order to understand the

The Wright Man

unique and basic mores of the people. It is also important to read what happened in this area before and after 1861. Very briefly, after the "gun shoot" on St. Helena Sound around Hilton Head Island, in 1861, when President Abraham Lincoln threatened to send troops to the area to frighten the wealthy, aristocratic slave holders who wanted South Carolina out of the Union, he did just that. As the guns roared, the whites fled, leaving in the Beaufort-St. Helena confines almost 10,000 enslaved who hadn't been taught to read or write and could only speak English with a strong African-based dialect.

President Lincoln initiated the Port Royal Experiment. He wanted the valuable cotton picked and he wanted to determine if the former slaves could be taught to read and write. The saga began in the spring of 1862, when two white women, Laura Towne and Ellen Murray were recruited by the Philadelphia-Port Royal Commission to travel to St. Helena Island to establish a school for the "contrabands," as the former slaves were called. They came and both taught school (Laura also visited the sick, having had some medical training) for over forty years. Both died on St. Helena Island.

The first school was opened in 1862 at Oaks Plantation House, one of the deserted plantations then occupied by Northerners. Classes were held on the veranda. Both adults and children, hearing of the school, trekked through the woods to join the class. Before long, the school outgrew the space and moved to the nearby Brick Church on Lands End Road. The church, built by the enslaved in 1855 for whites, and now taken over by Blacks, made an ideal school for weekday use.

Later in 1862, Charlotte Forten, of the well-to-do Forten family of Philadelphia, came to the Island. An African American who was trained as a teacher, she volunteered to join Laura and Ellen. On Charlotte's first day on the Island, October 27, 1862, she wrote that, "we heard the children read and spell. I noticed with pleasure, how bright, how eager to learn, many of them seemed. They sang beautifully in their rich, sweet, clear tones."

Charlotte's journal notations stress, primarily, her teaching experiences—both children and adults—her strong affinity for nature, trees, and flowers; her community work and her love for music.

In September 1862, President Lincoln sent word that he would issue an Emancipation Proclamation on January 1, 1863. Consequently, on December 28, 1862, General Rufus Saxton visited the Brick Baptist Church to invite the islanders to nearby Camp Saxton (the Smith Plantation) on Thursday, New Years day, for the reading of the Emancipation Proclamation. He also sought more young men to join the First South Carolina Colored Volunteers.

Forten writes in detail of the boat trip across to Beaufort on January 1, and over to the site of the camp. The sun was warm, the crowd gathered, eagerly, and the troops looked splendid in their dark coats and red pants. (All of the "colored" troops were issued red pants to clearly distinguish them from white troops.)

President Lincoln asked Dr. William Henry Brisbane to read the Proclamation. Dr. Brisbane had sold his slaves, moved north and became an abolitionist. With deep regret, he returned to South Carolina, bought back all of his slaves and freed them.

In March 1864, Laura Towne was successful in her efforts to secure a building for the school. They had outgrown the Brick Church. It was shipped in three sections by boat from Boston. During the next years, the campus grew and students and islanders constructed additional buildings. Charlotte Forten's health deteriorated and she was soon forced to return to Philadelphia.

The Wright Man

THE SCHOOL AND THE CENTER

By 1905, the need for industrial education led to the establishment of the trades in carpentry, blacksmithing, wheelwrighting, basket weaving, harness making, cobbling and mechanics. Agriculture was taught to students and community people. Teacher training courses also were offered, and the school became known as Penn Normal, Industrial and Agricultural School.

The year 1948 brought another change; the County and State took over responsibility of the education of Blacks on St. Helena and the surrounding islands. The Penn School Trustee Board allowed the classes to remain on Penn's campus until the public school was built. The last graduating class on the Penn School campus was in 1953.

In 1951, Penn School was transformed into Penn Community Services, Inc. Community development programs were initiated and facilities on Penn's campus were and are used to house conference groups. During this time, the Penn Nursery School and the Rossa B. Cooley Health Clinic were started.

Penn was the facility in South Carolina where bi-racial groups could meet during the 50s and early 60s, and it became a major retreat for civil rights groups. From 1961 to 1967, Dr. Martin Luther King, Jr., the Hon. Andrew Young and their staff met often to formulate strategies for social change in the South and the rest of the country. The historic March on Washington, D.C. was partly planned on Penn's campus.

Penn's current mission, guided by the Executive Director, Emory Campbell, is to preserve the Sea Island history, culture and environment through serving as a local, national, and international educational resource center, and by acting as a catalyst for the development of programs for self-sufficiency.

Penn Center has developed three main service programs and a conference center in an attempt to achieve the above goal:

HISTORY AND CULTURE PROGRAM

The History and Culture Program was established to collect, document, preserve and disseminate information related to the cultural heritage of Sea Island African Americans, a culture whose traditions and language are linked closer to West African heritage than any other black community in the Nation. The objectives of the program are achieved through the maintenance of a museum and archive collection and through the presentation of public programs. These resources and programs are designed to serve the educational needs of a national audience and to provide a rich resource for scholarly research.

PROGRAM FOR ACADEMIC AND CULTURAL ENRICHMENT (PACE)

PACE was established to assist Sea Island children, ages 5-17, in developing academic and social skills through a program of academic assistance, leadership training and cultural enrichment activities. The goals of PACE are achieved through three (3) program components: (1) After School Program, (2) Summer Enrichment Program and (3) the Teen Leadership Institute.

LAND USE AND ENVIRONMENTAL EDUCATION PROGRAM

The Land Use and Environmental Education Program was established to assist native Sea Islanders in preserving their land and culture in the face of a rapidly changing environment. The vision of the program is to preserve the culture and environment of the Sea Islands while providing economic opportunities and improved quality of life for residents. This vision is realized through three areas of activities, (1) Citizen Education, (2) Land Use Planning and Policy Reform and (3) Sustainable Economic Development.

The Wright Man

CONFERENCE CENTER

Penn Center's Conference Center provides accommodations and amenities for overnight stays and day conferences/meetings. Comprised of four (4) newly restored residential facilities and two (2) non-residential facilities, the Conference Center can accommodate up to eighty-five (85) overnight guests and provide meeting space for up to three hundred (300) people. The Conference Center is ideally suited and frequently used for educational, environmental and religious retreats and conferences.

Penn Center's director, Emory Campbell, is an example of a native son who left his early environment and later returned not only as a leader, but also as a visionary and proponent of constructive programs and policies. He was born in 1941 on Hilton Head Island, studied at the Michael C. Riley High School in Bluffton, and graduated in 1960 as class valedictorian. In1965, he earned his Batchelor of Science degree in biology at Savannah State College. Joining the Microbiology Department at the Harvard School of Public Health, he researched by day and tutored students in the evening.

After completing his M.A. degree from Tufts University in Boston, Campbell returned to South Carolina to work at the Comprehensive Health Agency for Beaufort and Jasper counties. In 1980, Campbell became the executive director for Penn Center. He vigorously embarked on a program to revive the Center's historical significance and to preserve the culture of the islands.

In 1988, the Board of Trustees launched a capital improvement campaign to renovate and improve existing facilities on the 50 acres. The campus is one of three land sites that comprise the 500-acre holding of the Center. The National Trust for Historic Preservation, the nation's leading preservation organization, awarded Penn Center its highest designation: Landmark Historic District, in 1974.

Aware of the fascinating history and learning of the programs and activities at Penn Center, the Michigan Support Group, for six years, supported the Center, not just with money, but with concern, involvement and frequent visits. It all began when Dr. Wright made that first visit to Penn Center in 1991. The (former) Museum, even though on a small scale, was utterly fascinating with its sincerity and simplicity. The grounds, the buildings, the trees and the history combine to present an awesome portrait of life as it was in times past, unfettered and uncluttered. The mystic aura of the surroundings is still there today.

Returning home, Wright immediately talked to a few close friends about the need for a Michigan Support Group for Penn Center.

In November 1992, Wright returned to St. Helena Island to attend the Annual Heritage Celebration. However, first he sought out Tom Barnwell, chairman of Penn Center's Board of Trustees, who lives on and owns several properties on Hilton Head Island. Wright asked Barnwell if the Michigan Support Group that he was organizing could help fund a development office at the Center. Barnwell asked the direct question, "what will it cost in your estimation?" Wright, caught off guard, answered, "fifty thousand dollars." Barnwell's response was, "Good. Come back when you have it." Wright had been challenged.

The Heritage Celebration opened on Thursday night with a fashion show, an array of ethnic food and church services at four of the Island churches.

On Friday, after the very informative and educational program, the crowds gather at the Brick Church Cemetery by the stately monuments dedicated to Towne and Murray (after death their bodies were returned to Pennsylvania for burial). "Echoes of Penn" sang beautiful St. Helena hymns and a speaker gave a short talk on these two loyal, loved and dedicated teachers.

The Wright Man

Well, at the end of the ceremony, Wright was visibly upset. What now? There was no mention of Charlotte Forten. About this time, Roberta Wright had read Charlotte Forten's Journal, and she and Wright knew of the sacrifices Forten had made, leaving her comfortable home, and coming to live on an island among "her people" who had never seen a Black lady done up in skirts just like Ms Towne and Ms Murray wore.

So, 1991 was the last time that Forten went unmentioned at the Annual Heritage Celebration. Everyone involved with the program was happy to include Ms Forten. By December 1992, Wright had asked his son, Wilbur B. Hughes, III (general manager and board member of Detroit Memorial Park Cemetery, Michigan's oldest African American Corporation) to have a granite marker made for Ms Forten. It was transported by car to St. Helena Island by the Wrights and presented at the Watch Night service at Brick Church on December 31, with a bus load of Michigan Support Group members attending. The Rev. Erwin Green dedicated the memorial marker and it was placed, and remains just outside the church door. Each year, the crowd now, also, gives a stirring tribute to Charlotte Forten, with a student extolling her contributions to Penn School.

The Michigan Support Group, according to Dr. Wright, should be listed as one of the great wonders of the world. Even before many members even visited the island, they picked up the gauntlet and marched forward.

The membership fee was $15.00 for individuals, $25.00 for families, and a Charlotte Forten membership established in 1993 in her memory was set at $130.00. (It had been 130 years since the Emancipation Proclamation was signed.) Membership meetings were held monthly at various locations in and around Detroit.

A chronological listing of the major MSG activities from January 1992 to 1998 includes the following:

1992

- January—Visit of Emory Campbell, Penn's executive director, to the Michigan Support Group organizational meeting in Detroit.

- January—Dr. Wright was invited to join the Penn Board of Trustees, which meets at the center

- February—Dr. Wright attended his first board meeting at Penn.

- June—Fund raiser by MSG for filming of the *Daughers-of the Dust* at the DIA, reception at Your Heritage House.

- July 18—First Annual Gullah Extravaganza at Detroit Yacht Club. "Goin' to the Lowlands." Special guests were entertainers, The Quimbys, from New Brunswick. GA.

- July—Joint bank account opened at S.C. National Bank (now changed to Wachovia Bank), with $10,000. Two signatures are required for withdrawal-Emory Campbell and Roberta Wright.

- Summer—First newsletter issued. Vol. 1, No. 1.

- Summer—MSG pledged $50,000 to Penn Center for the Development Directors Office.

- Auust—The MSG Anniversary Fund (later called Charlotte Forten Fund) was started, $130.00 for membership.

- August—Dr. William Pickard visited Penn and suggested to the MSG, an Emancipation Proclamation reenactment in honor of 130 years.

- September—Nancy Arnold's bus tour on Labor Day weekend to St. Helena.

- Fall—Newsletter published, Vol. 1, No. 2.

- September—Reporter and photographer from *Detroit Free Press* accompanied group to St. Helena, later wrote ROOTS and BRANCHES extensive coverage of trip (see Appendix).

- November 12-14—Nancy Arnold's bus tour to the Annual Heritage Days Celebration at Penn Center. Many MSG members attended.

- November 22—Pre-emancipation Day celebration in Michigan at Dr. William Pickard's residence. Special program between "antagonists featured pro-con arguments."

- December 31—Gathering of MSG members at St. Helena's Brick Church for Watch Night Service and dedication of memorial granite in honor of Charlotte Forten.

1993

- January 1—MSG guests gathered at Port Royal-Fort Frederick site for reenactment of the reading of the Emancipation Proclamation.

- January 1—"Evening with Charlotte Forten" at the Hilton Head Hilton Hotel. Natalie and Ron Daise were the performers—Natalie Daise was "Charlotte Forten."

- January 2—Hilton Head Hilton Hotel. Closing dinner party-Natalie and Ron Daise—Gullah performers.

- February 6—First Annual Meeting of the MSG.

- Spring—A *Tribute to Charlotte Forten, 1837-1914,* written by Roberta Wright-presented to all Charlotte Forten members.

- April—General membership meeting held at Plymouth United Church of Christ, Detroit.

- May 15—Herbert DeCosta. Penn board member from Charleston. S.C. visited MSG meeting in Detroit.

- May 30—Gullah Fish Fry held at Dr. Pickard's farm in Linden, Michigan—large crowd attended.

- Spring—Audrey Johnson nominated by MSG to apply for Development Director Job at Penn.

- Summer—General Membership meeting and meeting of the Executive Committee.

- July 18—"Goin' to the Lowlands II" at Detroit Yacht Club. Natalie and Ron Daise came to city to perform.

- Summer—Newsletter. Vol.1, No.3.

- October—Audrey Johnson selected as Penn's first Development Officer by the board of trustees of Penn Center.

- October—Fund raiser at Detroit's Warehouse Club, sponsored by Linda Watters and Gwen Esco Davis.

- November 3—Audrey Johnson began work at Penn Center.

- Winter—Vol. 1, No. 4 Winter newsletter.

- December—Karen Fisher announced 750 members belonging to MSG: 160 of whom were Charlotte Forten members.

- December 18—All members were thanked for their efforts at a "Membership Appreciation Party" at Dell Pryor Gallery, sponsored by Watters and Esco-Davis.

- Dr. Wright resigned as Penn board member and Penn board elected MSG member, Patricia Anderson Smith as new representative on the board.

1994

- January 17—General Membership Meeting.

- March-General Membership Meeting, election of officers at meeting held at the Museum of African American History.

The Wright Man

- April—General Membership Meeting, installation of officers at Plymouth United Church of Christ.

- February—Pat Smith's first board meeting at Penn.

- March-June—Fish Fry Committee meetings at James Howard's residence.

- March—MSG Committee to Canada to meet with Dr. Bryan Walls and family to discuss June 19 party on grounds of the John Freeman Walls Historic Site in Puce, Ontario.

- Spring—Newsletter. Vol.1, No.5.

- June 17—Received Emory Campbell's written report of activities of the Development Director, Audrey Johnson.

- June 19—MSG's Juneteenth Fund Raiser Celebration at Walls Historic Site in Puce. Mrs. Johnson attended and gave brief report to crowd.

- June 20—Press conference at MAAH for Mrs. Johnson to give report on 6 months at Penn.

- July and August—Executive Committee meetings. Discussion and decision to have raffle.

- August 16—Executive Committee Meeting-Edith Giles and Kathy Bradfield distributed tickets.

- August 17—Leonard Davis gave report on plans to have fund raiser at Repertory Theatre, *Kate's Sister,* January 14.1995.

- November 1994—Bus trip sponsored by Michigan Support Group Annual Heritage Weekend, St. Helena.

- December 1994—Bus trip—MSG-to Hilton Head Island and Penn Center, Emancipation Proclamation Celebration on Jan. 1.1995 (See program and detailed report). $50.000 payment for development director completed.

1995

- Jan. 1—See detailed report on Emancipation Proclamation program.

- Jan. 14—Detroit Repertory Theatre-fund raiser—*Kate's Sister.*

- February-April—Meetings, preparation for June 18, 1995 Fish Fry.

- May 18—Members travel to Port Royal. S.C. for celebration of award of National Historic Place.

- June 18 —Fish Fry, Dr. William Pickard's farm. McPickwood—Report by Audrey Johnson, development director.

- August-November—MSG agreed to furnish Pine Grove Cottage's five bedrooms. Articles and furniture collection began.

- November 9-11—Heritage Days Celebration in St. Helena.

- December 31, 1995—Watch Night Service. Brick Baptist Church, St. Helena.

- December 1995—$59,000 total so far paid for development director's office.

1996

- Jan. 1—Unveiling of plaque and reenactment of reading of Emancipation Proclamation at Camp Saxton, Port Royal. S.C.

- Jan. 1—Dinner, Fellowship Hall, Brick Baptist Church.

- Jan. 2—*Passed Over*—Play at Repertory Theatre, sponsored by Michigan Support Group.

- Feb. 4—Meeting to discuss Pine Grove Cottage. nomination of officers, discussion of *Deliverance,* a painting by Arianne King-Comer. Dr. Wright paid the $1,000 cost with donations from Ann Flanders, Mildred Fuller-Broxton, Fred D. Robinson, and Beatrice Henderson.

- March 11—Election of officers.

- March 11—Swearing in of officers by Hon. Craig Strong Leonard Davis, DDS, new president and Karen Fisher, vice president

- March to April 22—"gathering of furniture" storage at James Howard's residence.

- April 22—Packing by Florence Mills and committee and truck loaded and on to South Carolina.

- April 24-27—Patricia Smith at Penn Center to meet truck and arrange furniture.

- May 14—Meeting of MSG. "Deliverance" painting taken to meeting and donated to the new museum at Penn Center—Pine Cottage Committee reports.

- June 2—St. Helena Island-Pine Cottage. Arnett, Benezet. and Hampton House—end of Phase I—Open House attended by Wrights.

- July—Party at Norma & Leonard Davis' home for James Howard's committee for their dedication to the furnishing of Pine Grove Cottage.

- August to December—general meetings, discussion of furniture also sent to the Retreat House at Penn Center. The MSG also discussed ways it can assist with the Cafeteria restoration. As a summer 1996 fundraiser, members were seeking more Charlotte Forten members.

In 1997-1998, the activities of the MSG escalated, first, by a "Stay-at-Home" Tea which was very successful. Wright had turned the presidency over to Leonard Davis, DDS, who served well. The next year, however, Davis and his wife, Norma, were preparing to move to Charleston, S.C. for the winter. They moved in November and vice president Karen Rozier Fisher was elevated to the presidency. Dr. Karl Gregory, a long time member and supporter of Penn Center was elected vice president. The faithful and reliable Barbara Williford stayed on as recording secretary. In 1998, Aurelia Baxter and Florence Mills became co-chairs of the important membership committee and Paralee Day co-chaired the Gullah Fish Fry committee, chaired by Sarah Giddens.

Almost every listing on every page, involved many hours and effort on the part of Dr. Wright and the members of the Michigan Support Group. Charles Alexander played a major role in the success of the project with the typing, layouts, graphics, newsletters, etc. He was with the Michigan Support Group, continuously, from 1992 to its final days in 1998.

Although Wright feels that there are stories about the MSG/Penn experience that need to be told, he especially feels a "one-liner" in no way describes two of his favorite MSG accomplishments. One is the behind the scene "elbows and butts" scenario relating to the furnishing of Pine Cottage. The other relates to the year-long, almost daily work performed in order to award the "National Historic Place" plaque at the site of the reading of the Proclamation of Emancipation.

As you've read, Charlotte Forten's journal gave fairly explicit directions regarding the site. Many islanders, because of years of "handed-down stories and myths" informed Dr. Wright that the actual reading of the Proclamation took place somewhere on St. Helena Island, under a large oak tree. Because St. Helena has literally thousands of huge, beautiful, oak trees, he always jokingly asked for a better description of the tree. Wright commends Roberta for studying the journal and conferring with the librarian at the Beaufort County library and for locating the site. The State of South Carolina archivists confirmed the exact location after receiving Roberta's request for their investigation.

THE REENACTMENTS

The reenactments of this historical event, the reading of the Emancipation Proclamation, by Penn Center and Michigan Support Group on January 1, 1993; January 1, 1995; May 18, 1995; January 1, 1996, January 1, 1997, January 1, 1998, and January 1, 1999, at the original site, have shown the effects of the commemoration by the reawakening of the public to the true meaning of the 1863 celebration.

The first reenactment planned by Penn and the Michigan Support Group began on December 31, 1992, with a Watch Night Service at St. Helena's Brick Baptist Church when the Charlotte Forten memorial was presented.

On the following day, January 1, 1993, reenactment of the Emancipation Proclamation of January 1, 1863 was performed at the waterfront, Camp Saxton site, before an enthusiastic crowd wih great success. During this initial reenactment, it was noted that there was nothing there to indicate that here was the birthplace of freedom for African Americans.

Since the U.S. Naval Hospital now leases the land, a regular flow of calls and letters were exchanged with U.S. Naval officers. As host, the U.S. Navy, cooperated to the fullest by providing chairs, a public address system and naval personnel to make the occasion an outstanding success. Program participants included: Captain Ron Finke and Senior Chief Robert Bible of the Department of the Navy, who were most helpful for the reenactment; Mr. Tom Barnwell, chairman, board of trustees, Penn Center; Emory Campbell, Penn Center executive director; state senator McKinley Washington; state representative William Keyserling; Dr. William Pickard, MSG; Rev. A.C. Redd, trustee, Penn Center; Beaufort Mayor David Taub, who read the Emancipation Proclamation that was originally read by Rev. William Henry Brisbane, M.D.; and Wright, trustee of Penn Center and president of MSG. Dr. Pickard, after visiting Penn Center, had brought back to the

MSG, the idea of going forward with the celebration. It was a great occasion.

The reenactment was blessed with a noonday temperature of 71 degrees, a cloudless sky and the soothing sounds of the waves of the Beaufort River lashing the nearby coast. The MSG realized later that they were some 30 to 50 yards from the actual site, but the tabby shell remains of Fort Frederick, built in the 1700s, formed a spectacular background for the ceremony. The dinner following the program was held at the Hilton Head Hilton Resort. Natalie Daise presented "An Evening With Charlotte Forten" on January 1, and on January 2nd Natalie and Ron Daise, Beaufort residents, entertained the audience with Gullah skits and stories. The celebration was well covered by all area newspapers.

NATIONAL HISTORIC PLACE DESIGNATION

Michigan Support Group efforts, between January 1993 and January 1995, were directed toward seeking a National Historic Place designation at the site. The absence of a marker designating the grounds as special was most evident and gave impetus to the work.

A preliminary application to the South Carolina Department of Archives and History was completed and forwarded in February 1994. U.S. Naval Hospital personnel provided a statement prepared in the past by the Navy in regards to the property in discussion. A significant portion of that statement reads thusly:

> After the American Revolution in 1779, the inhabitants of the Beaufort area again resumed their agricultural and mercantile pursuits. Sea Island cotton was the principal agricultural crop and, until the start of the Civil War in 1861, its production greatly enriched the local planters and merchants. Following its abandonment, the land on which Fort Frederick was located became part of the John Joiner Smith Plantation. At an unknown date, Smith

erected a house and outbuildings on the property. During the Civil War, Beaufort was used as the chief base for the Federal South Atlantic Blockading Squadron and headquarters of the U.S. Army in the South. Beaufort was occupied by Union forces from November 1861 until the end of the conflict.

The John Joiner Smith plantation, now the site of the Naval Hospital, figured prominently in the Civil War. For a portion of the war the 1st South Carolina Volunteers, a regiment made up of black soldiers, camped on the grounds surrounding the house. Their bivouac was named Camp Saxton, after General Saxton, the federal military governor for the Beaufort area. On January 1, 1863, General Saxton had several thousand local freed slaves brought to the camp on the Smith plantation. At this meeting they were first officially informed of the Emancipation Proclamation and the document was read to them. This emotional ceremony lasted three hours and included prayers and speeches in addition to the reading of the Proclamation. This then was the first site in South Carolina where slaves were officially freed from their bondage by Union forces.

Construction on the Naval Hospital was started in 1946 and completed in 1949. No buildings constructed prior to 1946 are now present on Naval Hospital lands.

On September 10, 1993, Mr. Andrew Chandler, National Register specialist, South Carolina State Historic Preservation Office, sent articles, listings, and a catalog designed to assist with the application in response to our request. The application was completed and mailed along with photographs of the site.

On April 7, 1994, a letter was received from Mr. Chandler regarding the National Register. This most significant letter suggested that Penn Center and the Michigan Support Group should also pursue a listing in the National Register of Historic Places (in addition to the State designation). Chandler pointed out that not only were the words of the "document" (Emancipation Proclamation) first heard here, but it was also the site of the organization of the First South Carolina

Volunteers, the earliest federally authorized Black unit to fight for the Union.

Contact was made with Old Fort Jackson in Savannah, Georgia, regarding troops for the upcoming reenactment. Sgt. Murry Dorty responded and from that time on, the planners depended on Sgt. Dorty to prepare his troops for action. He did so in January 1995, May 1995, and again, in January 1996. In 1996, the First S.C. Colored Volunteers shared the platform with the 54th Massachusetts troops from Charleston, South Carolina. On January 1, 1997, 1998 and 1999, Joseph McGill, director of Penn Center's History and Cultural Affairs Program led the troops in maneuvers for the ceremony.

On October 14, 1994, a letter was received from Dr. George Vogt, state historic preservation officer, regarding a pending November 18, 1994 meeting to vote on the Michigan Support Group's application. Malcolm Dade, of Columbia, South Carolina, now chairman of the Penn Center trustee board, represented the Michigan Support Group at the meeting in Columbia. The vote of approval was unanimous, reported Dade.

Spirits were high at the time of the January 1, 1995 celebration because it appeared evident that approval would be forthcoming. Numerous letters were sent announcing the event. South Carolina state senator, McKinley Washington and representative William Keyserling sent letters of support. Plans were made for a special dinner to be held at the Hilton Head Crystal Sands Hotel. Frankie and Doug Quimby, of Brunswick, Georgia, were invited as entertainers for the New Year's Day party.

The New Year's Eve Watch Night Service at Brick Baptist Church was well attended by regular members and MSG members, who came by charter bus. The January 1 program at the site proceeded smoothly. Murry Dorty's troops were precise, the speeches meaningful, and the audience was pleased. Media coverage, as before, was extensive, with releases in local papers and in Columbia's *STATE*.

When word was received in writing that federal approval was awarded on February 2, 1995, personnel at the Navy Hospital anxiously planned a May 18 celebration in conjunction and with the approval of Penn Center and the Michigan Support Group. The Navy invited its top brass from Washington, D.C., including the Surgeon General. Students from the Robert Smalls Middle School in Beaufort attended. The program was videotaped by the Marine Corps photographer and the Marine Corps Band played several selections.

Toward the end of the program, artist Arianne King-Comer was introduced. She had been commissioned to depict on canvas, the 1863 scene at Camp Saxton. The presentation was outstanding. Detroit mortician, Rebecca Barksdale, in attendance at the ceremony, offered to cover the cost and paid for the commemorative plaque which was to be ordered from the South Carolina Department of Archives and History.

Looking forward to the January 1, 1996 celebration, the MSG invited Wallace Alcorn, minister and Ph.D., who lives in Austin, Minnesota, to come to South Carolina to read the Proclamation during the program. Dr. Alcorn is the great, great grandson of Dr. William Brisbane. His response in September 1995 indicated that he was unable to attend but would like to be invited for the January 1997 event. Dr. Alcorn prepared and sent a three-page statement documenting the illustrative life of Dr. Brisbane.

With final approval in hand, MSG members set about to order the plaque. A "city style," full-size form was selected and the wording was prepared. It was agreed that one side of the plaque would honor the First Public Reading of the Proclamation of Emancipation and the other side would commemorate the 1st S.C. Colored Volunteer Regiment. The contact person in Columbia was Dr. J. Tracy Power, National

Register specialist, who assured us that the plaque would be engraved and delivered to the site in time.

On December 31, the Watch Night Service was held at Brick Baptist Church. On January 1, 1996, persons from near and afar met at the Naval Hospital auditorium to witness the unveiling of the beautiful commemorative plaque. It was later placed on the grounds across from the hospital and at the Beaufort River site of the original reading.

Murry Dorty and his troops presented the reenactment and platform guests gave honor to the occasion. The painting, "Deliverance," depicting the scene of the original event, by artist Arianne King-Comer, was described and presented to the audience. A group of students from Penn's PACE Program sang the St. Helena Hymn. Relatives of Dr. Mansfield French, Mary and Bill Compton of Beaufort were in attendance. Dr. French played an extremely prominent role in the 1863 ceremony and in the lives of the Blacks on St. Helena Island.

The program was followed by dinner at Brick Church's Fellowship Hall. Festivities ended with a tour of Penn's Museum and the four newly renovated buildings, and to the display "Expressions of Indigo" by Arianne King-Comer.

The January 1, 1997 program followed the tradition of previous years, beginning with Watch Night Service at Brick Baptist Church. Penn Center's efforts to make this New Year's Day program special were rewarded. A primary factor was the plaque, now installed. The guests were impressed and felt joyful about the award. Then, too, the program was highlighted by the appearance and participation of the Reverend Dr. Wallace Alcorn of Minnesota. He delighted the crowd with stories about his great, great grandfather, Dr. Brisbane, who read the Proclamation on January 1, 1863.

The January 1, 1998 program brought the usual excitement and a large crowd to the Port Royal site. Joseph McGill, Penn's museum director, led the troop in their re-enactment of the proceedings of 1863. Speeches by the board chair, Malcolm Dade, executor director, Emory Campbell, and Dr. Wright were well received. South Carolina State Senator Glenn F. McConnell, elegant in a top hat, read the Emancipation Proclamation. The U.S. Naval Hospital personnel, as usual, worked diligently to erect the podium, sound system, and to direct traffic.

The January 1, 1999 celebration highlight was the reading of the Proclamation by Dr. Lawrence S. Rowland, professor of history at the University of South Carolina-Beaufort. Additionally, members of the 54th Massachusetts Re-enactment Regiment, a group established to preserve the history of African American involvement in the Civil War, presented a re-enactment of the 1st South Carolina Volunteer Infantry's participation in the first reading of the Emancipation Proclamation. They were led by Joseph McGill, who recently accepted the position as executive director of the African American Heritage Foundation in Cedar Rapids, Iowa. Other program participants were students of Walter Mack's PACE program; the Rev. Horace Williams, Jr.; U.S. Naval Hospital Captain, Elizabeth Barker; and Port Royal mayor, Samuel Murray.

Dr. Wright's other special pride and joy was unquestionably a true labor of love for all who participated. Pine Grove Cottage, which faces Martin Luther King Drive and is adjacent to the new museum, is strikingly beautiful. The Michigan Support Group selected the building to furnish in a manner that was classic and elegant, and most of all, authentic to the era of the early 1900s.

In comparison to the other stately buildings on the campus, such as the Hampton, Arnett and Benezet houses, Pine Grove Cottage is small. Consequently, the Michigan Support Group was able to assume responsibility for the entire building. It is difficult to say which MSG member expended the most energy toward this project. That, in itself, is a tribute to the group.

Pine Grove Cottage's five bedrooms were adopted by five members, who left "no stone unturned" in furnishing the rooms. These Good Samaritans were Dorothy Mann. Martha Morris, Patricia and Mark Smith, Aurelia Baxter and James Howard. Howard also provided storage space in his palatial home for several months until the furniture was loaded into the moving van. In addition, he donated rattan furniture for the beautiful Retreat House.

During these months, Patricia Smith "burned up" the highways searching for just the right linens and accessories for the cottage. Pine's other rooms, the kitchen, the living room, and the conference room were likewise adopted and adorned. Each room has a small metal plaque designating the donor. Michigan Support Group honored the Drs. Wright by naming the conference room in their honor.

Other highly treasured and valuable antique furniture and furnishings were donated by Paralee Day, Norma and Leonard Davis, Florence Mills, Barbara Williford, and Ida Drewery. Cash and furnishings were contributed by Ernest Mitchell, Edith Bell, Martha Jackson, Dr. Barbara Hughes Smith, Alma M. Brown, Eula Jackson, Kathy Bradfield, Mildred Fuller-Broxton, Titus McClary, Ruby Thompson, Matthew McNeely, Brunetta Vinson, Frances Deckard, Margaret Larrie, Sarah Giddens, Joyce Hurst, Maryhelen Amaker, the Oakland County Chapter of the Links, Inc., Karen Fisher, Tinnie Morman, and Natalia Tanner Cain, M.D.

Pine Grove Cottage sits as a proud jewel, lovingly polished and enhanced by the adoration and devotion of the Michigan Support Group.

In 1998, the Michigan Support Group, as originally structured, came to an end. At the September 14 meeting, members agreed to discontinue meeting as a group. An Advisory Committee, chaired by Alice Brown, was formed to serve as a liaison between Penn and the former MSG members.

The Wright Man

On October 15, a party was held at the Dunbar Memorial Museum on Frederick Douglass and honor was paid to all members and former members.

MSG presidents — Leonard Davis, DDS; Dr. Karl Gregory; Karen Fisher; and Wright

Wright and Dr. Margaret Burroughs at AAMA meeting in Chicago

Sgt. White and diner — Burton, South Carolina

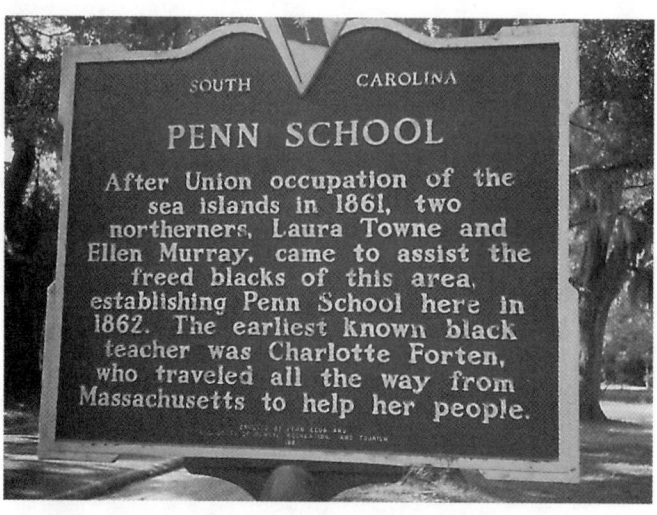

SOUTH CAROLINA

PENN SCHOOL

After Union occupation of the sea islands in 1861, two northerners, Laura Towne and Ellen Murray, came to assist the freed blacks of this area, establishing Penn School here in 1862. The earliest known black teacher was Charlotte Forten, who traveled all the way from Massachusetts to help her people.

Plaque at Penn Center — St. Helena Island, S.C.

The Wright Man

Tom Barnwell, Penn Center Chair, to Wright — "Show me the money"

Wright to Barnwell — "MSG has the money"

7 | 24

EMANCIPATION DAY

On New Year's Day 1863 this plantation owned by John Joyner Smith was the scene of elaborate ceremonies celebrating the enactment of the Emancipation Proclamation. Hundreds of freedmen and women came from Port Royal, Beaufort, and the sea islands to join Federal military and civil authorities and others in marking the event. After the proclamation was read, the 1st South Carolina Volunteers (Colored), the first black regiment formed
(Continued on other side)

The Plaque, front and back, a recognition of the importance of the site

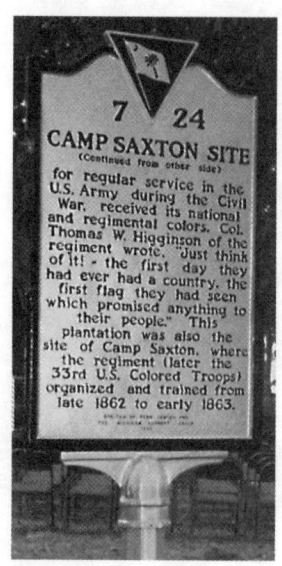

7 | 24

CAMP SAXTON SITE
(Continued from other side)

for regular service in the U.S. Army during the Civil War, received its national and regimental colors. Col. Thomas W. Higginson of the regiment wrote, "Just think of it! - the first day they had ever had a country, the first flag they had seen which promised anything to their people." This plantation was also the site of Camp Saxton, where the regiment (later the 33rd U.S. Colored Troops) organized and trained from late 1862 to early 1863.

Museum and Penn Center supporters:
Catherine Routt, Ernestine Rosemond, R. Wright and Valerie Proctor

The Annual Celebration of the reading of the
Emancipation Proclamation Port Royal, S.C. — soldiers at attention

Presenting the Charlotte Forten memorial
Wright; Emory Campbell, Penn's executive director; Brick Church's pastor, Rev. Erwin Green

Brick and the live oaks

The Wright Man

Echoes of Penn — Brick church cemetery

The ring shout
Lula Holmes of St. Helena Island and friends

Dr. Wright addressing the crowd at the Camp Saxton site
Port Royal, S.C.

Barbara Hughes Smith and Joseph Wendell Smith visiting Penn Center

The Wright Man

Beautiful Pine Cottage, Penn Center

The "Elbows and Butts" brigade
MSG members worked tirelessly to ship furniture to Pine Cottage and the Retreat House, Penn Center

MSG final meeting at the Dunbar Memorial Museum Bldg
Sarah Giddens, James Howard, Brunetta Vinson, Tinnie Morman, Patricia Smith, Aurelia Baxter

October 15, 1998 — Members pledged to continue support of Penn Center

The Wright Man

Dr. Wright's penchant for staying involved, for constantly attacking issues that he determines are fundamental, is ingrained in him. In the late 1960s, after opening the Detroit museum, he began to realize the need for the establishment of museums elsewhere, for the betterment of the lives of African Americans. He sought out Dr. Margaret Burroughs, artist, author, teacher, collector, traveler and lecturer, to share his thoughts about what needed to be done. Dr. Burroughs, along with her husband, Charles, had established DuSable Museum in Chicago in 1961. Like Wright, she envisioned the museum as a way to give Black children a sense of identity.

Burroughs and Wright, who came to be known as the mother and father of the African American museum movement, invited a group of six museum representatives to meet at Detroit's museum to form a National Black Museums Association. The group more than doubled in size each year and with the help of nationally known and respected artist, E. Barry Gaither, the first office was established. The site was the Museum of the National Center for Afro-American Artists in Boston, which Gaither directs.

The organization, renamed as the African American Museums Association (AAMA) met annually in various cities, establishing guidelines and developing a comprehensive survey of Black museums. In 1988, over one hundred people attended the annual meeting; the AAMA was becoming a force in the museum world, its effect on the museum movement was phenomenal.

The AAMA office moved to Washington, D.C. and later to Wilberforce, Ohio and the membership grew to over four hundred. In Chicago, in 1996, as an expression of the respect and love of the members for the founders, a fund was established in the name of Burroughs-Wright Scholarship. The many persons who worked diligently to promote all of the organization's meetings and programs are listed in the book's Appendix. Also listed is the 1999-2000 board of directors and the individual and organization members.

At the 1998 meetings in Birmingham, Alabama, co-hosted by the National Conference of Artists, the organization adopted a new name, the African American Association of Museums (AAAM). The keynote speaker was Robert G. Stanton, director of the National Park Service. Nominated by President Clinton, Stanton is the first African American to be appointed director of the 81-year-old National Park Service. Also at the meeting Detroit was selected as the site of the 1999 meeting. At Dr. Wright's previous suggestion, AAAM selected Penn Center, St. Helena, S.C. for the annual meeting in the year 2000. Rita Organ, curator of the Charles H. Wright Museum of African American History, was elected president of AAAM.

Aside from Wright's interest in seeing the museum movement flourish, he has a special affiliation with Canadian museums, as evidenced by his frequent visits across the border. Some of the Canadian museums associated with the African American Association of Museums are as follows:

Akwaa-Harrison Galley, Toronto, Ontario
Black Cultural Center for Nova Scotia, East Dartmouth, Nova Scotia

Hiram Walker Historical Museum, Windsor, Ontario

North American Black Historical Museum and Cultural Center, Amherstburg, Ontario

The Ontario Black History Society. Toronto, Ontario

Panafrican Development Society, Toronto, Ontario

Buxton Historic Site & Museum, North Buxton, Ontario

John Freeman Walls Historic Site, Puce, Ontario
Josiah Henson House, "Uncle Tom's Cabin," Dresden, Ontario

Dr. Wright has exchanged ideas with some of these organizations, especially the museums in Puce, Amhertsburg, Dresden, and North Buxton. The John Freeman Walls Historic Site ((Proverbs Heritage Organization) where the "Underground Railroad had its end," is in Puce, Ontario. Founded by Dr. Bryan E. Walls, it is truly a family operation, and a must to see.

The historic plaque on the grounds reads: In 1846 John Freeman Walls, a fugitive slave from North Carolina, built this log cabin on land purchased from the Refugee Home Society. This organization was founded by the abolitionists, Henry Bibb, publisher of the *Voice of the Fugitive,* and the famous Josiah Henson. The cabin subsequently served as a terminal of the underground railroad and the first meeting place of the Puce Baptist Church. Although many former slaves returned to the United States following the American Civil War, Walls and his family chose to remain in Canada. The story of their struggles forms the basis of the book, *The Road That Led To Somewhere,* by Dr. Bryan E. Walls. The refrain from the book's introduction is as follows:

"The Road That Led to Somewhere"
by Dr. Bryan E. Walls

The Road that Led to Somewhere
Has brought us all the way to where we are
Follow the side of the tree that the moss grows on
And the light of the north star

REFRAIN

Black is black and white is white
What they did for us help set things right
They jumped the broom to show their might
We the descendants feel no shame
One was voted into the Halls of Fame
Carry on the Walls proud name
We from John the slaves descendant
Wishing harm and ill to no one
Both countries ill are being amended
We're just as good as anyone
Canadian fruits of U.S. roots
Free to grow because you had to run
Free to cross both countries
Never again to have to flee
Prejudice, hate and bigotry
John you were a slave and downtrodden
For what you did can't be forgotten
We love your Road to peace and harmony
Jane you were white and a lady
From your love there came a baby
The story of our family history

The road we travel's not the same
Thank you John and thank you Jane
Thank you God for bearing us their name.

The North American Black Historical Museum and
Cultural Center is located in the area where many slaves came
across the Detroit River and into Amherstburg because it was

the narrowest point at which to cross. This made Amherstburg one of the Underground Railroad's largest terminals for coming into Canada. In the summer, many fugitives swam the river with their few belongings tied to their backs. During the winter months, many who saw snow and ice for the first time, crossed the frozen river with great difficulty. Most brought with them new energy for developing prosperous farms and businesses, and focused their many skills into meaningful trades, like building churches, schools, and homes.

It was because of his deep concern for the past, that Melvin Simpson founded the museum in 1964 in Amherstburg. He wanted to uncover and preserve the record of the rich heritage of Black people. In 1966, a major effort was undertaken to gather information and to establish appropriate research. The pastor and members of the Nazery A.M.E. Church raised money to build a hall adjacent to the church for the Black museum. In 1971, five members of the A.M.E. Church purchased the adjacent property. A log house on the land later became part of the museum complex. The North American Black Historical Museum became incorporated on October 20, 1975.

Dr. Wright visits the Buxton Historic Site and Museum (formerly the Raleigh Township Centennial Museum) every year on Labor Day.

On the Sunday of this weekend, residents and visitors are treated to a re-enactment designed to portray a significant event in the early years of the Settlement's history. Bryan Prince, Roberta Wright's cousin and mastermind of the annual re-enactments, along with a committee of devoted volunteers, has given special attention to the Sesquicentennial Celebration, 1849-1999. In addition to this, 1999 marks the 75th Annual Labour Day Homecoming Celebration. In February of 1999, the Government of Canada designated the Buxton Settlement as a "National Historic Site" to recognize its special significance in the history of the country.

The town of Merlin, adjacent to North Buxton, is where Roberta Wright's mother, grandparents, and twelve aunts and uncles were born and raised. Buxton was a settlement of woods and fields through which passed the "unseen" railroad. North Buxton is a unified community located about an hour's drive from Windsor. A beautiful country setting cemetery borders North Buxton's main road. Stand, for example, at the graves of Dennis and Jane Frances Robbins. Contemplate Dennis' story, the details of which are on file at the nearby Buxton Historic Site and Museum.

Originally named Dennis Calico, he was given his freedom on condition that he marry his master's slave mistress, who'd borne several of the white man's children. Partial documentation has been uncovered showing that this owner's surname was Tyson. In fact, the last child born into slavery was named James Tyson. However, several years before coming to Canada in the 1850s, Dennis had assumed the name Dennis C. Robbins. He died in 1871 at age 66.

The Josiah Henson House in Dresden, Ontario, is also a favorite of Dr. Wright. In this house lived the Reverend Josiah Henson (1789-1883) whose early life in slavery provided much of the material for Harriet Beecher Stowe's novel, *Uncle Tom's Cabin.* Born in Maryland, Henson escaped in 1830 to Upper Canada. In 1844, he and a group of abolitionists purchased 200 acres in this vicinity and established a vocational school known as the British American Institute for fugitive slaves. A sawmill and grist mill were built, and a considerable number of former slaves settled here. After emancipation was proclaimed in 1863, many returned to the United States, but Henson continued to occupy this house until his death in 1883, and is buried nearby.

The Henson home, popularly known as "Uncle Tom's Cabin," is now a museum, and it, along with other buildings from the old "Institute," is filled with many original displays of items pertinent to the era, including the pulpit from the

British Methodist Episcopal Church, where Josiah Henson ministered to the spiritual needs of his colonists for many years. Barbara Henson Carter, curator of Uncle Tom's Cabin Museum, is the great, great granddaughter of Mr. Henson.

In June 1989, Dr. Wright was a guest at the 200th Anniversary Celebration of Josiah Henson's birth. Dr. Wright entitled his speech, "Will the Real Josiah Henson Please Stand Up." The Honorable Lincoln M. Alexander, Lt. Governor of Ontario, was one of the celebrity speakers.

Although the Canadian museums are constantly visited by residents of Canada, tour buses from "the states" cross the border with regularly scheduled trips to visit these historic sites.

During the years 1965 to 1986, while busy with the Museum, the African Medical Education Fund, and the African American Museums Association, Dr. Wright never neglected his medical practice. He was at the beck and call of his patients, day and night. By retirement, the count of babies delivered was over 5, 000. However, the serious illness of his wife, Louise, leading up to her death on September 13, 1985, left him in despair. He provided love, encouragement, support, and hope to her, until the end. Dr. Wright regularly attended services at Central Methodist Church, in downtown Detroit, and had unquestionable spiritual security to help him through this crisis.

Fortunately, the medical office personnel and physicians at 50 Westminster had always maintained harmonious relationships. Back in 1975, Dr. William Bentley, Wright's partner, entered into a agreement with Dr. Thomas Batchelor, then medical director of Comprehensive Health Services of Detroit, so that Bentley, Dr. R.S. Rangarajan, the other partner; and Dr. Wright would take over the obstetrics-gynecology services at CHSD (now the Wellness Plan).

The three partners, and for brief periods, Dr. Samuel Edwin, Dr. Barry Burgess and Dr. Dennis Means worked well together. Wright had purchased the building before moving his medical practice and his family there. Just prior to 1985, the partners discussed the subject of retirement quite frequently and finally by 1986, the office was closed. After some 40 years of practice, this was not an easy move for Dr. Wright. He had moved his family to Nicolet Street in downtown Detroit in the late 1970s.

Dr. Rangarajan, the youngest of the three, took over the medical directorship of Comprehensive Health Services of Detroit and Drs. Bentley and Wright spent the next few months answering patients' questions and moving and storing medical records. Dr. Bentley, having suffered from a vascular disease for some years, died in the early 1990s. His death was a serious blow to "Rajan" and Wright and to his many, many friends.

Dr. Wright, at the insistence and advice of his cousin, Sharon Smith, who lived in California, had a computer sent to him. He soon learned the technique and spent much of his time typing letters, his daily log, and more letters. Some letters were to friends, but some were "Letters to the Editor." He was an ardent reader and seldom let incorrect facts or articles that denigrated African Americans, go unheeded.

In August 1986, the day before the opening of the second annual African World Festival at Hart Plaza, Dr. Wright fainted while walking to the post office. First reports—actually rumors—were that he had suffered a heart attack. "This was not true," says Wright, but the doctor couldn't readily determine the problem. Some who know Dr. Wright well, think that in the press of activity preparing for the festival, he just hadn't eaten. Food was not a priority for him, and living alone, he had no one to monitor his eating. In fact, his salvation often was and is Eloise Shannon, who keeps him supplied with his favorite sweet potato pie, and Frances Curtis, who regularly sends rolls and other goodies. Then too, Dr.

Wright could cook one "dish"—cabbage. He cooks a "mean" pot of cabbage, enhancing it with turkey sausage, onions, and red peppers.

In June 1986, a group of doctors—fellow physicians—planned and carried off a hilarious roast for Dr. Wright at the Roostertail. He was "burnt to a crisp" by Dr. Harcourt Harris; Dr. William Bentley; Mr. Robert Shannon; Dr. Lionel Swan; Hon. Erma Henderson; Dr. Charles Vincent; Dr. Cecil Jonas; and others.

It was there, that Wright met Roberta Greenidge Hughes. Her friend, Vivian Johnson, had asked her to attend, stating that Dr. Wright wished to discuss "the papers" of her father, Robert I. Greenidge, M.D. At the roast, Roberta approached Wright, and they agreed to meet at a later date for lunch. At lunch, at Restaurant Chic Afrique on Woodward Avenue, Wright was sadly disappointed when Roberta admitted she had not visited the Museum on West Grand Boulevard. Needless to say, she made a visit before the week was out, joined the Million Dollar Club, and wrote letters to some of her friends to solicit memberships. They began dating in 1987, and married in August 1989. After the Museum's move in 1987 to the new site, Roberta assisted Wright with all of the "history programs," and activities at the Museum.

Even though retired from his medical practice, Dr. Wright maintained the kind of fast paced schedule that belies his age. It is probably safe to say that Dr. Wright, who has traveled throughout Europe, Africa, Central America, the Caribbean, the United States, and other countries, has never been on "vacation" as we know the word.

One such example was his trip to Puerto Rico. Wright had purchased a time share and scheduled a February 1990 visit. Wife, Roberta, packed beach clothes. They were never used; but motor trips throughout the island did prove interesting. During the visit to Aquadilla, on the northwest coast of Puerto Rico, Wright announced that it was where Columbus made landfall in 1493, after his second transatlantic voyage. Since Wright had researched the events of the previous 500 years, he asked some of the local people standing around, "What happened to all of the Trianos and Aranak Indian tribes who greeted Columbus in Puerto Rico in 1493?"

One young man told Wright that they were carnivores and "ate each other up." Wright responded with the observation that they all seemed to disappear after Columbus' arrival. "What did he do to increase their appetite for each other?" asked Wright. They stopped smiling and became defensive. One of them dismissed Dr. Wright and turned away, saying, "Aw, you know how those Spaniards were." "Don't go away," Wright said, "Wait and tell me about them." But that was the end of the conversation. Wright, of course, was speaking in Spanish to the locals.

Another instance was the "vacation" trip in 1991 to Hilton Head Island, South Carolina. By then, Roberta, herself, had lost the meaning of the word, and the trip was to research African American cemeteries in the low country. A side trip to St. Helena Island, S.C. resulted as read in Chapter 10.

With both Wrights writing, it seemed necessary to attack the problem of publication.

Charro Books was organized in 1991, at the time of the publication of, *The Birth of the Montgomery Bus Boycott.* The name, *CHARRO,* is a compilation of Charles and Roberta. It was started for the prime purpose of structuring the publication of the books written by the two of them. Consequently, through the years they have had to turn down literally hundreds of requests for assistance in publishing other's books. They both know the difficulties of publication. Dr. Wright's previous book, *Paul Robeson: Labor's Forgotten Champion,* was published by Dr. James Jay. *Lay Down Body: Living History in African American Cemeteries,* by Roberta Wright and Wilbur B. Hughes, III, was published in 1996 by Visible Ink Press. However, his and Roberta's other books were self-published.

The Wright Man

Work stopped on the "Mandela" book that Dr. Wright had been writing when he began concentrating on the 100th Anniversary of the National Medical Association (NMA).

It all started around 1993 when Wright began to ask his fellow physicians what they were planning for the July 1995, 100th anniversary. From the responses, it became clear that nothing was being written. He informed the NMA board and officers that he would write such a book and have it completed by the anniversary. He sought assistance about the contents but received no response.

In July 1994, Wright attended the 99th annual NMA meeting in Orlando, Florida and announced that the story of the NMA would be completed as promised. It was a difficult task because Wright wanted to include material that required extensive research. The book arrived from the printers just a few days prior to the July 1995 meeting. Although Wright regrets he did not have a final editing, he, nevertheless, knows that the book is informative, unique, controversial, shocking, and educational.

In Atlanta, one of the first visitors to the booth where the books were being sold, was Dr. Leonidas H. Berry, a former NMA president and outstanding internist. He immediately informed Dr. Wright that the book was unauthorized, was not endorsed by the NMA and that Wright must so inform the purchasers. He announced that "they" would be writing the history.

During the entire conference, few, if any members or officers of the board visited the booth or encouraged sales. Although the president-elect had been enthusiastic, he too, faded in the crowd. Wright also sent word to the alumni associations of all of the Black medical colleges present that he would give them a portion of each sale, but that didn't generate any interest. Fortunately, many of the conference participants did purchase and later praise the book.

The 1996 annual meeting in Chicago proved to be a more pleasant experience. Dr. Henry Moses of Meharry Medical College invited Wright to share Meharry's booth. A significant number of sales were made.

Besides being a writer, Dr. Wright is a voracious reader. Regularly, he "devours" the local daily papers, the *Michigan Chronicle,* the *Michigan Citizen,* the *New York Times,* daily and Sunday editions. Let's not forget the *Crains* and also the *Monitor* that he picks up at the rear entrance of the Museum or at the market. He is a "clipper" and like hoards of newspaper cutters, he has collections of articles crammed into files and boxes in various and sundry places.

One story that fascinated Wright concerned freedom, a word that he cherishes. Freedom: the condition of being free, independence; frankness, outspokenness, exemption from a defeat or duty, etc. Consequently, when Dr. Wright became familiar with the "Pass to Freedom," he arranged to have a quantity of "passes" made for sale to the museum membership. The story that fascinated and interested him reads thusly:

In 1724, there were three times as many Negroes as whites in Carolina. This was so because to encourage the importation of slaves in Carolina, white settlers were offered several acres of land for male and female slaves brought into the colony. Severely restricted laws were passed and the enslaved were regularly whipped and punished.

It was amidst such conditions that a Negro girl, named Elisabeth Welb was born, about 1825, near Neuss River, North Carolina. In the small community of Neuss, northeast of Raleigh, Elisabeth grew to womanhood. Though little else is known about her, it has been determined that she was a free woman. Elisabeth was issued a "Pass to Freedom," a small rectangle of durable cotton cloth bearing her name and birthplace and boldly imprinted with the word, "Free."

Elisabeth apparently worked in the area as a domestic, one of the few kinds of employment available to a free Black woman at the time. As she worked, she carried her pass, prepared to produce the certificate if anyone should question her right to conduct her own affairs. At some time during the mid 1800s, Elisabeth chose to part with her pass, which she had cherished and preserved. She decided her Pass to Freedom was to be her legacy to her children and her children's children. Unable to give her son other heirlooms or even a recorded family history, she gave him her pass. It was to serve as a means of continuity, a reminder that although he had roots in slavery, he and his children were free.

As a young man and woman, Elisabeth and her husband's dreams were realized when their son, Virgil Richardson, made his way north. He carried little else with him but his mother's "Pass to Freedom." Leaving by night with a close friend, he boldly approached the captain of a northbound ship, asking for work. The two were hired on the spot and earned their passage to Boston. Virgil met and married well-educated Rachel Kellogg and soon became a successful merchant.

Rachel and Virgil's eldest daughter, Mary Eugenia Hamilton, a gifted musician who lived to celebrate her 93rd birthday and other future birthdays, handed down the pass to her own daughter, Mary Florence, who was also a musician, Mary Florence (Peek) handed down the pass to her eldest daughter, Eva Louise Peek, who is the present holder of Elisabeth Welb's pass. Now, Mrs. George M. Allen, Louise has carried on the spirit of her great-great grandmother, with an impressive record of public service and achievement in the Boston area.

As Elisabeth Welb had looked upon her "Pass to Freedom" as a legacy to her descendants, Louise Allen saw the pass as much more than cloth and ink. To her, it was and is a symbol of the rights of all men and women, a guide to all, as members of the human family, to a greater awareness of the need for freedom, justice, and equality. She permitted the original cloth and ink pass to be reproduced and shared with the American people in the 1970s. Dr. Wright's favorites are the silver medallions that can be worn as necklaces and those made into key chains. The necklaces are worn with dignity and pride by many unrelated descendants.

In addition to being a reader, a writer, and the constant initiator of new ideas, new programs, and new projects, there is more to our "biographee." But that other side still reveals, as one might expect, a man with a seriousness of purpose.

Wright has a great curiosity regarding technology, space, and even astronomy. As a car passenger at night, he frequently startles the driver when he excitingly exclaims: "Look, there are the seven sisters, and there is the big dipper..." He joined the computer age in the early 1980s and prefers the computer to the television, which he watches only occasionally. Wright has been cited for his skill in playing table tennis. Moses D. Nicholson remembers that in the early sixties, Wright was one of the top players at the old Grand Army of the Republic (GAR) Center on Grand River Avenue. Wright assisted at the center in helping to make a young teen a national champion. Another of Wright's talents relates to conceiving cartoons. He regularly describes funny and appropriate cartoons relating to current events and is annoyed that he can't draw. At one time Wright prepared a "portfolio" of ideas and tried to interest a young artist in transforming those thoughts into cartoons. The artist dismissed Wright quickly and summarily.

Wright also is an opera buff. Whenever he can catch radio or television broadcasts of operas such as *La Traviata, Turandot, Barber of Seville, The Magic Flute* and others, he listens intently. His enthusiasm regarding this type of drama that is frequently replete with tragic and fatal consequences, or when "Alfredo is smitten and undone at the sight of Violetta..." brings smiles to his otherwise unexpressive countenance. This engrossment began while a student in medical school. A few fellow opera

The Wright Man

buffs from nearby Fisk University joined him to listen to the Metropolitan Opera of the Week. He was enthralled with the music and looked forward to those Saturday afternoon sessions.

Wright's appearance has changed very little through the years and he is easily recognized by persons who have not seen him of late. His weight fluctuates only slightly; he tips the scale at around 150 or 155 pounds. This, even though he has a great passion for sweets, and eats deserts daily. He will eat his, and yours if it is left unguarded. One of Wright's favorite spots for "homemade cakes" and cobblers is the Lewis Latimer Cafe at the Museum.

The old saying, "what you see is what you get," well fits Dr. Wright. There is no pretense, no false façade, no arrogance. For sure, he is aware of his prominence; he is constantly praised by admirers, friends and strangers, but it does not inflate his ego.

Wright never hesitates to challenge his friends and associates to write their stories. He has little patience with people who have interesting lives and important missions that would enhance the history and the story of African Americans, but who won't write about them. When Wright received shares of Detroit Memorial Park Association stock and attended his first annual stockholders meeting, he immediately asked who was going to update their present history booklet. He reminded the board members that it must be done and that the Association's 70th anniversary was approaching. The book, *Detroit Memorial Park Association-The Evolution of an African American Corporation,* by Roberta Wright, resulted and was published in 1993.

Dr. Wright has a special and natural fondness for his daughters and son-in-law, William Griggs, as mentioned. He also loves and admires his stepdaughter, Dr. Barbara Hughes Smith; her husband, Joseph W. Smith and their children—his grandchildren. This love and admiration extends to his stepson, Wilbur B. Hughes, III; his wife, Adawork Hughes and their children—his grandchildren. And these feelings flow freely to his godsons, David Smedley, Brian Smedley and wife, Evita. David's pride and joy is his sculpture of the "Sankofa Bird," which has been adopted by Howard University for its Legacy of Leadership Award. Because a photo of the sculpture is herein included, it seemed important to tell the interesting story of the Sankofa symbol and bird sculpture in the Appendix. Wright enjoys his extended family immensely and spends considerable telephone time with them. But the love of his life is his granddaughter, Louisa. He boasts about her skills and ability with the computer and her good grades at school. In return, she gives much love to "Pompa," as she has always called him.

Dr. Wright's "want to do" list runs the gamut of ideas. Major among these is the desire to rewrite and expand his 1984 book, *The Peace Advocacy of Paul Robeson.* He also wants to see a major catalog of the Museum's Core Exhibit. Realizing this would not be his project, he knows his contributions to the catalog would be valuable. Also, Dr. Wright has great interest in the Conference Center at Penn Center since it's the nation's only African American National Historic District. He is pleased that at his request, the African American Museums Association chose to have its annual meeting at the center in the year 2000.

It is disturbing to him, however, that beautiful Penn Center, this marvelous historic site, has to continually "beg" for funds. He hopes that a world class building, a major auditorium and meeting facility will be a priority—built by and financed by some of the country's African American entrepreneurs. Wright is a member of Plymouth United Church of Christ and lists the senior minister, Nicholas Hood, III and his father, Nicholas Hood, II, pastor emeritus, as two of his favorite people. Dr. Wright could well sing the old spiritual:

There's a little wheel a-turnin' in my heart,
There's a little wheel a-turnin' in my heart,
In my heart, in my heart,
There's a little wheel a-turnin' in my heart.

Oh, I feel so very happy in my heart,
Yes, I feel so very happy in my heart,
In my heart, in my heart,
Oh, I feel so very happy in my heart.

Oh, I don't feel no way tired in my heart,
No, I don't feel no way tired in my heart,
In my heart, in my heart,
Oh, I don't feel no way tired in my heart.

*U of M engineering student, Deidre Proctor (remember 1987 photo) at 1997 Opening
with Dr. Wright and from left: Roberta Wright, Dr. Barbara Hughes Smith;
Deidre's parents, Fred and Kim Proctor*

Wright and daughter, Dr. Carla Wright

Dr. Mark Smith and Patricia Smith

The Wright Man

Adawork and Wilbur Hughes visiting Museum

The Hughes return with children (Wright's grandchildren), Alexandria Brooke Hughes and Christian Wright Hughes

Wright and daughter, Carla Wright, M.D., and Barbara Hughes Smith and Joseph W. Smith

Councilman Rev. Nick Hood, III, Wright, and Samuel Thomas

The Wright Man

Doris Chenault Hood, Rev. Nicholas Hood, II, Elmer Anderson, and Nathan Hood

Harold Varner, architect, and the Wrights

Wright and Ingida Asfaw, M.D.

Ruth Goens, sculpturer, and Nate Shapiro

The Wright Man

The Wrights and Betty Price

Wright and the Hon. Erma Henderson

Wright and Dr. Charles Adams, Hartford Church, sermon in honor of Robeson

Former Robeson Scholarship Awardees
Robert Shannon, at podium and from left:
Mrs. Martin, mother of Monique Martin Johnson, 1981; Wilbert McCormick, 1976;
George Ahmad Goff, 1987; Lori L. Hall, 1990; and Wright, seated

The Wright Man

From left: Larry C. Latimore, Northwestern High School principal; Mamie M. Humphrey, retired principal, Osborn High; Robert Shannon, retired educator; Linda Spight, principal Mumford High; Emeral Crosby, principal Pershing High and committee co-chair; Jacqueline A. Hughes, principal Northern High; Irma J. Hamilton, principal Renaissance High; Walter R. McLean, principal Redford High; Beverly A. Gray, principal Martin Luther King High; and the Wrights, seated

Shannon, Wright, Dr. Crosby and Robeson awardees

313

Christian W. Hughes and W.B. Hughes
Robeson painting in background by Leroy Foster is part of Committee's exhibit

Museum supporters, Dr. Marvin Greene and Erma Greene

The Wright Man

Horace and Yvonne Rodgers with Wright

Charles Wright and son-in-law, William Griggs, at birthday party

Guests at 80th birthday — "A Family Affair"

Dorothy Mottley congratulates Wright

The Wright Man

Joyce Essien, M.D., of Atlanta, Georgia

Wright and the birthday cake

N.S. Rangarajan, M.D. and Shanthi Rangarajan

Dr. Roslyn McClendon, Wright, Charles Shannon, Yolanda Shannon Bates, Stephanie Griggs, Carla Wright, M.D. and Robert Shannon, Jr.

The Wright Man

Winifred & Lewis Wright of Cleveland, Wright's cousins and Wright

Birthday party by "Virgos," Larry Smith and Judge Craig Strong. "Virgo" Wright honored.
From left: Lillian Key, Smith, and the Wrights.
Back row from left: a friend, George (The King) Cunningham, Jr., Hon. Leona Lloyd; Hon. Leonia Lloyd;
Hon. Craig Strong; Patricia Gardner; Leo "Grits" Rice; and Leon Gardner

Wright and Wilbur Hughes in Oakland, California greeting two guests

World famous artist and sculpturer of Mexico visiting the museum.
Francisco Mora and wife, Elizabeth Catlett and seated, Terrence Hicks.
From left: Robert Norwood; Robert Stamps; Rozenia Johnson; acting president, Ernest Duncan; Rita Organ; Wright; Coraleen Rawles;
Michele Parchment; Patricia Carrolle; Roberta Wright; Dale Mott; and Harry Harrison

The Wright Man

Josephine Harreld Love, director, Your Heritage House

Ernest Duncan, Wright, and Hubert W. Massey

Doris Chenault Hood; Ambassador Andrew Young; Dorothy I. Height,
chair & president emerita of NCNW; Roberta Wright, Feb. 11, 1999 in Museum boardroom.
Leroy Foster painting in background.

Dr. Barbara Smith (center), daughter of Dr. Charles H. Wright, accepted a special award in her father's honor,
presented by Judge Craig S. Strong (left) and jazz pianist James Tatum, JFTA president. Michigan Chronicle photo

The Wright Man

AAAM Executive Committee Meeting in Detroit, Jan. 30, 1999.
From left: Habeebah Muhammad, Anacostia Museum, AAAM secretary; Linda Stephens, American Jazz Museum, 18th & Vine, Kansas City, MO; William Billingsley, AAAM Operations manager, Wilberforce, OH; Carolyn Adams, Virginia Museum of Fine Art; Deborah Mack, Underground Railroad & Freedom Center; Peggy Mortez, director of Bronzeville Children's Museum; Rita Organ, Charles H. Wright Museum curator and AAAm president; Dr. Charles Wright, AAAM founder & Museum founder; Robert Haynes, Oakland, CA African American Museum & Library; and Bill Gwaltner, National Park Service, Fort Estes, CO

Dr. Wright and Shirley Northcross

Osceola McCardy of Hattiesburg, MS at the museum surrounded by Martin Luther King, Jr. High School visitors

Louise Wright Griggs of Chicago — Wright's granddaughter

The Wright Man

Dr. Wright's granddaughter, Christina Barbara Hughes of Richmond, VA

Wright's Godsons; Dr. Brian Smedley & Professor David A. Smedley, both of Washington, D.C.

Sankofa sculpted by David Smedley

Margaret Dudley and Kevin Davidson share podium

The Wright Man

Wright and Councilman Clyde Cleveland, longtime museum supporter

Dr. Wright; Bob Eaton, Daimler Chrysler; Earl Graves, Black Enterprise;
Frank Fountain, Daimler Chrysler; Roy Roberts, General Motors

327

Hon. Andrew Young; Helen Love; Dr. Wright; Bernice Grier, Mayor Young's sister;
Dr. Jefferson; Juanita Clark, Mayor Young's sister; Ernest Duncan

Wright's grandchildren, Blythe Lelia Allen and Brett William Allen

The Wright Man

Chapter 1

1. Interview with Lovie Page Pinkston, August 8, 1992
2. Interview with Charles Wright, 1989
3. Ibid.
4. Ibid.
5. Ibid.
6. Ibid.
7. Edwards, G. Franklin. *The Negro Professional Class,* Glencoe Press. 1959.
8. Rogers, Jr., Furman. "History of Houston County," Master Thesis, Alabama Polytechnic Institute, 1952, p. 198.

Chapter 2

1. Interview with Hugh Blanding, August 8, 1992
2. Interview with Felix James, October 1992
3. Rose, Arnold. *The Negro in America,* N.Y.: Harper & Brothers, 1944, p. 111
4. "Out of the Mud." *Time,* Vol. 37, January 20, 1941, p. 57

Chapter 3

1. Coser, Rose L. *Life in the Ward,* East Lansing: Michigan State University, 1962, p. 19
2. Burling, Temple, Lentz, Edith and Robert Wilson. *The Give and Take in Hospitals.* New York: G.R. Putnam & Sons, 1956, p. 79
3. Davie, Maurice. *Negroes in American Society.* New York: McGraw-Hill, 1949, p. 329
4. Interview with Charles Wright, 1990
5. Ibid.
6. "Negro Health," *Time,* Vol. 35, No. 15, April 8, 1940, p. 44

7. Ibid.
8. Interview with Charles Wright, 1992
9. Capeci, Dominic. *The Harlem Riot of 1943.* Philadelphia: Temple University, 1977, p. 106
10. Ibid.
11. Bontemps, Arna. "The Two Harlems," *The American Scholar,* Vol. 14, Spring 1945, p. 172

Chapter 4

1. Babson, Steve. *Working Detroit: The Making of a Union Town,* New York: Adama
2. Capeci, Dominic. *Race Relations in Wartime Detroit,* Philadelphia: Temple, 1984, p. 37
3. Widick, B.J. *Detroit: City of Race and Class Violence,* Quadrangle Books, 1972, pp. 123-124
4. Capeci - Op Cit., p. 37
5. Pringle, H.F. and K. Pringle, 1948, "The Color Line in Medicine," *Saturday Evening Post,* p. 15
6. Ibid., p. 72
7. Interview with Charles Wright, 1980
8. Interview with Carla Wright, September 5, 1992

Chapter 5

1. Reitzes, Dietrich. *Negroes and Medicine,* Cambridge, MA: Harvard University Press, 1958, p. 161
2. Ibid., pp. 156-157
3. Interview with Charles Wright, 1998
4. Reitzes, OP. Cit., p. 144
5. Correspondence with Charles Wright
6. Ibid.
7. Wright, Charles. "The Progress of Negro Medical Specialists in Detroit," Typescript, 1962, pp. 1-3
8. Report, Detroit Commission on Community Relations
9. Reitzes, Op. Cit.
10. Interview with Charles Wright
11. Ibid.
12. Wright, Charles. "The Progress of Negro Medical

Specialists in Detroit," Typescript, 1962

13. Ibid.
14. Reitzes, Op. Cit.
15. Lackey, Lawrence, "Detroit Medical Society in Civic & Community Activities. "Journal of N.M.A., November 1963, pp. 485-487
16. Conot, Robert. *American Odyssey,* New York: William Morrow, 1972
17. Ibid.
18. Letter to Congressman Dingell
19. Interview with Charles Wright
20. Dr. Lackey, Op. Cit.
21. Dr. Rangarajan, May 24, 1993
22. Ibid.
23. Speech, Dr. Joshua Williams

Chapter 6

1. Isaac, Harold. The New World of Negro Americans, New York: The John Day Company, 1963, p. 105.
2. Ibid.
3. Ibid.
4. A flyer, undated
5. A Policy Statement, Typescript
6. Ibid.
7. Frazier, E. Franklin, *Black Bourgeoisie,* January 1962
8. Junod, Veolanie I. ed. *The Handbook of Africa,* New York University Press, 1963
9. Ibid.
10. Interview with Charles Wright
11. Ki-Zerbo, Joseph. "African Personality and the New African Society" in William John Hanna, ed. *Independent Black Africa,* Chicago: Rand, McNally & Co., 1964, pp.53-54
12. Interview with Charles Wright, 1993
13. Low, Theodore. *The Museum as a Social Instrument,* New Metropolitan Museum of Art, 1942, p. 15

Chapter 7

1. Fager, Charles. *Selma,* 1965, p. 16
2. Interview with Charles Wright, September 16, 1993
3. Ibid.
4. Interview with Nadine Battle, 1993
5. Fager, Op. Cit.
6. Wright, Op. Cit.
7. Wright, Ibid.
8. Ibid.
9. Communication with Attorney Hobart Taylor
10. Wright, Ob. Cit.
11. Widick, B.J. *Detroit: City of Race and Class Violence,* Quadrangle Books, 1972
12. Interview with Anita Kitson, 1993

The Wright Man

BOOKS

Alabama: A Guide to Deep South (1941). Compiled by Writer Program of WPA. New York: Richard R. Smith

Angelou, Mayo (1997). "Alone" in *Oh Pray My Wings Are Gonna Fit Me Well*. New York: Random House

Artist Showcase (1988). Afro-American Museum Support Group

Babson, Steve. *Working Detroit: The Making of a Union Town*. New York, Adama

Bontemps, Arna (Spring, 1945). "The Two Harlems" *The American Scholar*. Vol. 14, pp. 167-172.

"Booker T. Washington, Moderate Negro View." (1967) in Leslie Fishel and Benjamin Quarles (eds.) *The Negro American, A Documentary History*. Glenview, Illinois: Scott, Foresman, p. 344

Boyd, Dr. Melba Joyce (1997). "This Museum Was Once a Dream" in *The Spirit in the Words*, published by Chrysler Corporation

Bukowczyk, John (1989). *Detroit Images*. Detroit: Wayne State University Press

Burling, Temple, Lentz, Edith and Robert Wilson (1956). *The Give and Take in Hospitals*. New York: G. P. Pumam & Son

Capeci Dominic (1977). *The Harlem Riot of 1943*. Philadelphia: Temple University

Capeci, Dominic (1984). *Race Relations in Wartime Detroit*. Philadelphia: Temple

Conot, R. (1974). *American Odyssey*. New York: William Morrow

Coser, Rose L (1962). *Life in the Ward*. East Lansing: Michigan State University

Davie, Maurice (1949). *Negroes in American Society*. New York: McGraw-Hill

Douglas Conner (1985). *A Black Physician's Story*. Jackson University Press

Dollard, John (1937). *Caste and Class in a Southern Town*. New Haven: Yale University Press

Doyle, Don (1985). *Nashville Since the 1920s*. Knoxville: The University of Tennessee Press

Drake, and H. Clayton (1945). *Black Metropolis*. New York: Harper and Row

Edwards, G. Franklin (1959). The Negro Professional Class. Glencoe: Free Press

Folk, John H. and Lynn D. Dierking (1992). *The Museum Experience*. Washington: Whalenbeck Books

Frazier, E. Franklin, (1957). *Black Bourgeoisie*. New York: Free Press

Frazier, E. Franklin (1946). *The Negro Family in the United States*. Chicago: University of Chicago Press

Furman Rogers Jr. (1952). "History of Houston County." Master Thesis: Alabama Polytechnic Institute

Gallagher, Buell (1938). *American Caste and the Negro*. Columbia University Press

Gamble, Venessa (1989). "The Negro Hospital Renaissance: The Black Hospital Movement, 1920-1945," in Diana E. Long and Janet Golden *The American General Hospital*. Ithaca: Cornell University Press

Hamilton, Charles (1992). *Adam Clayton Powell, Jr.* New York: Atheneum

Hayden, Robert C. and Jacqueline Harris (1976). *Nine Black Doctors*. Addison-Wesley

Hero, Alfred (1959). *Americans in World Affairs*. Boston. World Peace Foundation

House, Gloria (1989). "Mandala for Mandela," *Rain Rituals*. Detroit: Broadside Press

Junod, Violanie I. ed. (1963). *The Handbook of Africa*. New York University Press

Katzman, D. M (1973). *Before the Ghetto: Black Detroit in*

The Wright Man

Nineteenth Century. Urbana: University of Illinois Press)

Ki-Zerbo, Joseph (1964). "African Personality and the New African Society" in William John Hanna, ed. *Independent Black Africa*. Chicago: Rand McNally & Co.

Kovanis, Georgea and Tracey Dawkins (1987). "Donor 'Adopts' New Museum." *Detroit Free Press*

Landy, Bart (1978). *The New Black Middle Class*. Berkeley: University of California

"Life of Josiah Henson," narrated by himself, Boston, Arthur D. Phelps (1849) Re-published by Uncle Tom's Cabin Museum, Dresden, Ontario, Canada (1965)Lincoln, C. Eric *The Black Muslim in America*

Lomax, Louis (1952). *The Negro Revolt*. New York: Harper

Low, Theodore (1942). *The Museum As a Social Instrument*. New Metropolitan Museum of ArtMcKinney, C. Guita (1980). *Sweet Rain*. New York: Lupa Publication

Maynard, Aibre de L. (1978). *Surgeons to the Poor*. New York: Appleton-Century-Crofts

Morais, Herbert. *The History of the Negro in Medicine*. New York: Publisher Co.Morton, Dr. Verona (August 1984). "Black Through During Chautaugua Era." *The Galley*. Detroit: Museum of African American History

Murray, Florence (1942). *The Negro Handbook*. New York: Wendell Malliet and Co. Museum Anniversary Booklets: 1983, 1984, 1990

Myrdal, Gunner (1944). *An American Dilemma*. New York: Harper

Negro Hospitals: A Compilation of Available Statistics. (1931). Julius Rosenwald Fund

Packard, Vance (1959). *The Status Seeker*. New York: Harper

Peck, William H. (1991). *The Detroit Institute of Arts: A Brief History*. Detroit: Founders Society Detroit InstitutePoindexter, Hildrus (1973). *My World of Reality*. Detroit: Balamp Publishing

Peyton, Thomas R. (1950). *Quest for Dignity.* Los Angeles: William Lewis

Reitzes, Dietrich (1958) *Negroes and Medicine.* Cambridge, MA: Harvard University Press

Rich, W. (1991). "Detroit: From Motor City to Service." in H.V. Savitch and John C. Thomas. *Big City Politics in Transition.* Newbury Park: Sage Publications

Rich, W. (1989) *Coleman Young and Detroit Politics.* Wayne State University

Rose, Arnold (1944). *The Negro in American.* New York: Harper & Brothers

Summerville , James (1983). *Educating Black Doctors.* University of Alabama Press

Taylor, Larry (Fall, 1974). "A Study of National-International Linkages Among Black Detroit Leaders," in Hartman, David ed. "Immigrants and Migrants: The Detroit Ethnic Experience," *Journal of University Studies,* Vol 10, No. 2-4, 1-425.

"The Pass to Freedom." Phoenix, Arizona: Combined Public Relation Services (1975)

Warner, Lloyd W., Meeker, Marcia and Kenneth Eells (1971). *Social Class in America: A Manual of Procedure for the Measurement of Social Status.* Chicago: Science Research Associates (1949). cited in M. Truzzi, *Sociology: The Classic Statements.* New York: Random House

Walker, Helen (1949). The Negro in the Medical Profession. Charottleville: University of Virginia

Watson, Fred Sheton. *Hub of the Wiregrass: History of Houston County, Alabama, 1903-1977.* Anniston: Higginbothan, Inc.

Work, Monroe. *The Negro Yearbook, 1935-1938.* Negro Year Book Publishing Co. Tuskegee Institute, Alabama

Widick, B.J. (1972). *Detroit: City of Race and Class Violence.* Quadrangle Books

The Wright Man

Wright, Charles H. *Paul Robeson in Detroit*. (Prepared for the Museum of African American History)

Wright, Charles H. (1975). *Robeson: Labor's Forgotten Champion*. Detroit: Balamp

Wright, Charles H. (1984). *The Peace Advocacy of Paul Robeson*. Detroit: Harlo Press

Wright, Charles (1995). *National Medical Association Demands Equal Opportunity*. Detroit: Charro Press

Wright, Roberta Hughes and Wilbur B. Hughes, III (1997). *Lay Down Body: Living History in African American Cemeteries*. Detroit: Visible Ink Press

Periodical and Newspaper Articles

"Detroit NAACP Opposes New Segregated Hospitals" *JNMA*, 46 (1954), p.68

"Haynes Memorial Medical Hospital" *JNMA*, 42 (1950), 187

"Negro Health," *Time*, Vol. 35, No. 15 (April 8, 1940), pp. 41-44

"Negro Nurses and Physicians" *Modern Hospital*, LXIII, (October 1944), 41-42

"Negroes Plan Branch School" *Dothan Eagle*, Vol. 24, July 1926

"Out of the Mud" *Time*, Vol. 37 (January 20, 1941), pp. 56-57

"Private Hospitals: Odd Law Make Them Detroit's Biggest Negro Business." *Ebony*, October 1950, 37-41

Adam, Charles (March 31, 1990). "When Two Elephants Fight." *Michigan Chronicle*, p. 2

Allison Henderson and Lionel Swan (1969). "Negro Physicians in Michigan" *JNMA*, 61, 448-452

Askari, Emilia and Cook, Christopher (March 19, 1990). "Black History Museum's Founder Quits" *Detroit Free Press*, p. 1B

Boyd, Robert (January 29, 1960). "To Bar Bias" *Detroit*

Free Press, p. 1

Davidson, Arthur (September 1957). "A History of Harlem Hospital" *Journal of the National Medical Association*, Vol. 56, No. 5 pp. 374-380

Davidson, William (January 13, 1962). "Our Negro Aristocracy" *The Saturday Evening Post*, p. 10+

Dothan Eagle, (October 8, 1981). Vol 11, No. 13 p. 1

Fortune, F.W. (May 1939). "The Negro Physician" *JNMA*, Vol. XXXI

Josaitis, Mark (May 29, 1985). "Museum is tall on hope, short on money" *Detroit Free Press*, p. 1A

King, Jr. Martin Luther (1968). "The Role of the Behavioral Scientist in the Civil Rights Movement" *Journal of Social Issues*, Vol. XXXIV

Lackey, Lawrence (November 1963). "Detroit Medical Society in Civic and Community Activities," *Journal of National Medical Association*, pp. 485-487

Lochbiler, Peter (June 20, 1975). "Angry U. of D. Trustee Resigns in Dispute Over Dental School," *Detroit News*, p. 1b

Michigan Chronicle (August 8, 1959) p. 5

Miller, Kelley "The Historic Blackground of the Negro Physicians" *Journal of Negro History*, Vol. 1, (April 1916)

Pringle, H.F. and Pringle, K (1948). "The Color Line in Medicine" *Saturday Evening Post*, p. 15+

Richard, M.P. (1969). "Ideology of Negro Physicians: A Test of Mobility and Status Crystallization" *Social Problems*, Vol. 17 (Summer), pp. 20-29

Riggs, Flodean "African History Museum Members Dissatisfied" *Michigan Citizen*, (November 10, 1989), p.10

Spilerman, Seymour (1970). "The Causes of Racial Disturbances: A Comparison of Alternative Explanations." *American Sociological Review*, 34,

The Wright Man

627-645

The Voice of the Negro, (December 18, 1914) Vol. 3, No. 14

The Voice of the Negro, (February 5, 1915) Vol. 3, No. 20

Thompson, W. Arthur and Robert Greenidge (1963). "Negro in Medicine in Detroit." *JNMA,* 55, 475-484.

Walker, Monroe (December 3, 1980). "Old Hospital For Blacks to Be Restored." *Detroit News,* p. 1B

Watson, Susan (March 20, 1990). "Why Wright Cut Cord on His Museum," *Detroit Free Press,* p. 18

William, M.D., Joshua (May 21, 1977). "Speech on Clinic Day," pp. 1-13

Wilson, Danton (July 15, 1989). "Mayor Young Speaks Out on Museum of African American History," *Michigan Chronicle,* p. 1, 4A

Wright, Charles (1978). "Travesty on the Oath of Hippocrates," *Journal of the National Medical Association,* Vol. 70, No. 4, p. 233

Wright, Charles (June 16, 1988). "Nelson Mandela, Freedom-Fighter, Turns 70." *Michigan Chronicle,* 1A, 4A

Wright, Charles and Carla Wright (August 15, 1984). "Obstetric Care in a Health Maintenance Organization and A Private Fee-For Service Practice: A Comparative Analysis," *American Journal of Obstetrics and Gynecology,* Vol. 149, No. 8, 848-856

340
The Wright Man

Index

A

B

C

The Wright Man

The Wright Man

APPENDIX

Museum Volunteers and Staff
Museum Trustees
News Articles & Statements
AMEF Students
Artists
AAAM Members
The Play, "Were You There?"
Robeson Scholars
Wright's Vita

347

MUSEUM VOLUNTEERS & STAFF

Dr. Wright is extremely appreciative of all of the men and women who assisted with his many projects, especially the African Medical Education Fund, the African American Museums Association, the Robeson programs, and the Michigan Support Group for Penn Center, St. Helena Island. However, because the Museum of African American History depended so heavily, for so many years, on a vast number of volunteers during 1965 and into the 1990s, we are including the names of some. These are persons who served as museum office assistants, chairs and members of anniversary committees and other programs, auxiliary and support group members and others who helped in various and sundry ways.

The volunteers often work side-by-side with museum staff persons—administrative, support and maintenance—who are the lifeline of the museum at all stages of its existence. Staff invests a great deal of time in designing exhibitions and programs that will communicate ideas to the public. The work of the support services and the need for maintenance of the exhibits and of the entity in general is immeasurable. However, with all of these functions working well, the result is a powerful museum with experience that results in multiple kinds of learning for all.

As written previously, it is not possible to name all of the staff persons who served the Museum, beginning as IAM (International Afro-American Museum) to the Museum of African American History. However, they are to be commended for their contributions to the success of the Museum

Volunteers not only serve as support for museum staff, but they frequently, necessarily, have more contact with visitors than anyone on the staff. Consequently, this is an awesome responsibility and one that cannot be taken lightly. Good personal interaction increases the likelihood that a museum experience will be memorable. Studies show it is not uncommon for children to remember qualities of volunteers, years after the experiences.

Volunteers at the museum have exhibited a true love, concern and dedication to perform their duties displaying knowledge and intelligence.

Many, probably most, of the volunteers are busy persons with jobs or other interests in addition to the time spent at the museum.

Some of the volunteers listed herein were a part of membership groups, with specific activities to plan and carry out. Others worked as individuals with schedules designating days and hours of work. When Dr. Wright's sister, Willie Pearl Battle, was director of volunteers, she developed a well-run system of operation and held the respect of the large group. At her death, Ruth Stephens led the volunteers and worked diligently with the men and women until the time of the move to the third museum site on Warren Avenue.

Conducting tours was just one of the many contributions the volunteers, from 1965 to 1996, performed. They also provided according to their skills, experience and interests, clerical support to staff, including assistance with special events.

Some of the volunteers highlighted in the museum newsletters: Barbara Stewart, Brunetta Vinson, Mildred Pitts, Mariel Wardell, Barbara Williford, Cordella MacRae, and the trio, Doris Blevins, Louise C. Smith and Roberta Bass. The trio has been especially involved with African World Festivals and field trips to other cities, and they have been with the museum for many years.

Other long time volunteers highlighted: Kathy Bradfield, Geraldine Bryant, Lennie Morrison, Lovie Pinkston, Eugenia Rucker, Pauline Sims, Bedia Thomas, and Marilyn Wall.

After the move to the Warren Avenue building in April 1997, the volunteer office structure was changed to better accommodate the needs of the larger facility.

An article written in anticipation of the move to the larger facility reads thusly:

> Volunteering is a give and take process. Volunteers give their time and talents and in exchange they take back with them experiences, knowledge, friendships and in lots of cases FUN! The Museum of African American History offers this to its volunteers along with an opportunity to learn and enjoy the African American history and culture. With the expansion of the new MAAH, we need more volunteers to serve in the listed capacities.
>
> If you would like to receive experience and knowledge working in a museum or would simply like to establish new friendships and have some fun in the process while learning more about African American history and culture, please join us as a volunteer.
>
> Volunteer Positions
> • Information Center Representatives
> Greet visitors and answer questions
> • Museum Teachers
> Conduct and lead tours
> • Membership Recruiters
> Solicit members by phone and letter writing
> • Administrative Support
> Assist with typing, filing and answering phones
> • Research Assistants
> Research genealogy and assist with writing
> • Museum Store Assistants
> Arrange merchandise and help customers
> • Collections Assistants
> Help re-pack, re-hang and clean collections items
> • Education Representatives
> Speak to school groups and develop educational materials

The terms, "teachers," "educators," and "support" persons have replaced "volunteers" and "docents." The director of these support persons is now a member of staff.

Some of the museum volunteers including persons who served on various committees and who were active during the years 1965 to 1996 are listed herein, followed by a listing of more recent volunteers.

Rev. Charles Adams
Oliver Agee
Alice Agee
Kathleen Akins
Rev. Daniel Aldridge
Mary Alexander
Hon. Alex Allen
Charles Allen
Doris Allen
Marcus Allen
Vincent Allison
Essie Andrew
Rev. Wendell Anthony
Nancy Arnold
Margaret Ashworth
Leon Atkins
Johnnie Mae Atkinson
Dr. Alvin Aubert
Joy Austin
Bridget Baker
Emma Baker
Carl Baldruf
Julia Baldwin
Barbara Banks
Don H. Barden
Deborah Barney
Jude Kay Barr
Benita Barton
Roberta Bass
Alonzo Bates
Pearl Wright Battle
Emmett Baylor, Jr.
Lillian Beard
Mary Bell
Julius Bender
Felicia Bennett
Douglas Bethune
Elizabeth Bethune
Juanita Bilinski

Francois Billingsley
Dave Bing
Gloria Black
Alberta Blackburn
Catherine Blackwell
Hon. James Blanchard
Dorothy Bledsoe
Geraldine Bledsoe
Doris Blevins
Matthew Blount
Betty Borman
Betty Boyd
Cleophus Boyd
Kathy Bradfield
Johnetta Brazell
Dr. Nellie Brodis
Jim Bridge
Dr. Nellie Brodis
Bobbie Brooks
Bishop P.A. Brooks
Angelo Brown
Cordelia (Betty) Brown
Johnnie Brown
Linda Brown
Lillian Brown
Marie Brown
Sharon Brown
York Brown
Karen Brown
Roberta Brown
Shirley Brown
Jasper Bruce
Kathy Bryant
Geraldine Bryant
Beatrice Buck
Juanita Burks
Mrs. Burrington
Elizabeth Burris
Dr. Margaret Burroughs

Pharfeania Butler
Duryea Calloway
Rev. Earl Calloway
Mildred Cameron
Great Hour of Caring
Betty Carter
Jeanette Carter
Mark Carter
Rev. James Carver
Willie Cash
Dr. Yvonne Catchings
George Cathcart
Mr. and Mrs. Perry Chaney
Erma Chennevert
Adolpus Christian
Annette Clardy
William Clark
Gwendolyn Clark
Yvonne Clements
Sandra Clemons
Bonita Burton Cobb
Edward M. Cody
Keiler L. Coleman
Hon. Barbara Rose Collins
Edna Colungo
Gladys Cook
Kimberly Cook
Ruth N. Cook
Hon. Wendy Cooley
Elbert Cooper
Robert Cooper
Gwendolyn Copeland
John W. Copeland
Paula Cozart
Jim Crewell
Lynne Crittendon
Hon. George Crockett
Wardell Croft
Lindsay Crooks

Museum Volunteers & Committee Members-1965-1996

Deirdre Cross
David R. Curry
Olivia Curry
Dr. Austin Curtis
Frances Curtis
George Cushingberry
Ada Cyrus
Malcolm Dade
Gerald Daniel
Tyrone Davenport
Boddie Davis
Joyce Davis
Nerissa Davis
Jerry Davis
Charles Davis
Erma Davis
Irene Davis
Sandra Davis
Morlean Day
Merlinda Day
Congr. Ron Dellums
Donald Dennard
Betty DeRamus
Norman Dillard
Ernest Dillard
Margo Diomands
Sister Marie Dolores
Lawrence Doss
Robert Douglas
Walter Douglas
Leonard Douglas
Helen Drake
Barry Dressel
Ida Drewery
Cullen Dubose
Margaret Dudley
Rev. Robert Dulin
Kay Dumas
Dr. Dewitt Dykes
Sherman Eaton
Esther Gordy Edwards
Dennis Evans
Barbara Favors
Helen Felton
Charles Fennicks
Deborah Feranadze
Carol Flemings
Gwendolyn Flowers
Hazel Forest

Rachael Fowler
Willa Fry
Kathy Frye
Virginia Fuller
Rosetta Gadson
Dorothy Galloway
Francis Gamble
William J. Gammage
Marie Gardner
Roland Gardner
Diana Gassoway
Sabre Gathers
Patricia Noni Gee
Verda Gentry
Michelle Gibbs
Clyde Giles
Larry Givens
Elsie Gordon
Edward Gordon
Gloria Graves
Joy Graves
Carrie Gray
John Green
Williedean Green
Rev. Havious Green
Carrie Grey
Joann Griffin
Vivian Griffin
William Griggs
Stephanie Griggs
Gwendolyn Gurley
Emmett Hagood
Clarence Hall
Elliott Hall
Emma Hall
Judy Hall
Austerine Hambrick
Micheal Hamlin
Linda Handy
Ann Haney
J. Edward Hannah
Mrs. Harbin
Barbara Harding
John Hardy
Phyllis Hargrove
Ken Harris
Cynthia Harris
Betty Hart
Anna Marie Hayes

Sarah Haygood
Aaron Hedgepath
Grace Henderson
Hon. Erma Henderson
Henderson Hendrix
Shannon Henry
Jayne Henry
Joseph Henshaw
Ronald Hewitt
Wayne Hicks
Aaron Hicks
Gregory Hicks
Ernestine Hicks
Dorothy Holloway
Dr. Elizabeth Hood
Hon. Nick Hood II
Charles Howell
Imani Humphrey
Ted Hunt, Jr.
Bill Hunter
Teola Hunter
Robert Hurst
Billie Hurtle
Jim Ingram
Jean Ingram
Wanda Jackson
Nancy Jackson
Joseph James
John James
Leno Jaxon
Dr. Arthur Jefferson
Hiawatha Jemison
Norita Jennings
Ann Johnson
Arthur Johnson
Dr. Charmaine Johnson
Cassandra Johnson
Frances Johnson
Kathryn Johnson
Lotus Johnson
Luvenia Johnson
Nan Johnson
Phyllis D. Johnson
Sharon Lewis Johnson
Loretta Jones
Lovell Jones
Rev. Matthew Jones
Naomi Jones

Museum Volunteers & Committee Members-1965-1996

Clemmie Jones
Rev. Joseph Jordon
Njei Kai
Micheal Kan
Mona Lisa Kelly
Hon. Damon Keith
Dr. Jessie Kennedy
Henry King
Che Korega
Golda Krolik
Ruby Larkin
Margaret Larrie
Reginald Larrie
Wil Lassiter
Gaytra Lathon
Kenneth Laws
Barbara Lee
Hazel B. Lee
Angelo Leonard
Thelma Leonard
Thelma Leslie
Rev. James Lewis
Betty Lewis
Walton Lewis
Denise Lewis
Howard Lindsay
Johnnie Mae Little
Hon. Leona L. Lloyd
Hon. Leonia J. Lloyd
Dr. Herbert Locke
Ernest Lofton
James Logan
Thelma Logan
Hon. William Lucas
Thelma Luster
Ron Lyons
Cordelia MacRae
Naomi Long Madget
Hon. Maryann Mahaffey
Loris Jean Manus
Andrew Manier
Loris Jean Manus
Barbara Mapson
Beverly March
Marvel Mardell
Bella Marshall
George Martin
Fred Martin

Maxine Martin
Melody Martin
Treese Martin
Walter Mason
Greg Mathis
William Matney
Ceola Maxwell
Barbara Turner Mays
Robbie McCoy
Aubrey McCutcheon
Jacque McDaniels
Arielle McEvans
William McGill
Rosse McKay
Hattie M. McKinney
Carol McMurtry
Dr. Marjorie Peebles Meyers
Valeria Micheals
Rosella Miller
Cecil Miller
Agnes Miller
Willia Miller
Franklin Mills
Shirley Milton
Cynthia Mitchell
Lilyann Mitchell
Shirley Monger
Mrs. Monk
Ken Moon
Dr. Dorothy Moore
Hon. Marion Moore
Eunice Moore
Vera Morgan
Tinnie Mormon
Lennie Morrison
Jean Morton
Bernice Morton
Dr. Verona Morton
Laura Moseley
Dorothy Mottley
Shahida Muasi
Ayesha Muhammed
Khadijah Muhammed
Georgella Muirhead
A-Alkebu Mutope
Naomi Nelson
Vivian Nevins
Wallace Newton

Margaret Noble
Marilyn Nunn
Joe O'Connor
Warris Omar
Cleophia Orr
Ethel Owens
Doris Parker
Mary Lou Parks
Damon Parson
William Patrick
Deon Patterson
Cora Pearson
Rev. J.J. Perry
Marie Peterson
Elaine Phillinganes
Lovie Pinkston
Mildred Pitts
Bethesda Points
Williams Poplack
Dr. John W. Porter
Latrielle Powers
Viola Preston
Bryant Price
Ernestine Ramsey
Julie Ramsey
James Ramsey
Sadie Ramsey
Pennie Ranier
Classie Rawles
Allen Rawls
Brenda Rayford
Rosemary Reed
Charles Reeves
Phillip Rhodes
Elaine Richardson
Roe Richardson
Leroy Richie
Ernestine Ricks
June Ridley
Anna Riggins
Maurice Roberts
Les Roberts
Dr. Phyllis Robinson
Vertie Rogers
Virgil Rollins
Dr. Mary Ross
Vivian Ross
Yvonne Roundtree

Museum Volunteers & Committee Members-1965-1996

Juanita Rucker
Eugenia Rucker
Gloria Rucker
Johnathon Rucker
Yvonne Rush
Regina Sanders
Hon. Nellis Saunders
Hon. Nelson Saunders
Helen Shannon
Robert Shannon
Nate Shapiro
Khadejah Shelby
David Shelton
Pauline Sims
Dr. Mildred Singleton
Richard Singleton
Dr. Earnest Singleton
Mattie Smedley
Yvonne Smith
Beverly Smith
Coretta Smith
Dorita Smith
Dorothy Smith
Audley Smith
Dorothy H. Smith
James Smith
Dr. Mark Smith
Louise C. Smith
Ruth Smith
Myzell Sowell
Walter Spears
Owsley Spiller
Henry Stallings
Marie Starks
Ruth Steele
Robert Stephens
Ruth Stephens
Barbara Stewart
Marilyn Stewart
Kris Stodgell
Horace Stone
Clarence Stone
Craig Stone
Lolie Stoudamire
Mardell Stricklen
Joan Strong
Brenda Strong
Manila Strong

Hon. Craig S. Strong
Clarence Studevant
Josephine Sullivan
Dwight Sullivan
Robert Synder
Herbert Tabor
Dennis Talbert
Alice Tarter
Karla Tatum
Deborah Taylor
Mary Taylor
Elaine Terrell
Samuel Thomas
Hon. Edward Thomas
Vincent Thomas
Bedia Thomas
Elnora Thomas
Rosalind Thomas
Ann Thompson
Leo Dell Thompson
McKinley Thompson
Marian Thurman
Joyce Tibbs
Oretta Todd
N. Tounsel
N. Townsley
Doretha Traylor
Eric Tucker
Arthurine Turner
Marie Turner
Barbara Twyman
Jane Ulmer
Hilda Vest
Donald Vest
Martha Vincent
Charles Vincent, M.D.
Brunetta Vinson
Sha'lsta Wahid
Georgia Wahid
Hon. Myron Wahls
Louvert Waldon
Stanley Waldon
Geneth Ray Walker
Marion Walker
Charles Walker
Deborah Walker
Debra Walker
Marilyn Wall

Ted Wallace
Juvena Walls
Al Ward
Bea Ward
Margaret Ward
Mariel Wardell
Paula Wardell
Lorraine Warren
Dorothy Washington
Floyd Washington
Jacqueline Washington
Kenneth Washington
Loretta Washington
Homer Waterman
Ida Watson
Nellie Watts
Deirdre Weir
Patricia West
Delores Wharton
Rosa Lee Wheeler
Laurette Whisett
Jerry White
John White
Augustus White
John Williams
Adrienne Williams
Ramona Williams
Doris Williamson
Barbara Williford
Wanda Willis
Danton Wilson
Porterfield Wilson
Reginald Wilson
Barbara Wilson
Robert Wolf
Helen Wright
Paul Wright
Denise Wright
Patricia Yancy
Hon. Coleman A. Young
Margaret Zarif

Some of the persons listed who served as volunteers or worked on anniversary or support committees continued their affiliation with the museum as it made the transition into the third site, a much larger facility. However, there were many new faces, some of whom are listed here:

Deirdre Adgers
Gloria Alexander
Herbert Alexander
Linda Allen
Lillie Allison
Abdul M. Aquil
Deirdre Arnold
Sharon Bartell
Percy Baxter
Vanessa Blanding
Shawn Blanks
Yvonne Bond
Janice Boston
Teresa Crocker Brown
Patricia Brown
Wanakee Brown-Berlin
Ora Brown Davis
Fontella Buddin
Juanita Williams Bush
Margaret Butler
Toni Cade
Julie Calloway
Audrea Calloway
Maggie Clayborn
Jacqueline Curtis
John F. Davis
Paralee Day
Stanley de Jongh
Lawrence Dilworth
Mary Doyle Lasseigne
Dawna Dunlap
Jacqueline Garrett
Barbara Garrett
Elaine Gilbert
Vernetta Glass
Brenda Godfrey
Rogenia Goza
Kimberly Green
Petiste Graves
Helen Groves
Charity Hall
Cathy Hardaway
Dorothy Hardeman

Deborah Hardin
Regina Hardy
Athenia Harris
Johnnie Hatch
Leola Hatton
Senora Hawk
Anne Henry
Mary Belle Hicks
Barbara Mockenhull
Emma Holmes
Shirley Horne
Marvin Hughes
Zelma Hughes
Mosezella Idleburg
Sharon Jackson
Audrey James
Linda Jenkins
Brenda Jeter
Annie Mae Johnson
Ruth Ann Johnson
Alexander Johnson
Almeta Johnsson
Gloria Jones
Mary F. Jones
Denise Kennedy
Eric Leonard
Darlene Leonard
Diane Lewis
Marcee Lloyd
DeLores Lundy
Michael Lundy, Jr.
Jamiel Martin
Jeffrey Martin
Nzingha Masani
Marjorie Mason
Tresscella McGuire
Chiquita McKenzie
Lauren McKnight
Betty McMillion
Frantz Michel
Rosetta Miller
Idrander Moore
Howard Moore

Terrie Mosley-Lang
Obioma Onwuzulike
Willie Parker
Juanita Parnell
Chey Payne
Anne Peoples
Crystal Pickett
Eddie Pierce
Rose Mary Pierce
Mellanese Posey
Monica Posey
Alva Randall
Joanne Robertson
Wendell Shackleford
Freddie Shannon
Rosalind Simmons
Torrey Smith
William Snellings
Miriam Solomon
Lula Stallworth
M. Louise Stanton
Diane Stephens
Gail Stith
Josephine Sullivan
LaDonne Thomas
Shirley Thompson
Veronica Thompson
Deborah Tripp
Joyce Tucker
Edith Turner
Barbara Twyman
Vincent Tye
Marion Walker
Bernadette Walker
Ramona Ward
Cynthia Watters
Edna Weaver
Mary E. Wells
Elaine Williams
Rasheda Williams
Patricia Wilson
Toccarra Woods
Winifred Young

If we have neglected to include you on this list, we apologize and wish to let you know that we appreciate any volunteer service you may have given the museum.

CURRENT MUSEUM STAFF

Shelia Bail
Jackie Breeden
Patricia Carrolle
Cathy Carter
Patrina Chatman
Crystal Coleman
Kevin Davidson
Bemidele Demerson
Ernest Duncan
David Egner
Audrey Gaylor-Wright
Carla Glamb
Dean Hamm
Toya Hankins
Harry Harrison
Desirnai Hicks
Terrence Hicks
Felecia Hunt-Taylor

Lisa Johnson
Rozenia Johnson
Beverly Jones
Ellen Jones
Dawn Langford
Almee Lloyd
DeLores Lundy
Meghan Magee
Charles Martin
Donyale Martin
Darren Matthews
Michelle Merritt
Ledia Mims
Stacey Minyard
Dale Mott
Robert Norwood
Charles Organ

Rita Organ
Michele Parchment
Will Phillips
Randy Pullin
Coraleen Rawls
Tyjuana Ruff
Lola Rushin
Michelle Segue
Equilla Slaughter
Dorita Smith
Sean Talbot
Anthony Tyler
Margaret Ward
Dwane Watkins
Dawn Williams
Hillary Williams
Thaddeus Williams
Bernard Wilson

Appendix II

MUSEUM TRUSTEES

The Museum has had only three chairpersons in its long history. Dr. Wright served as chair from 1965 to his resignation in 1990. At that time, Eugene Gilmer took the reins and led the board until 1995 when Dr. Arthur Jefferson became chair. Listed are most of the members of the Board of Trustees from 1965 to the present time. The current Board, however, is also listed separately.

Appendix III

NEWSPAPER ARTICLES AND SELECTED STATEMENTS

A sampling assortment of arresting and provocative articles is included. Most were written by others, but the first article is one of the numerous articles that Dr. Wright wrote, resulting in his being fired.

The news editors at Alabama State College in Montgomery, at Meharry Medical School in Nashville, Tennessee, and at Harlem Hospital in New York City, all thought Wright's articles too inflammatory. Each time, he was asked to "cease and desist." The time period of Wright's newspaper career extends from 1937 to the 1950s.

Following is the "Bama Brief" article. Decide for yourself.

```
AN EDITORIAL
Bama Briefs
(Fall of 1937)
```

I just don't know what this Old World is coming to, nobody is concerned with the other fellow. This is not just true in everyday life, but it is the same in the world in general.

Emperor Haile Selassie went to the League of Nations, in Geneva Switzerland, to obtain help against Benito Mussolini who invaded his country five years ago. The League of Nations listened, but did nothing to help him. Now, a little man with a black mustache is making it hard for the jews in Germany. The jews are crying to the world for help, but nobody is willing to try to stop Adolph Hitler. Each year his treatment of the jews is worse than the year before, yet nobody seems to care.

The Negro has been oppressed by the white man, here at home, for hundreds of years. Many Negroes have told of this treatment but again, nobody seems to mind. Unless one group becomes concerned about what happens to another group the outlook for this "Old World" is not so good.

(Excerpts from an editorial written for the Student Newspaper at Alabama State College, Montgomery, Alabama, 1937).

— CHARLES H. WRIGHT

Although there were many outstanding newspaper and magazine articles, the one by Betty DeRamus of the *Detroit News*, April 1998, goes right to the grain, probably because of their mutual close friendship.

Renaming museum is a fitting tribute to Dr. Wright
BETTY DeRAMUS

When Dr. Charles H. Wright first set up Detroit's original Afro-American museum, he sometimes shared his bold, broad-shouldered dreams with me. I had no choice but to lie still and listen. He was my gynecologist.

Stretched out on a table waiting for the touch of cold instruments, I would obediently accept materials and information about the museum. Dr. Wright was my physician, which put him right up there with mama, daddy and macaroni and cheese. Besides, I couldn't very well dash out wrapped in a short sheet.

Make no mistake about this. Dr. Charles H. Wright always has been an obsessed man. A single-minded man. A man so driven by his vision that no stop signs, detours or roadblocks could slow him down.

Yet I'm pretty sure that even he never dreamed that the International Afro-American Museum he set up in 1965 on West Grand Boulevard would become the largest facility of its kind in the world.

All he wanted to do was create something that would bring together people of all races and ethnic backgrounds, show them what they had in common and build big strong blocks of black pride.

All he wanted to do was heal minds and hearts as well as he healed bodies.

This is why he supported the museum with his own money and community contributions until receiving the city of Detroit'' help to erect a new building in 1987 on John R and Frederick Douglass.

"A history museum brings us to our common denominator," he once told The Detroit News. "We are all children of God."

However, when long time Detroiters think about Dr. Wright, they often remember the mobile unit stuffed with historical materials that he used to send to Detroit public schools and ethnic festivals.

Thanks to the black inventors' exhibit I learned that Edmond Berger had created a spark plug in 1830, T.J. Marshall a fire extinguisher in 1872, Willie Johnson an egg beater in 1884, Garrett Morgan a gas mask in 1914, Joseph Hunger Dickinson a record player arm in 1918 and Garrett Morgan a traffic light in 1923.

I learned that Jan Ernest Matzelinger had revolutionized the shoe industry by inventing a machine for attaching soles on shoes in Lynn, Mass.

Since those days, my search for proof of black achievements has taken me from Nigeria to Havana, from Ethiopia to Rio de Janeiro. But nothing has ever recaptured the surge of pride I felt the first time I saw Dr. Wright's small, straight-from-the-shoulder inventors' display.

On Monday, it was announced that the $38.4-million Museum of African American History had been renamed the Dr. Charles H. Wright Museum of African American History.

Oh, happy day.

In 1990, Dr. Wright resigned from the museum, displeased, he said, because the late Mayor Coleman Young's administration was exerting too much control.

It was a bitter-sweet ending to a story of ceaseless struggle and unsurpassed achievement. I'm glad Detroit has decided to rewrite the script.

Wright, now 79, says he was "very pleased" by the decision to put his name on the museum.

So are the rest of us, doctor, including those 7,000 babies you delivered and all those patients whose bodies, minds and spirits you treated at the same time.

Detroit Free Press
3/9/63

His Judas Counts 'Dollars'

Like St. Augustine of old, Dr. Charles H. Wright of 59 Westminster, gives a lot of thought to theology when he hears the crying of babies.

The Fifth Century Augustine, inclined to be pessimistic at times, thought he detected an argument for original sin in the wailing of a baby.

Dr. Wright, who delivers babies in Detroit, finds his thoughts turned to just what the baby will be like when he grows up. Will he be a St. Peter, a Judas, or a Pilate?

•••

IN FACT, if you ever wonder what a doctor, who happens to be a little early on the scene, spends his time, Dr. Wright has the answer. He tries to figure out — on paper — just what the people Jesus knew would say or do if they were born today.

He's written a compact, easy to dramatize little homily, mixed with humor and some profound ideas about getting along in life, based on the crucifixion and people Jesus knew.

He's mixed it with modern interpretative dances and spirituals and called it "Were You There?", a name of haunting Negro spiritual that pops up now and then in the drama.

It'll be "premiered" 8:30 p.m. Friday, March 22, at the Detroit Art Institute and the proceeds will go to the non-profit African Medical Education Fund, Inc., which is dedicated to training better doctors for Africa.

•••

"I WORKED on it in hospitals while waiting for patients to deliver," says Dr. Wright, president of AMEF and a member of St. Andrew's Presbyterian Church.

He tries to get across the meaning of Lent and the Cross—people should be concerned with others and live day by day for God, and not the "almighty dollar."

"Most people who go to Passion plays come away amused and entertained and miss the significance of it," he said. "A Passion play is usually given in stilted language and costumes and they think they've seen something like the battle of 1812."

Judas, a dancer, in Dr. Wright's play counts dollar bills, not shekels.

And St. Peter, roused up a bit, says in a language that at least the good doctor is used to—"We don't have birth certificates, but you do have my word for it!"

Detroit Free Press
1/6/66

Funds and Lore Sought
Detroit Group Pushes Negro History Museum

Retrieving the past for a people stripped of their history can be an exercise in heartbreak.

But a Detroit gynecologist, Dr. Charles H. Wright, is convinced the job can be done. He heads a group of Detroiters which intends to open a museum of Negro history financed by private contributions.

"For generations the Negro has been told he has no history," said Dr. Wright. "So as soon as a Negro dies all his possessions are often thrown out with the rubbish.

Dr. Charles Wright

•••

"THIS IS the kind of attitude we have to change. We think there are valuable documents stored in trunks and basements all over the area.

"And since people have learned of our project they have come to us with them — some dating from the Civil War." he said.

The theme of the museum will be the Negro's struggle for equality. Exhibits would date back to before the Civil War and forwards through this civil rights conflict in the modern South.

Since the International Afro-American Museum Committee was formed in Detroit last fall, co-sponsoring organizations have sprung up in New York and San Francisco, said Dr. Wright.

"It's going to take an astronomical sum of money to put this thing across," he said. "But I feel it is a must if the American Negro is to view himself in the perspective of history.

"And we also feel that he (the Negro) must

finance the project himself. If he is going to identify with the museum he must be part of its creation and not have it handed to him on a silver platter by the Federal Government."

...

THE COMMITTEE'S fundraising goal for 1966 is a modest $25,000 enough to hire a full time executive director and a small staff.

Permanent headquarters will be opened by the end of January at 1549 W. Grand Blvd.

A native of Dothan, Ala., Dr. Wright has lived in Detroit for 12 years. He was recently named Man of the Year by the local chapter of Omega Psi Phi Fraternity.

Dr. Wright is president of the African Medical Education Fund and was voted Doctor of the Year by the Detroit Medical Society in 1963.

The doctor also dabbles in dramatics and one of his plays, "Were You There?" will be presented March 31 and April 1 at the Detroit Institute of Arts Auditorium to raise funds for the museum.

Detroit Free Press
2/10/71

DETROIT DOCTOR'S CRUSADE

Museum Tells the Black Experience

BY FRANK ANGELO
Free Press Managing Editor

An editor meets such interesting people. For example:

Dr. Charles H. Wright, a medical man who delivers thoughts on what's good for a city like Detroit as easily and expertly as he delivers babies.

In fact, when the slim Meharry College graduate sat for the kind of probing interview which he likes to reserve for patients, he had just completed a stint that started with a 3 a.m. appearance in the delivery room of Hutzel Hospital.

ACROSS the editor's desk, however, the talk centered on his enthusiasm for the International Afro-American Museum, an organization for which he feels deeply as the many mothers he knows feel for their new-born.

Dr. Wright is black. And he is proud and articulate and, like so many black people these days, a bit angry that he has continually to explain himself and verbally battle for the kind of recognition he justly feels should come naturally.

DR. Charles H. Wright: "We want to present the facts of events and stop the repitition of misinformation."

It was apparent when he walked into the office that he was suffering from a slight fever of belligerency. His first few words left no doubt.

"It's hard to understand," he started, "why when white men talk of building museums in this city, they get attention. But the fact that we have a museum that's a going concern, that is doing an outstanding job of serving the community, gets not a line in the paper."

No doubt about it. The editor was being told in polite terms that his racial bias was showing.

But just a moment, Dr. Wright. Such questioning of motives is not entirely fair. Newspaper people often simply aren't aware of what's going on. They have a big city to cover and it's not possible to be on top of everything.

"Well, it's hard to believe, but . . . okay . . ."

So, now that we have established a little better understanding, what about the museum?

"It opened on March 10, 1965, in part of what was then my office building. We're still there on the corner of West Grand Boulevard and Warren, only the museum has expanded greatly.

"We present the black experience from Africa to America in microcosm with a limited budget ($35,000) a year.) The public is invited at no charge and we put a lot of emphasis on attracting student groups for guided tours, illustrated lectures, etc., for a small fee.

"We want to present the facts of events and stop the repetition of misinformation. I'm convinced that distortion of history got us into our present situation, but we've got to deal with history to change people's attitudes."

A WORTHY objective, Dr. Wright, but more specifically, how can your museum help?

Through special efforts. Next Sunday (Feb. 14)

we're opening an exhibit centered on the Montgomery (Ala.) bus boycott. Mrs. Rosa Parks, who started it all, will be on hand for the unveiling of a portrait of herself and her family. It's done by Leroy Foster, and it's outstanding.

"I'll bet you didn't realize that Mrs. Parks had a family? And I'll bet you think that she refused to move on a spur-of-the-moment impulse?

"The fact is that Mrs. Parks knew exactly what she was doing, that she had been secretary of the NAACP for years, had observed countless court cases in which people had been punished for not moving to the back of the bus, was offended by what she saw and finally made up her mind to do something about it.

"This is the kind of factual material we emphasize . . . The fight for freedom doesn't rest simply on emotional, impulsive moves. It rests on commitment, deep, bed-rock solid."

There was much more because men who feel bitter don't turn off very easily. But it seemed Dr. Wright felt a bit better as he departed. He had made a few points.

And this man who deliberately chose Detroit as his home town, for the moment, will be satisfied to have all Detroiters go to and support the International Afro-American Museum located at 1549 W. Grand Boulevard at Warren (Phone: 899-2500). And certainly he'll be disappointed if you miss the exhibit that opens Sunday at noon and runs for six weeks.

Detroit Free Press   1/21/71

Auto Official Doctor Join Board of U-D

The University of Detroit has added two new lay members to its board of trustees.

Walter T. Murphy, executive director of North American public relations for the Ford Motor Co., and Dr. Charles Wright, a gynecologist and obstetrician who is founder of the International Afro-American Museum in Detroit, return the board to a membership of 16.

They replace G. Mennen Williams, who became a justice of the Michigan Supreme Court, and the Rev. Father Jules J. Toner, director of novices for Colombiere College in Clarkston, Mich. Both men resigned.

Detroit Free Press   6/29/66

Arts Commisson Picketed at Reorganization Meeting

The Detroit Arts Commission held its reorganization meeting Tuesday as five pickets who said they represented the Association for the Study of Negro Life and History, Detroit branch, marched on the sidewalk in front of the Detroit Institute of Arts.

Dr. Charles Wright, spokesman for the five pickets, said the group was left out of planning for the dedication ceremony for the African Art Gallery held Saturday in the institute's new South Wing.

•••

HE DEMANDED that the association, which worked with the Founders Society in the initial planning of the gallery, be allowed to participate fully "in future planning and implementation of such plans."

Arthur Coar, president of the Detroit Branch of the Association for the Study of Negro Life and History, said the association "did not in any way authorize this disgraceful action."

Coar said in a statement:

"The association deeply regrets this incident and disclaims any responsibility for the actions and statements of these individuals.

In its business meeting, the commission unanimously named Lee Hills, executive editor and publisher of the Free Press, its new president, replacing Lawrence Fleischman, who is moving to New York.

Hills, who was sworn in as a member of the commission earlier in the day, is a member of the Friends of Modern Art and has been a patron member of the Founders Society since 1959.

Elected vice president of the commission was Ralph T. McElvenny, president of Michigan Consolidated Gas Co.

Also serving on the commission are Douglas F. Roby, Mrs. Edsel B. Ford, Harold O. Love, Stanford C. Stoddard and Mrs. Harry L. Winston.

•••

OUTSIDE THE institute, pickets carried various signs, including three with political overtones.

One claimed Mayor Cavanagh had bested former Gov. G. Mennen Williams, his opponent in the Democratic primary for the U.S. Senate, by relegating Williams' African art gifts to the African gallary to the basement during the dedication week.

Cavanagh laughed off the suggestion, saying Williams' art would be a fine addition to the gallery.

Williams was in Grand Rapids Tuesday. In a heated discussion with museum officials, his aides protested the idea, which was given by the pickets, that Williams had any knowledge of the protest march.

"It's true we tried to call him at Mackinac Island last night and again today but couldn't reach him," said Dr. Wright. "But we think it's strange his things are in the basement."

•••

THE WILLIAMS art was planned as a part of the June 25 dedication, but the schedule was changed.

"It was impossible to get the huge collection sorted and cataloged," said Willis Woods, institute director. "Some of it has been here five months, some is still coming in. The governor told us we were free to pick whatever we wanted.

"He has not contacted us and made no comment on our change in schedule."

Fleischman, outgoing president of the commission, said the Williams' part of the showing was canceled simply because it was decided that no one donor would be singled out during the week-long South Wing dedication.

Board Chairman Eugene Gilmer and museum Executive Director Marian Moore.

Michigan Citizen   12/23-29/90

Founder questions city control of MAAH

By Derrick C. Lewis
Staff Writer

The Museum of African American History's annual meeting held Dec. 11, was marked by a question of city versus membership control of the museum.

Museum founder Dr. Charles Wright called the question on the procedure of appointing board members, pointing out museum members used to vote on seven members from the private sector to serve on the board, and the city would appoint eight for a majority.

He says over the years the board changed its by-laws to allow the city to appoint all of the board members.

Board Chairman Eugene Gilmer says this arrangement came about when the museum agreed to accept city funding. The museum received almost $900,000 in grants from the city this year, out of a total of $1,046,125.

Fourteen members currently serve on the board, and most were appointed by Mayor Coleman Young. The tenure of board members is two years, and it is the mayor's perogative on whether to re-appoint or not.

SOME MEMBERS expressed concern that the Young appointed board is not representative of the museum's 3,000 members.

Wright said this was a reason for his resignation as board chairman this year. He served as the museum's board chairman for twenty-five years.

Museum member Hazel Lee says a lot of people will not have anything to do with the museum, financially, until there is a reconciliation between Wright and the board.

Gilmer indicated Wright's support of the museum should be a sign of a reconciliation.

Wright says he supports the museum by paying dues, but there has been no reconciliation. He says he does not know what is going on at the museum.

WRIGHT ALSO ASKED Gilmer about the future of the museum, saying it was not discussed during presentations by him and museum Executive Director Marian Moore.

Wright was referring to negotiations the museum is having with the Detroit Institute of Arts, the Science Center, and the Center of Creative Studies to determine whether the museum building will be sold to the city and relocated elsewhere.

Gilmer would not comment on the museum's position, saying the negotiations are continuing and a report to the membership will be given when the board receives further information.

Museum of African American History founder Dr. Charles Wright thinks the mayor's appointed board is not representive of museum membership

About 150 people attended the annual meeting which included a slide presentation presented by Moore, which gave a glimpse of events given by the museum during the year.

Moore pointed out more than 489,587 people attended museum events during the fiscal year. Some events hosted by the museum was the Museum's 25th Anniversary Celebration in March which included the awarding of the Paul Robeson scholarship to student Lori Hall, who is currently attending Hampton University.

THE MUSEUM HOSTED the Winds of Freedom exhibition, a youth oriented project, featuring more than 100 works of art by area students;

The 7th Annual African World Festival, attended by nearly 310,000 people, which earned the museum $102,703, and;

Held a march with the city of Detroit to honor African National Congress leader Nelson Mandela.

The museum also revealed it's first edition of *African American News,* a newsletter which will circulate four times a year to keep members informed of events at the museum.

The financial report indicated the museum received $1,388,786 in total revenue for 1990, compared to $1,132,122 in 1989. The museum received $24,461 in private contributions, $50,096 from the membership, $16,689 in interest and dividends, and $148,712 from "other revenues."

Expenses for 1990 was $1,671,302, an increase of $421,009 from 1989. A beginning of the year fund balance of $992,885 covered the revenue deficiency.

Artist's Statement on the "Sankofa Bird" sculpture
(Legacy of Leadership Award)

The Sankofa symbol

The Sankofa is an Akan symbol found on the Adinkra, a ceremonial cloth worn by the royalty and spiritual leaders of the Asante people in Ghana. Like many Adinkra symbols, Sankofa images are based on the observation of nature, human attributes, vets, and cultural exchanges. The original Sankofa image is based on the behavior of preening birds. It is a representation of a bird whose head is turned rearward to groom its back or tail feathers.

The bird is said to be looking back into its past to fetch lessons from earlier experiences. It may need to revisit these lessons before moving on. The Sankofa is literally translated as: "It is not taboo to go back and retrieve if you forget" and may have layers of meaning. The recollection of history and the retrieval of collective wisdom from our heritage is necessary to understand how to direct ourselves for the future.

Two other Sankofa images resemble open ended heart shapes with spirals either on top or both top and bottom. recently, a Sankofa image was found on a coffin at the enslaved African Burial Ground Excavation in New York City. Howard University is spearheading this project.

The Sankofa Bird sculpture

Sankofa symbols are essentially two-dimensional graphics. My sculptural interpretation conceptually fuses the Sankofa image and swirling qualities with my own proces for developing three-dimensional form. As with the symbols, it is an spiraling form of an abstract bird whose head is facing rearward when seen from certain perspectives. From other vantage points it appears to be a bird looking forward. One must move around the sculpture, looking at it from various perspectives in order to fully enjoy its total imagery.

With the award at eye level, the front of the sculpture appears as a large "S" in its overall shape (sort of like Superman's emblem). As you move around it on the right side there will be a point where the bird appears to be looking backwards. Move around it some more and you'll discover a bird facing forward. Moving around the bird on the left side will also result in a bird looking both back and forward. An astute observer may discover a yin-yang (Tai-Chi) egg in the belly of the bird from the back. It appears in the area of physical material and empty space made by connecting the lines of the edge of the wing and the interior of the body. hope the unique experience of different images offered by the Sankofa Bird sculpture relates to you as the layers of meaning that can be interpreted from the Sankofa symbol.

— David Smedley

ARTISTS

Listed are some of the artists who, as described in the story, were part of a program in the spring of 1983, called "The Artists Showcase." The museum's response was that, "We, of the Afro-American Museum of Detroit have had a rich and rewarding relationship with the artists in the community." This began in the late 1960s, when funds from donated art helped "save the day."

Alice Agee
Oliver Agee
Oni Akilah
Kwasi S. Asante
Anthony Bacon
Milton Bennett
Richard Bennett
Cleveland Bohler
Michael Bowen
James H.M. Boyce, Jr.
Henri Ambaji King
Ronald L. Latham
James A. Lewis
Jon Onye Lockard
Naomi Long Madgett
James H. Malone
James H. Mathis
Walter Morgan
Hartwell Nance
Harold Neal
Pauline Norman

Joseph Norris
Latonia R. Nunn
Carol Owens
Aaron Ibn Pori-Pitts
Lorraine W. Powell
Dudley Randall
Wilbert Riser
Edward Broom
Elwyn Bush
Council Cargle
Yvonne P. Catchings
LaRon Carlisle
Ora Carter
Paul Collins
Matthew Corbin
Kevin L. Davidson
Katherine T. Ellis
LaVerne Flake
Leroy Foster
Randolph Gear
Oscar M. Graves

Pervis A. Hawkins
Dorothy Holloway
Leno Art Jaxon
Clarissa Johnson
Lester Johnson
Desmond Jones
Arthur Roland
Otto M. Sanders
Ron Scarborough
William Sanders
Onita Jackie Sanders
Dwight Smith
Isabelle N. Stanton
Cledie Taylor
Robert Tomlin
Howard Weathington
Bennie White, Jr.
John Williams
Walter Williams
Shirley Woodson
James L. Wright
Robert Wright

Appendix V

AFRICAN AMERICAN ASSOCIATION OF MUSEUMS

The story in Chapter Eleven traces the history of the African American Association of Museums from its inception in the 1960s. Dr. Margaret Burroughs of Chicago, joined Dr. Wright after hearing of his desire to bring together representatives from the few Black museums existing in the United States. The idea was to form an organization that would become a forum for the sharing of ideas, experiences and programs, and encouraging others to start museums.

The lists include the 1999-2000 board of directors elected at the August 1998 meeting in Birmingham, Alabama, and lists of individuals and organizations associated with the AAMA.

AFRICAN AMERICAN ASSOCIATION OF MUSEUMS (AAAM) BOARD OF DIRECTORS

Rita Organ
President
Charles H. Wright Museum of
    African American History
Detroit, MI

Bill Gwaltney
2nd Vice President
Rocky Mt. National Park
Estes Park, CO

Edna Diggs
Treasurer
National Afro American
    Museum
Wilberforce, OH

Lina Stephens
Council
18th & Vine Museums
Kansas City, MO

Deborah Mack
Council
National Underground Railroad
    Freedom Center
Cincinnati, OH

Robert Haynes
Council
African American Museum &
    Library
Oakland, CA

Lawrence Pijeaux
1st Vice President
Birmingham Civil Rights
    Institute
Birmingham, AL

Habeebah Muhammad
Secretary
Anacostia Museum
Washington, DC

Carolyn Adams
Council
Virginia Museum of Fine Art
Richmond, VA

Terrie Rouse
Council
Afro American History &
    Cultural Museum
Philadelphia, PA

Peggy Montez
Bronzeville Children's Museum
Evergreen Park, IL

William Billingsley
Association of African American
    Museums
Wilberforce, OH

AFRICAN AMERICAN ASSOCIATION OF MUSEUMS (AAAM)
EXECUTIVE DIRECTORS & ADMINISTRATIVE PERSONNEL

Carolyn Adams
Community Affairs Director
Virginia Museum of Fine Arts
Richmond, VA

Wanda Aikens
Anacostia Museum –
    Smithsonian
Washington, DC

Beth Alberty
Director of Collections
Brooklyn Children's Museum
Brooklyn, NY

Carol J. Alexander
Executive Director
LaVilla Cultural & Heritage
    Association
Jacksonville, FL

Ana M. Allen
POSITIV!
Washington, DC

Betty Arenth
Interim Director
Sen. John Heinz Pittsburgh
    Regional History Center
Pittsburgh, PA

Amina Anderson
Executive Director
Black United Fund of Oregon
Portland, OR

Brooke Davis Anderson
Director
Diggs Gallery
Winston-Salem State University
Winston-Salem, NC

Barbara Andrews
Curator
National Civil Rights Museum
Memphis, TN

Harvey Bakari
Historic Interpreter
Colonial Williamsburg
    Foundation
Williamsburg, VA

T. Lindsay Baker
Director
Texas Heritage Museum
Hill College
Hillsboro, TX

Kathryn L. Beard
Wayne State University
Detroit, MI

Clayborn Benson
Director
Wisconsin Black Historical
    Society
Milwaukee, WI

Michelle Bibbs
Director of Development
DuSable Museum of African
    American History
Chicago, IL

Deirdre L. Bibby
Executive Director
The Amistad Foundation, Inc.
Hartford, CT

William Billingsley
Association of African American
    Museum
Wilberforce, Ohio

Althea S. Bolden
Executive Director
Harrison Museum of African
    American Culture
Roanoke, VA

Robert J. Booker
Executive Director
Knoxville, TN

Josie W. Brantley
Birmingham, AL

Claudine Brown
Program Director - Arts
The Nathan Cummings
    Foundation
New York, NY

Tamera Brown
Historian
Anacostia Museum
Washington, DC

Lawrence Burgess
Interpretive Specialist
National Capital Parks East
Washington, DC

Tracey H. Burns
Historic Site Manager
North Carolina Transportation
    Museum
Spencer, NC

Margaret T. Burroughs
Founder
DuSable Museum of African
    American History
Chicago, IL

Emory S. Campbell
Executive Director
Penn Center, Inc.
St. Helena Island, SC

Marian Carpenter
Curator of African American
    Materials
The Children's Museum of
    Indianapolis
Indianapolis, IN

Melvin Carr
Human Resources Officer
Missouri Historical Society
St. Louis. MO

Patrina Chatman
Registrar
Charles H. Wright Museum of
    African American History
Detroit, MI

Denise B. Christian
Executive Director
Crispus Attucks Cultural Center,
    Inc.
Norfolk, VA

AFRICAN AMERICAN ASSOCIATION OF MUSEUMS (AAAM)
EXECUTIVE DIRECTORS & ADMINISTRATIVE PERSONNEL

Carla B. Cleaves
Special Projects
National Civil Rights Museum
Memphis. TN

Leanne R. Cole
Troy State University,
  Montgomery
Montgomery, AL

Wayne Coleman
Archives
Birmingham Civil Rights
  Institute
Birmingham, AL

Karen Comer
Tubman African American
  Museum
Macon, GA

Vernon Courtney
Interim Director
National Afro American
  Museum & Cultural Center
Wilberforce, OH

Spencer R. Crew
Director
National Museum of American
  History
Washington, DC

Betty Cunningham
African American Museum
  Dallas
Dallas, TX

Kim Curry-Evans
Collections Manager
Scottsdale Museum of
  Contemporary Art
Scottsdale, AZ

Glenna Cush
Director of Promotions and
  Public Relations
Alpha Omega Information
  Systems, Inc.
Upper Marlboro, MD

Jacqueline K. Dace
Research Associate
Missouri Historical Society
St. Louis, MO

Kevin Davidson
Senior Designer
Charles H. Wright Museum of
  African American History
Detroit, MI

James J. Davis
Chief Protection Services
National Gallery of Art
Washington, DC

Victor L. Davson
ALJIRA, Inc.
Newark, NJ

Angelia Debnam
Program Administrative
  Assistant
Southeastern Center for
  Contemporary Art
Winston-Salem, NC

Edna C. Diggs
Curator
National Afro American
  Museum & Cultural Center
Wilberforce, OH

Richard K. Dozier
Tallahassee, FL

Clarenda Drake
Chief IR & VS
National Capital Parks East
Washington, DC

W. Marvin Dulaney
Director
Avery Research Center
Charleston, SC

Jim Dunn
Arcadia
Charleston, NC

Lucenia Dunn
National Council of Negro
  Women, Inc.
Washington, DC

James N. Eaton, Sr.
Founder & Director
Black Archives. Research Center
Florida A & M University
Tallahassee, FL

Allan L. Edmunds
Philadelphia, PA

Gwenndolyn Y. Elmore
Executive Director
The Arna Bontemps African
  American Museum &
  Cultural Arts Center
Alexandria, LA

Carol Enseki
Executive Director
Brooklyn Children's Museum
Brooklyn, NY

Coty Y. Evans
Curatorial Services
Birmingham Museum of Art
Birmingham, AL

Martie Evans-Charles
Gold Eye Production Company
Bronx, NY

George Ewert
Director
Museum of Mobile
Mobile, AL

Cassie Fahrney
Director Membership Services
AASLH
Nashville, TN

Frank Faragasso
Historian
National Capital Parks East
Washington, DC

Zora M. Felton
Chief of Education, Emeritus
Anacostia Museum-Smithsonian
  Inst.
Washington, DC

AFRICAN AMERICAN ASSOCIATION OF MUSEUMS (AAAM)
EXECUTIVE DIRECTORS & ADMINISTRATIVE PERSONNEL

Vilma S. Fields
Director
Chattanooga African American
  Museum
Chattanooga, TN

Jesse E. Fisher
Security & Operations Director
University of California Berkeley
  Art Museum
Berkeley, CA

Sheila M. Flanagan
Assistant Director
Museum of Mobile
Mobile, AL

John E. Fleming
Director
National Underground Railroad
  Freedom Center
Cincinnati, OH

Tuliza Fleming
National Gallery of Art
Washington, DC

Cheryl Fox
Curator
Banneker Douglass Museum
Annapolis, MD

Wonda L. Fontenot
Director
Wannamuse Institute
Opelousas. LA

Karen Franklin
Administration
National Afro American
  Museum & Cultural Center
Wilberforce, OH

Curtis J. Franks
Director Museum Education &
  Exhibits
Avery Research Center for
  African American History &
  Culture
Charleston, SC

Roland L. Freeman
President
The Group for Cultural
  Documentation, Inc.
Washington, DC

Brent D. Glass
Executive Director
PA Historical & Museum
  Commission
Harrisburg, PA

Prizgar Gonzolaz
Lushena Books, Inc.
Mind Power The Way of the
  Future
Chicago, IL

Deborah Gray
Executive Director
Tuskegee Human & Civil Rights
  Multicultural Center
Tuskegee, AL

Derek Anthony Gray
Exhibit Manager
Chattanooga African-American
  Museum
Chattanooga, TN

Jonathan Green
Jonathan Green Studios, Inc.
Naples, FL

Vivian P. Greene
Administrative Assistant
Chattanooga African-American
  Museum
Chattanooga, TN

Kim Miller Griffin
Education Specialist
National Afro American
  Museum & Cultural Center
Wilberforce, OH

William W. Gwaltney
Chief of Interpretation
National Park Service
Rocky Mountain National Park
Estes Park. CO

Aisha Habadah
NJIT
Bloomfield, NJ

John Hale
Superintendent
National Capital Parks East
Washington, DC

Kathe Hambrick
Museum Director
River Road African American
  Museum
Gonzales, LA

Sheila Hanagan
The Museum of Mobile
Mobile, AL

John Hankins
Development Associate for
  Community Affairs
New Orleans Museum of Art
New Orleans, LA

Tiffany M. Hardy
New York University
New York, NY

Amelia Harris
Exhibitions Specialist
Maryland Department of
  Housing & Community
  Development
Annapolis, MD

Ottawa W. Harris
Director
Black American West Museum &
  Heritage Center
Denver, CO

Robert L. Haynes
Senior Curator
African American Museum &
  Library
Oakland, CA

LeRoy Henderson, Jr.
Chattanooga African-American
  Museum
Chattanooga, TN

AFRICAN AMERICAN ASSOCIATION OF MUSEUMS (AAAM) EXECUTIVE DIRECTORS & ADMINISTRATIVE PERSONNEL

Melinda Herzog
Curator
Gov. Bill & Vara Daniel Historic
  Village
Waco, TX

Gerlinde Higginbotham
CSI Graphic Images
Worthington, OH

Urla Hill
Director
The Speed City Collection
San Jose, CA

E. Selean Holmes
Cultural Consultant
Cincinnati, OH

Benjamin Horowitz
Director
Heritage Gallery
Los Angeles, CA

Carroll Hynson, Jr.
Chairperson
Maryland Commission on
  African American Culture &
  History
Annapolis, MD

Catherine Ingram
Curator
National Park Service
Washington, DC

James L. Ingram, Jr.
Capital Interpreter
Colonial Williamsburg
  Foundation
Williamsburg, VA

Don Jackson
Board of Trustees
DuSable Museum of African
  American History
Chicago, IL

Kern M. Jackson
Minority History Specialist
Museum of Mobile
Mobile, AL

Emily James
Historic Interpreter
Colonial Williams Foundation
Williamsburg, VA

Isabel P.E. Jasper
Archives Administrator
National Afro-American &
  Cultural Center
Wilberforce, OH

Irene D. Johnson
Executive Director
Museum
African American Museum of
  Art
Deland, FL

Carroll Johnson
Exhibit Director
Library of Congress
Washington, DC

James W. Johnson
Director
Alabama State Black Archives
Normal, AL

Mirma A. Johnson
Curator/Education
National Civil Rights Museum
Memphis, TN

Teresa Johnson
Financial Manager
Smithsonian Institution
Washington, DC

Trudy Kelley
Supervisory Staff Coordinator
National Park Service
Washington, DC

Richard T. Kemp
CEO
Afro American Mail Order Co.
Burlington, VT

Regina L. Kennedy
Security Supervisor
Birmingham Museum of Art
Birmingham, AL

Eric Key
Executive Director
The Kansas African American
  Museum
Wichita, KA

Niami Kilkenny
Director
Program in African American
  Culture
National Museum of American
  History
Smithsonian Institution
Washington, DC

Jacqueline P. King
Manager of Community
  Relations
High Museum of Art
Atlanta, GA

Anthony Knight, Jr.
Museum & Historic
  Preservation Consultant
Town of Eatonville
Deltona, FL

Vicki Kopf
Southeastern Center for
  Contemporary Arts
Winston-Salem, NC

Stephanie W. LeDuff
Ohio Historical Society
Columbus, OH

Twyta Lang-Gordon
Motherland Imports
Los Angeles, CA

Raymond Langston
Chairman of Board
Highland Beach Historical
  Commission
Frederick Douglass Museum
Annapolis, MD

Jackie Lewis-Harris
St. Louis Arts Museum
St. Louis, MO

AFRICAN AMERICAN ASSOCIATION OF MUSEUMS (AAAM)
EXECUTIVE DIRECTORS & ADMINISTRATIVE PERSONNEL

Doris H. Ligon
Director
African Art Museum of
  Maryland
Columbia, MD

Brian C. Little
Director
Black History Museum &
  Cultural Center
Richmond, VA

Lyn Logan-Grimes
Columbus Museum of Art
Columbus, OH

Lillian W. Lovett
Historic Site Manager
The Newsome House
Newport News, VA

Gail S. Lowe
Anacostia Museum
Washington, DC

Merceria Ludgood
Former Board Member
Museum of Mobile
Mobile, AL

George S. Martin
Deputy Chief, Administration
National Gallery of Art
Washington, DC

Nona R. Martin
Education Director
African American Museum in
  Philadelphia
Philadelphia, PA

Cameron Martindale
Vice President for Institutional
  Advancement
Troy State University -
  Montgomery
Montgomery, AL

Rhonda L. Matheison
Director of Finance &
  Operations
High Museum of Art
Atlanta, GA

Christy S. Matthews
Director of Interpretive
  Programs
Colonial Williamsburg
  Foundation
Williamsburg, VA

Joan Maynard
Executive Director
Weeksville Society
Brooklyn, NY

Joseph McGill, Jr.
Executive Director
African American Heritage
  Foundation
Cedar Rapids, IO

Sylvia Watts McKinney
Executive Director
Museum of Afro American
  History
African Meeting House
Brookline, MA

Philip Jackson Merrill
Nanny Jack & Company
Baltimore, MD

Carole Merritt
Director
The Herndon Home
Atlanta, GA

Regina Monteith
Director of Education
Historic Columbia Foundation
Mann-Simons Cottage
Columbia, SC

Peggy A. Montes
President
Bronzeville Children's Museum
Evergreen Park, IL

Earl D. Moore
Board of Trustees
DuSable Museum of African
  American History
Chicago, IL

Freda Walker Moore
Art Plus Tees & Mo
Garrisonville, VA

Juanita Moore
18th & Vine Museums
Kansas City, MO

Roscoe M. Moore, Jr.
Rockville, MD

Helen M. Moss
Community Outreach
  Coordinator
The Dayton Art Institute
Dayton, OH

Tara D. Morrison
Consultant
NPS/NCSHPO
Baltimore, MD

Habeebah Muhammad
Anacostia Museum
Washington, DC

James W. Myles
President
Provident Foundation
Chicago, IL

Inelle Nealey
Support Services
Schomburg Center for Black
  Research
New York, NY

Steven C. Newsome
Director
Anacostia Museum/Smithsonian
  Inst.
Washington, DC

Andrea Nichols
National Museum of African Art
Washington, DC

Elaine Nichols
Curator of History
South Carolina State Museum
Cola, SC

AFRICAN AMERICAN ASSOCIATION OF MUSEUMS (AAAM)
EXECUTIVE DIRECTORS & ADMINISTRATIVE PERSONNEL

Nancy Nolan-Jones
Director
African American Museum
Cleveland, OH

Patrick M. O'Brien
Morgan State University
Baltimore, MD

Toilynn O'Neal
Museum Coordinator
Art Consortium's African
   American Museum
Cincinnati, OH

Rita Organ
Curator
Charles H. Wright Museum of
   African American History
Detroit, MI

Diane S. Okwukwu
Alabama State Black Archives
Normal, AL

Maurice D. Parrish
Interim Director
The Detroit Institute of Arts
Detroit, MI

Margaret H. Peacock
Teacher
HABSE & Cleve. Hts. -
   University Hts. Schools
Cleveland Hts, OH

Wendi L. Perry
Curator
Missouri Historical Society
St. Louis, MO

Gene Peters
P.R.I.S.M & Tiques
South Farmingdale, NY

Bernadette M. Phifer
Curator
George Washington Carver
   Museum
Austin, TX

Lawrence J. Pijeaux, Jr.
Executive Director
Birmingham Civil Rights
   Institute
Birmingham, AL

Ju'Coby A. Pittman
Executive Director
Clara White Mission
Jacksonville, FL

Denita V. Powell
Program Assistant/Admin. Asst.
National Underground Railroad
   Freedom Center
Cincinnati, OH

Nicelle Price
Chattanooga African American
   Museum
Chattanooga, TN

Eleanor Qadirah
Board of Directors
United Arts Council
Salisbury, NC

G.B. Quinney
Director of Security
Birmingham Museum of Art
Birmingham, AL

Valena Randolph
Education Specialist
National Afro American
   Museum & Cultural Center
Wilberforce, OH

Beldon Raspberry
Director of Administration
Brooklyn Children's Museum
Brooklyn, NY

Ernestine A. Ray
Executive Director/Curator
Old Dillard Museum
Fort Lauderdale, FL

Edward Rigaud
Executive Director
National Underground Railroad
   Freedom Center
Cincinnati, OH

Beverly Robertson
Director
National Civil Rights Museum
Memphis, TN

Mary A. Robinson
Training Specialist
National Park Service
Stephen T. Mather Training
   Center
Harpers Ferry, WV

Kenneth G. Rodgers
Director
North Carolina Central
   University
Museum of Art
Durham, NC

Maureen J. Rolla
Administrative Director
Getty Leadership Institute
New York, NY

Benjamin C. Ross
Sixth Mount Zion Church
Richmond, VA

Patrick Ross
Riverdale, MD

Terrie S. Rouse
Executive Director
African American Museum in
   Philadelphia
Philadelphia, PA

Rosemary Sadlier
President
Ontario Black History Society
Toronto, ONT

Debby Saintil
Cambridge, MA

Rosalind Savage
Director
Banneker Douglass Museum
Annapolis, MD

AFRICAN AMERICAN ASSOCIATION OF MUSEUMS (AAAM)
EXECUTIVE DIRECTORS & ADMINISTRATIVE PERSONNEL

Cynthia Schaal
Director
Afro American Cultural Center
Charlotte, NC

Veela Sengstacke
Director of Marketing
Provident Foundation
Chicago, IL

Stacey Shelnut
Asst. Director Education
Baltimore Museum of Art
Baltimore, MD

Charlotte Sherman
Curator
Heritage Gallery
Los Angeles, CA

Steven Shwartzman
Program Officer
Institute of Museum & Library
    Services
Washington, DC

Charles F. Siles
Programs Curator
Louisiana State Museum
New Orleans, LA

Charles F. Siler
Program Curator
Louisiana State University
New Orleans, LA

Wylene Sims-Burch
Director
Howard County Center of
    African American Culture
Columbia, MD

Alonzo N. Smith
Research Historian
Program in African American
    Culture
National Museum of American
    History
Washington, DC

Anne Collins Smith
New York, NY

Emma C. Smith
National Conference of Artists
Washington, DC

Nikki A. Smith
Project Director
Maryland Museum of African
    American History & Culture
Crownsville, MD

Patrice Snead
Community Programs
    Coordinator
Minnesota Historical Society
Saint Paul, MN

Lawrence L. Spencer
Managing Representative
Art Partners
Columbus, OH

Shirl Spicer
Winston-Salem, NC

Monica Monique Spry
Historical Interpreter
Colonial Williamsburg
    Foundation
Williams burg, VA

Portia Stallworth
Administration
Birmingham Museum of Art
Birmingham, AL

Sharon Steinle
Manager
The Amistad Foundation, Inc.
Hartford, CT

Lina Stephens
18th & Vine Museums
Kansas City, MO

Rowena Stewart
Director
18th & Vine Museums
Kansas City, MO

Barbara Stratyner
New York, NY

Bettye J. Stull
The King Arts Complex
Columbus, OH

Karen E. Sutton
Old Dominion University
Baltimore, MD

Ted Swigon
Beverly Shores, IN

Dorothy Taylor
Black Heritage Coordinator
The Alabama Historical
    Commission
Montgomery, AL

Franzine K. Taylor
Head Ready Representative
Alabama Department of
    Archives & History
Montgomery, AL

Gilbert Taylor
Curator
IPS Crispus Attucks Museum
Indianapolis, IN

Paul Taylor
Professor
University of Maryland
College Park, MD

Eugene Thompson
Acting Registrar
America's Black Holocaust
    Museum
Milwaukee, WI

Eugene R. Thompson
Alexandria, VA

Jessie Thymes
Coordinator, Community
    Outreach
The Field Museum
Chicago, IL

AFRICAN AMERICAN ASSOCIATION OF MUSEUMS (AAAM)
EXECUTIVE DIRECTORS & ADMINISTRATIVE PERSONNEL

Tracey Tisdale Richardson
Sen. John Heinz Pittsburgh
Regional History Center
Pittsburgh, PA

Michelle Torres-Carmona
Scheduling & Exhibitor
   Relations Coordinator
Smithsonian Institution (SITES)
Washington, DC

Leo F. Twiggs
Executive Director
Stanback Museum &
   Planetarium
South Carolina State College
Orangeburg, SC

Sala Udin
Pittsburgh City Council
Pittsburgh, PA

Elaine Vinson
Director of Human Resources
Museum of Science and
   Industry
Chicago, IL

Lawrence T. Walker, Sr.
NSDAR
Washington, DC

Roslyn A. Walker
Director
National Museum of African Art
Washington, DC

Tyra S. Walker'
Museum Curator
National Park Service Museum
   Resource Center
Glenndale, MD

Margaret Thomas Ward
Librarian/Archivist
Charles H Wright Museum of
   African American History
Detroit, MI

Nancy Watts
History/Cultural Consultant

Ophelia Wellington
Executive Director
Freetown Village
Indianapolis, IN

Bernard Williams
Chicago, IL

Herbert T. Williams
Director
Community Folk Gallery
Syracuse, NY

Mel White
Director, African American
   Programs
Old Salem, Inc.
Winston-Salem, NC

Patricia A. Whitted
Security Supervisor
Birmingham Museum of Art
Birmingham, AL

Herbert T. Williams
Director
Community Folk Art Gallery
Syracuse University
Syracuse, NY

Kathryn Williams
Director
Museum of Afrikan History-Flint
Flint, MI

Vernetta M. Williams
Smithsonian Institution
Suitland, MD

Brenda Woods
Washington, DC

Thomas A. Woods
Director
Old World Wisconsin
Eagle, WI

Anotinette D. Wright
President
DuSable Museum of African
   American History
Chicago, IL

Charles H. Wright
Detroit, MI

Jeanne Zeidler
Hampton University Museum
Hampton, VA

ALABAMA

Alabama State Black Archives
Research Center & Museum
Normal, AL

Birmingham Civil Rights
Institute
Birmingham, AL

Birmingham Museum of Art
Birmingham, AL

Museum of Mobile
Mobile, AL

Tuskegee Institute National
Historic Site
National Park Service
Tuskegee Institute, AL

Tuskegee Human & Civil Rights
Multicultural Center
Tuskegee, AL

Southeastern Center for Afro-
American Architecture
Tuskegee Institute
Tuskegee, AL

ARIZONA

Scottsdale Museum of
Contemporary Art
Scottsdale; AZ

ARKANSAS

Delta Cultural Center
Little Rock, AR

CALIFORNIA

California African American
Museum
Los Angeles, CA

African American Museum of
Fine Art
San Diego, CA

African American Museum &
Library
Oakland, CA

Dunbar Hotel, Cultural &
Historical Museum
Los Angeles, CA

Ebony Museum
Oakland, CA

Heritage Gallery
Los Angeles, CA

Museum of African American
Art
Santa Monica, CA

National Minority Military
Museum
University of California
Davis, CA

COLORADO

Black American West Museum &
Heritage Center
Denver, CO

Rocky Mountain National Park
National Park Service
Estes Park, CO

CONNECTICUT

The Amistad Foundation
Hartford, CT

Wadsworth Atheneum
Hartford, CT

DISTRICT OF COLUMBIA

Anacostia Museum
Smithsonian Institution
Washington, DC

Frederick Douglass National
Historic Site
National Park Service
Washington, DC

Moorland-Springarn Research
Center & Library
Howard University
Washington, DC

National Museum of African
American History
Smithsonian Institution
Washington, DC

National Park Service
National Capital Region
Washington, DC

Smith-Mason Gallery
Washington, DC

FLORIDA

Afro American Museum of
the Arts
Deland, FL

Black Archives, Research
Center & Museum
Florida A & M University
Tallahassee, FL

Black Heritage Museum
Miami, FL

Clara White Mission
Jacksonville, FL

LaVilla Cultural & Heritage
Association
Jacksonville, FL

Museum of African-American
Art
Tampa, FL

Old Dillard Museum
Fort Lauderdale, FL

Joseph E. Zee Memorial
Library and Museum
Jacksonville, FL

GEORGIA

APEX Museum (Afro-
American Panoramic
Experience)
Atlanta, GA

Arts N Artifacts Gallery
Columbus, GA

Collections of Life and
Heritage
Atlanta, GA

Hammond House Galleries
Atlanta, GA

High Museum of Art
Atlanta, GA

The Herndon Home
Atlanta, GA

HISTORY AND ART MEMBER ORGANIZATIONS

Laney Walker Museum
Augusta, CA

Martin Luther King Jr. Center for
Social Change
Atlanta, GA

Tubman African American
Museum
Macon, GA

INDIANA

The Children's Museum of
Indianapolis
Indianapolis, IN

Conner Prairie
Fishers, IN

Crispus Attucks Museum
Indianapolis, IN

Freetown Village
Indianapolis, IN

ILLINOIS

Bronzeville Children's Museum
Evergreen Park, IL

DuSable Museum of African
American History
Chicago, IL

Field Museum
Chicago, IL

Isobel Neal Gallery
Chicago, IL

Museum of Science & Industry
Chicago, IL

Museum of Contemporary Art
Chicago, IL

KANSAS

The Kansas African American
Museum
Wichita, KA

Quindano Town Underground
Rail Road
Kansas City ,KS

KENTUCKY

African American Heritage
House
Louisville, KY

The Kentucky Derby Museum
Louisville. KY

LOUISIANA

Arna Bontemps African
American Museum &
Cultural Arts Center
Alexandria, LA

Black Arts National Diastora,
Inc.
New Orleans, LA

C.C. Haydell, Sr. MD Cultural
Arts Center
New Orleans, LA

Louisiana State Museum
New Orleans, LA

River Road African American
Museum
Gonzales, LA

Henry C. & Lydia G. Sindos Art
Gallery
New Orleans, LA

Wonnamuse Institute for Study
of Arts, Culture & Ethnicity
Opelousas, LA

MASSACHUSETTS

Afro-American Cultural Center
Springfield, MA

The Children's Museum
Boston, MA

Museum of Afro-American
History
Boston, MA

Museum of Afro American
History
Brooklie, MA

Museum of African American
History
Roxbury, MA

National Center of Afro-
American Artists
Boston, MA

Parting Ways Museum of
Afro-American History
Plymouth, MA

MARYLAND

African Art Museum of
Maryland
Columbia, MD

Banneker Douglass Museum
Annapolis, MD

Charles H. Chipman
Cultural Center
Salisbury, MD

Eubie Blake National Jazz
Museum & Cultural
Center
Baltimore, MD

Howard Cty Center of
African American Culture,
Inc
Columbia, MD

The Great Blacks In Wax
Museum
Baltimore, MD

James E. Lewis Museum of
Art
Morgan State University
Baltimore, MD

Maryland Museum of African
Art
Columbia, MD

Maryland Museum of African
American History and
Culture Project
Crownsville, MD

Baltimore Museum of Art
Baltimore, MD

MICHIGAN

Charles H. Wright Museum
of African American
History
Detroit, MI

Henry Ford Museum &
Greenfield Village Research
Center
Dearborn, MI

Michigan Ethnic Heritage
Studies Center
Detroit, MI

Motown Historical Museum
Detroit, MI

Museum of Afrikan American
History-Flint
Flint, MI

MINNESOTA

African American Cultural
Center
Minneapolis, MN

Minnesota Historical Society
Saint Paul, MN

MISSISSIPPI

Smith Robertson Black Cultural
Center
Jackson, MS

MISSOURI

Bruce R. Watkins Cultural
Center
Kansas City, MO

Vaughn Cultural Center
St. Louis, MO

St Louis Science Center
St. Louis, MO

18th & Vine Museums
Kansas City, MO

NEBRASKA

Great Plains Black Museum
Omaha, NE

NORTH CAROLINA

Afro American Cultural Center
Charlotte, NC

Diggs Gallery
Winston-Salem State University
Winston-Salem, NC

Martin Luther King Museum of
Black Culture
Eden, NC

North Carolina Central
University Art Museum
Durham, NC

North Carolina Transportation
Museum
Spencer, NC

Old Salem, Inc.
Winston-Salem, NC

Southeastern Center for
Contemporary Art
Winston-Salem, NC

NEW JERSEY

African Arts Museum
S.M.A.Fathers
Tenafly, NJ

The Newark Museum
Newark, NJ

Afro-American Historical &
Cultural Museum
Willingboro, NJ

Merabash Museum
Willingboro, NJ

NEW YORK

Afro-American Cultural Center
New York, NY

Aunt Len's Doll and Toy House
New York, NY

Black History Exhibition Center
Hempstead, NY

Brooklyn Children's Museum
Brooklyn, NY

Community Folk Art Gallery
Syracuse, NY

Schomburg Center for Research
in Black Culture
New York, NY

The Strong Museum
Rochester, NY

The Studio Museum in Harlem
New York, NY

Store Front Museum
Jamaica, NY

Weeksville & Bedford
Stuyvesant Historical Society
Brooklyn, NY

OHIO

Arts Consortium
Cincinnati, OH

Art Tatum African American
Resource Center
Toledo, OH

Charles White Gallery
Central State University
Robeson Cultural Arts Center
Wilberforce, OH

Cleveland African American
Museum
Cleveland, OH

The Dayton Art Institute
Dayton, OH

Dunbar House
Dayton, OH

The King Complex
Columbus, OH

Karamu House
Cleveland, OH

National Afro American
Museum & Cultural Center
Wilberforce, OH

National Underground Railroad
Freedom Center
Cincinnati, OH

Ohio Historical Society
Columbus, OH

OKLAHOMA

SANAMU African Gallery
Kirkpatrick Museum Complex
Oklahoma City, OK

HISTORY AND ART MEMBER ORGANIZATIONS

PENNSYLVANIA

Afro-American Historical &
Cultural Museum
Philadelphia, PA

Please Touch Museum
Philadelphia, PA

Sen. John Heinz Pittsburgh
Regional History Center &
Museum
Pittsburgh, PA

Selma Burke Art Center
Pittsburgh, PA

RHODE ISLAND

Center for the Study of Race &
Ethnicity In America
Brown University
Providence, RI

Rhode Island Black Heritage
Society
Providence, RI

SOUTH CAROLINA

Avery Institute of African
American History & Culture
Charleston, SC

Avery Research Center for
African American History -
College of Charleston
Charleston, SC

I.P. Stanback Museum &
Planetarium
South Carolina State College
Orangeburg, SC

Mann-Simons Cottage, Richland
County Historic Preservation
Columbia, SC

Old Slave Mart Museum
Sullivan's Island, SC

Penn Center, Inc.
Penn School Historic District
St. Helena Island, SC

South Carolina State Museum
Cola, SC

TENNESSEE

Beck Cultural Exchange Center
Knoxville, TN

Chattanooga Afro American
Museum
Chattanooga, TN

National Civil Rights Museum
Memphis, TN

TEXAS

African American Cultural
Heritage Center
Dallas, TX

Museum of African American
Life & Culture
Dallas, TX

George Washington Carver
Museum
Austin, TX

Gov. Bill and Vara Daniel
Historic Village
Museum Studies (Baylor
University)
Rio Vista, TX

Sutton's Black Heritage Gallery
Houston, TX

Texas Heritage Museum
Hill College
Hillsboro, TX

VIRGINIA

Alexandria Black Resources
Center
Alexandria, VA

Black History Museum &
Cultural Center
Richmond, VA

Crispus Attucks Cultural Center
Norfolk, VA

Colonial Williamsburg
Foundation
Williamsburg, VA

Hampton University Museum
Hampton University
Hampton, VA

Harrison Museum of African
American Culture
Roanoke, VA

The Newsome House Museum
& Cultural Center
Newport News, VA

Virginia Museum of Fine Arts
Richmond, VA

WISCONSIN

America's Black Holocaust
Museum
Milwaukee, WI

Old World Wisconsin
Engle, WI

Wisconsin Black History
Museum
Milwaukee, WI

WEST VIRGINIA

National Park Service
Harpers Ferry Center
Harpers Ferry, WV

Stephen T. Mather Training
Center
U.S. National Park Service
Harpers Ferry, WV

DR. WRIGHT'S PLAY: WERE YOU THERE?

The amazing saga of "Were You There?" is best explained by the introductory statement that follows. A sampling of letters is included. As with most of Wright's projects there was a relationship and correlation with another of his projects. In this case, the proceeds from the play were used to help support the African American Education Fund. The play met with great success, both on the stage and by way of television. Many years after its last performance, a request was made to Dr. Wright for permission to revive "Were You There?" on stage. A year 2000 production is scheduled.

WERE YOU THERE?   1965

INTRODUCTION

Charles H. Wright, M.D.

The first germ of an idea about Were You There? was born on a Sunday morning in the late fifties. The Fisk University choir was featured on a radio program of Negro spirituals, among which was "Were You There?" A golden-voiced baritone sang a solo portion of the spiritual with such conviction that one felt that he had indeed, been "there;" and if you had not been "there" you had missed one of the greatest experiences of a lifetime.

A closer look at the repertoire of spirituals revealed that many of them deal with the Crucifixion, in a variety of ways. Apparently the enslaved blacks identified very closely with the Master, in His hour of crisis. When these related spirituals are arranged in the proper sequence, they alone, will tell their own version of this greatest went in biblical history.

As the idea grew, it took the form of a musical drama, using the spirituals as a musical framework; if you have ever listened attentively to "Were You There?" and allowed yourself to become involved in its statement, it is easy to understand how this one song became and remained the cerebral theme of the entire effort.

Earlier in my life, I had seen a stage version of "Porgy and Bess". While it may be exciting stage fare, I found that it served to reinforce the popular "stereotype" of black people as slovenly, oversexed, irresponsible, near-do-wells. The worldwide popularity of this stage work does little to project a positive image of black Americans. "Carmen Jones" and other lesser-known religious-type presentations have, to a degree, presented the black man as something apart, not quite human, something that should be laughed at and pitied, but never respected.

Thus, for me at least, it became imperative that there must be created a work that would reflect our essential humanity. Whether such an effort would receive the same acceptability and support as the other kind was always a "moot" question. The answer to that question should have been a foregone conclusion.

Despite my impatience to get on with the job, there was never any illusion that I had the skills to do it myself. Many hours were spent in trying to interest learned members of the clergy to take the leadership in doing the biblical portion of the play. Some of these men held advanced degrees in theology and liberal arts, and seemed eminently qualified to assist in such a project. My recruitment efforts failed. One of the clergymen was so discouraging that I tried to forget the "whole thing."

Some three years later, having failed to recruit or forget, a final effort was made to convert an idea into a reality. A call was sent to three of my patients to come to my office for an after-office-hours conference. These three were Katherine Ellis (dance teacher), Vicotria McCants (music teacher), and Jane Ulmer (science teacher, actress). They listened attentively, offered guarded encouragement, and quite certain that they could not meet the requirements themselves, went away to seek "qualified assistance." At our third meeting these ladies had to confess that they, too, had not been able to interest anyone in working with the project. Moreover, the possibility of doing so seemed very remote.

For a long time no one spoke, hoping to avoid this moment of truth. Finally, someone blurted out, "We'll have to do it ourselves!" The tension was broken, but fear persisted. At that moment we had no firm plans. Each of us accepted firm assignments that night; and we set out on an unchartered sea.

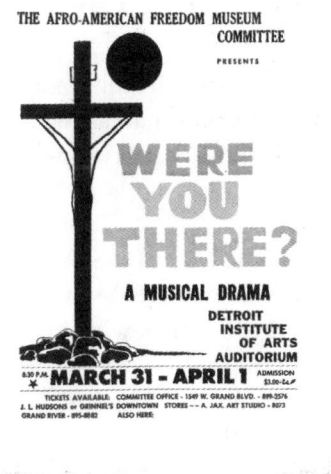

THE AFRO-AMERICAN FREEDOM MUSEUM
COMMITTEE

PRESENTS

WERE YOU THERE?

A MUSICAL DRAMA

DETROIT
INSTITUTE
OF ARTS
AUDITORIUM

6:30 P.M. **MARCH 31 - APRIL 1** ADMISSION $3.00-2¢

TICKETS AVAILABLE: COMMITTEE OFFICE - 1549 W. GRAND BLVD. - 899-2576
J. L. HUDSONS or GRINNEL'S DOWNTOWN STORES - - A. JAX. ART STUDIO - 8073
GRAND RIVER - 895-8882   ALSO HERE:

Gun College Newsletter-May 1963

DETROIT FELLOW TURNS PLAYWRIGHT - PRODUCER TO AID STUDENT FUND

Dr. Charles H. Wright, at left in the picture, is president of the African Medical Education Fund, Inc. a tax exempt, non-profit organization established in 1960 by the Detroit Medical Society to raise funds to render financial assistance to any needy medical student who agrees to practice in Africa. Recently he wrote and produced a three-act religious play "Were You There?" in which the story of Easter was retold for modern man using the media of song and dance as well as words. Negro spirituals provided the musical framework of the play. Pictured with Dr. Wright is Woodie King, Jr., drama critic for the Detroit Tribune and professional actor and director, who directed the play.

Inspiration for this activity stemmed from the efforts of a young Nigerian who was accepted as a student by the Toronto Medical School just two months before the fall 1960 term was to start. He was working in Detroit at the time and turned to local physicians for financial help to take advantage of this opportunity. He had very little cash or other resources of his own but managed to put together two to three hundred dollars, a microscope, and a few other useful articles. With there he set out for

Toronto, serenely certain that some day he would be a doctor! Motivated by this optimism, and by their knowledge of the needs of the African peoples for medical help, the Detroit Medical Society organized the African Medical Education Fund, Incorporated. The young man whose personal problems served to trigger this activity is now a junior medical student and has received full financial support from this Fund. Next year another African will enter the University of Indiana Medical School with full help. "Full help" for these students is about $2000 annually.

"WERE YOU THERE"

Wright's soul-searching drama is staged in a television studio centered around an arrogant, sadistic TV producer craving for power, B.J., played with depth and professionalism by Council Cargle, a Detroit teacher and professional actor.

B.J. reluctantly consents to the other six cast members taking time off to participate in the traditional Good Friday Services, the Tre Ore, with intentions of his remaining in the studio to catch up on his heavy backlog. Instead, he falls asleep and is revisited by his staff . . . who indeed WERE THERE at the crucifixion.

In B.J.'s dream, Delores Porter emerges as a great actress as Mary Magdalene, and as Mary in the modern scene. Ernest L. Hudson proves himself a skilled actor with unique character in his portrayal of Peter Simmonds in the modern scene and as Peter Simon in B.J.'s dream. The part of Judas adds excitement to the production as Donald Hayes brings this Biblical character to life before your very eyes, and Leon K. Smith, a businessman and accredited actor, brings another viewpoint of Pontius Pilate in the dream - and portrays with zest aid skillfulness, Mr. Ponti in the setting. Anthony Wellington Perkins, a Wayne State University drama student, is sharp and exciting as the Biblical figure Joseph of Arimethea and as Joe in the studio. Roy Adams, also a Wayne State University student, draws praise in his outstanding portrayal, with patience, of Nicodemus and Nick in the modern scenes.

Cargle, in his sure-footed performance of B.J. definitely commands the audience's attention during the drama, exhibiting great skill and range. Delores Porter is as graceful and patient and vivid as Mary Magdalene as she is in her real life career of speech instructor in a Detroit Public School.

Brazeal Dennard's Chorale group greatly enhances the drama, complimented by timely choreography directed by Kathryn Ellis. Along with Ellis are the dancers: Gina Ellis, Jennifer Myles, Deborah Richardson and Carla Wright, daughter of the playwright. The Ellis solo dancers include: Kathryn Ellis as Mary Magdalene, Bobby Peters as Peter, and Albert Sammons, Jr., as Judas.

Attributed to the success of "Were You There," is the outstanding camera direction of WTVS Director of Production, Jack Costello, assisted by John D. Carter, Jr., as stage director. After viewing the TV production last Easter season, a Detroit critic wrote" . . . the direction and camera work showed an admirable sophistication that begs for more frequent exercise . . . There is an excellent balance among close-up, medium and long shots and the blocking seems extremely well coordinated . . . Particular mention should go to Miss Porter, Smith and Hudson . . . Co-ordination between Costello and dialog director John D. Carter, Jr. seemed of the highest degree."

Dr. Charles H. Wright conceived the idea last year to bring his already acclaimed play to television, and naturally being a member of the board of trustees for Channel 56, he discussed the possibility of a TV production with station manager, James N. Christianson and Jack Costello.

"Were You There" is a color production of WTVS - Channel 56, directed by John D. Carter, Jr., with television direction by Jack Costello; videotape editor Jim Steed; produced and written by Dr. Charles H. Wright. Funds for the television production were provided Channel 56 by a public service grant from 14 Detroit clergymen, businessmen, community leaders and the IAM.

Channel 56 shot the teleplay in five sessions over a three-week period, a total of about 40 hours. It first began as a four camera show, but ended up with three cameras, and wag edited in four days, meeting the scheduled airing date last Easter Season.

In the televised production Of this classic Easter story, total theatre comes forward through comedy, pathos and skillful dramatic ability, exhibited by this professional cast projecting the author's purpose . . . to exhibit the true meaning of Easter. Told in drama, song and dance, WERE YOU THERE is worth not missing.

Promotion and publicity for the soul-searching teleplay was handled by Lilyann Mitchell, now the Director of Publicity and Promotion for Channel 56, with Bedia Thomas assisting as Production Secretary.

A noted Detroit Designer Noni Gee, proprietor of a unique boutique, "Ujaama Shoppe," designed all the colorful costumes in the Biblical scenes. Still photography was done by James Jemison, Henry Roundfield and Lloyd Winston.

Paintings seen in the drama are the courtesy Of Devon Cunningham and Henri Umbajki King.

Most unique, feathering the cap of Detroit, "Were You There" was written, produced and cast by and with all Blacks from the Detroit community. The IAM co-sponsored the TV production along with the Black community. The lAM is the only museum of its kind in the country, holding exclusive rights to the production.

Mrs. Margaret Ashworth is acting President of the Board of Trustees, while IAM founder, Dr. Charles H. Wright, serves as its Chairman of the Board of Trustees.

Ref: Lilyann Mitchell Date: March 9, 1973
Director of Public Relations/Promotion
WTVS - Channel 56

AFRICAN MEDICAL EDUCATION FUND

During the existence of the AMEF program, there were many persons who expended numerous hours, almost daily, to make it a success. Officers listed during one period were Charles H. Wright, M.D., president; Horace Bradfield, M.D., vice president; Ethelene Crockett, M.D., secretary; and Roblyn Arrington, M.D., treasurer. Project committee members listed were Welford Hill, M.D., chairman; Juanita Collier, Ph.D.; Congressman Charles C. Diggs, Jr.; Clarence Green, M.D.; Mrs. Welford Hill; Phillip Lenud; Nimrod Sherman, M.D.; Evelyn Sublett; Mrs. Lionel Swan; and Mrs. Malcolm West. A partial listing of the students who participated in the program, their place of origin, and the medical school attended is provided. Also included is a copy of the second annual program, announcing one of their very successful benefit parties.

African Medical Education Fund partial list of students:

NAME	COUNTRY OF ORIGIN	MEDICAL SCHOOL
U. Kalu	Nigeria	George Washington University
N. Nwaneri	Nigeria	Howard University
E. Otchere-Agyei	Ghana	Howard University
N. Udoh	Biafra	Howard University
G. Geh	Cameroon	University Florida-Gainsville
C. Folabit	Cameroon	La Faculte Libre de Medicine
Z. Moko	Cameroon	Howard University
A. Nyong'o	Kenya	University of Michigan
E. Sawyer	Liberia	Wayne State University
R. Tshibangu	Zaire	University of Rochester
M. Tuma	Cameroon	Wayne State University
W. Adebayo	Ghana	Howard University
B. Ekeledo	Nigeria	Michigan State University
E. Imoke	Nigeria	Michigan State University
C. Nchekwube	Nigeria	Howard University
N. Ntshona (Miss)	South Africa	Howard University
O. Ogunbase	Nigeria	Wayne State University

African Medical Education Fund

K. Oyefule	Nigeria	Howard University
T. Mawoyo	Rhodesia	University of Lagos
C. Uddoh	Nigeria	Temple University
D. Fofung	Cameroon	Howard University
L. Mahomva	Rhodesia	Meharry or Howard University
R. Balogun	Nigeria	University of Michigan
A. Iwuagwu	Nigeria	Wayne State University
E. Famutimi	Nigeria	Georgetown University
F. Izuora	Nigeria	Midland Lutheran College
U. Okoro	Nigeria	Howard University
S. Mutswairo	Rhodesia	St. George University
C. Chidi	Biafra	Case Western Reserve
S. Martin	W. Cameroon	Washington University
M. Mitoko	Kenya	Yale University
S. Kpadenou	Togo	Wayne State University
N. Ongele	Kenya	Howard University
C. Ezendu	Biafra	University of Cincinnati
I. Obuzor	Nigeria	Howard University
E. Moyo	Rhodesia	Howard University
C. Agore-Iwe	Nigeria	Howard University
P. Sende	Fr. Cameroon	Howard University
E. Fondo	W. Cameroon	Howard University
E. Adedeji	Nigeria	Howard University
J. Ibeaja	Nigeria	Howard University
P. Obiaya	Nigeria	Washington University
N. Azikiwe	Nigeria	St. Louis University
G. Adegbile	Nigeria	Howard University
K. Buahene	Ghana	Royal University Malta
E. Buanausi	Malawi	University of Hamburg
J. Okorie	Nigeria	Howard University
C. Adeoye	Nigeria	Loma Linda University
S. Soremekun	Nigeria	University of Toronto
S. Adebonojo	Nigeria	University of Pennsylvania
J. Adio	Nigeria	University of Michigan
A. Muchori	Kenya	Indiana University
I. Asfaw	Ethiopia	Indiana University
E. Emembolu	Ngeria	Howard University
J. Kazigo	Uganda	Howard University
Nnamdi Dike	Nigeria	Howard University

The African Medical Education Fund

Cordially Invites You to Attend its

Second Annual

𝔅𝔢𝔫𝔢𝔣𝔦𝔱 𝔗𝔥𝔞𝔫𝔨𝔰𝔤𝔦𝔳𝔦𝔫𝔤 ℭ𝔞𝔟𝔞𝔯𝔢𝔱

on Wednesday, November the Twenty-fifth
nineteen hundred and sixty-four
at nine o'clock

Latin Quarter

3067 East Grand Boulevard
Detroit, Michigan

DONATION: $5.00 per person
(tax deductible)

MUSIC: Jimmy Wilkins Orchestra

COMMITTEE

Mrs. Welford T. Hill, Chairman	Mrs. Robert Mines
Mrs. Malcolm E. West, Co-Chairman	Mrs. Raymond Nero
Mrs. Fred Aldridge	Mrs. William T. Patrick
Mrs. Alwin Barefield	Mrs. Marie Poston
Mrs. George Blackwell	Mrs. Harry Riggs
Miss Annie Burns	Mrs. Luther Rosemond
Mrs. Volna Clermont	Mrs. Irving Ruben
Mrs. Chester Cobb	Mrs. Nimrod Sherman
Dr. Juanita Collier	Mrs. Oliver Smith
Mrs. Ivan Gaskill	Mrs. Joshua Smith
Mrs. Carlos Gayles	Mrs. Lionel Swan
Mrs. Clarence Greer	Mrs. Charles Whitten
Miss Trudy Haynes	Mrs. Joshua Williams
Mrs. Marshall Hill	Mrs. Delford Williams
Mrs. Kenneth Hylton	Mrs. Willette Womack
Mrs. Lawrence Lackay	

The purpose of the organization is to assist in the training of doctors who will practice medicine in Africa. Anyone who has been accepted by an A-Class medical school, and who is in need of financial assistance, is eligible if he agrees to practice medicine on the continent of Africa immediately after his formal training is ended.

For Tickets Call — WE. 3-3279
TO. 8-4860

Dr. Wright's bio-resume lists several of his accomplishments that are not included in the book's main chapters. We particularly want the reader to note the listings of his lectures and appearances, the honors and awards and the journal articles, books and papers he has written.

EDUCATION

Meharry Medical School, 1939-1943, M.D.
Alabama State College, 1935-1939, B.S.
Southeast Alabama High School, 1932-1935

Post-doctoral Training

Certified by American College of Surgeons; 1955
Certified by American College of Obstetrics-
Gynecology; 1955
Resident; Obstetrics-Gynecology; Harlem Hospital,
N.Y.; 1950-1953
Assistant Resident; Pathology; Cleveland City
Hospital; Cleveland, Ohio; 1945
Assistant Resident; Pathology; Harlem Hospital; New
York; 1944
Intern; Harlem Hospital; New York; 1943-1944

PROFESSIONAL HISTORY

Medical Practice Status

Retired, 1986
Assistant Clinical Professor of Obstetrics-Gynecology;
Wayne State University School of Medicine;
1969-1983
Specialist; Obstetrics-Gynecology; Detroit, Michigan;
1953-1986
General Medical Practice; Detroit, Michigan; 1946-
1950

Hospital Affiliation Status

Hutzel Hospital; Detroit, Michigan; Senior Attending;
Emeritus
Harper-Grace Hospital; Detroit, Michigan;
Emeritus Attending
Sinai Hospital; Detroit, Michigan; Senior
Attending; Emeritus

ORGANIZATIONS

Professional
National Medical Association
Detroit Medical Society
Michigan State Medical Society
Wayne County Medical Society
American Medical Association; 1947-1953 (resigned)

Non-Professional
President; Charro Books
President; Michigan Support Group of Penn Center;
    Detroit, Michigan; 1992 - Present
Trustee; Penn Center of the Sea Islands; St. Helena
    Island, South Carolina; 1991
    Chairman; Board of Trustees; Museum of
    African American History; 1965-1987

LECTURESHIPS
Book signing and lecture; Wayne State University
    med. Students, interns and residents
Eleventh Annual Senior Banquet; speech and book
    signing; minority medical students; University
    of Michigan; April 20, 1996
Minority Medical Students Reception; speech and
    book signing; University Club; Michigan State
    University; April 12, 1996
Celebration of Black History Month; guest speaker;
    Riverview Hospital; February 21, 1996
"Tribute to African American Physicians in American
    Health Care" Guest speaker and book signing;
    Detroit Renaissance Club; February 14, 1996
Heritage Celebration of Penn Center; lectured
    groups; November 1995
Lecture/Book Signing; signed 300 books; Museum
    of African American History; September 2, 1995
The Centennial Convention of the National Medical
    Association (at its birthplace); book signing for
    delegates; Atlanta, Georgia; July 29, 1995
Celebrated Juneteenth program by Michigan Support
    Group at McPickwood farm in Linden,
    Michigan; spoke to group about Penn Center;
    June 19, 1995
During a meeting at the site in Port Royal, S.C., where

the Emancipation Proclamation was first read in public on January 1, 1863, representatives of the state (S.C.) and the federal government agreed with our suggestion and declared the site "A Historic Place;" May 18, 1995

Met with Mr. James Patton, president of The Wellness Plan, who offered and provided financial support to publish the book, *THE NATIONAL MEDICAL ASSOCIATION DEMANDS EQUAL OPPORTUNITY: Nothing More, Nothing Less,* May 1995

Participated in a session on Adult and Community Education, an enrichment program; February 22, 1995

Spoke to students at Osborn High School, "For a Good Future, Preserve the Past," February 16, 1995

Addressed the Student National Medical Association Region V Conference on "Cultural Identity, Education and Inspiring Committee of Color," Kellogg Center, Michigan State University, October 22, 1994

"100th Anniversary of National Medical Association;" Medical Faculty Conference; University of Michigan; November 16, 1993

Consultant Lecture; African American Museum of Ann Arbor Interest Group; May 2, 1993

"Rev. Martin Luther King and the U.A.W." Trade Union Leadership Council; Detroit, Michigan; February 27, 1993

Re-enactment of Emancipation Proclamation on its 130th Anniversary at the original site; Port Royal, South Carolina; January 1, 1993

"Dedication of Historic Marker to Charlotte Forten;" St. Helena Island, South Carolina; December 31, 1992

Tribute to Leroy Foster; presentation of Oscar Graves Award; Fox Theatre, May 20, 1992

"Health Care in Cuba," panelist, Michigan Chapter of U.S. Peace Council, Midwest Labor Institute, April 2, 1992

Retirement Dinner, Catherine Obing, R.N., guest

speaker, Embassy Suites Hotel, March 27, 1992

Malcolm X Forum, Discussion of Penn Center of South Carolina, March 25, 1992

"Penn Center, A Landmark Historic District;" Gray Panthers, Oak Park, Michigan; March 20, 1992

National Honor Society, guest speaker, Southwestern High School, March 19, 1992

"Life & Times of Dr. Martin Luther King," keynote speaker, Booker T. Washington Business Association, February 19, 1992

Black History Discussion; Thompson Middle School, Southfield, Michigan; February 10, 1992

"Health and Social Justice;" Dr. Martin L. King Seminar; Emory University School of Public Health; Atlanta, Georgia; January 22, 1992

Family Reunion Banquet; Brockman, Kilgore, Smith & White families; University of Detroit Mercy; July 6, 1991

"Spirit of Survival," Black History Network; Museum of African American History; September 28, 1991

Graduation Ceremony; guest speaker; Nataki Talebah Schoolhouse; Summer 1991

Career Day program; with 50 children regarding career plans; Weatherby School; May 21, 1991

Testimonial to Oscar Graves & his contribution to the Museum of African American History; speaker; May 20, 1991

Morehouse Medical School Graduation; representing Community Health Services of Detroit; Atlanta, Georgia; May 1991

Museum of African American History Volunteer & Award Program; May 1, 1991

"Voice of the Century;" Paul Robeson birthday lecture; tape presentation; Midwest Labor Institute; April 7, 1991

"Paul Robeson & Jeros, A Long-Term Relationship;" talk to Docents; Wayne State University, Community Arts Auditorium; March 1991

Lecture: MAAH; Black History Program; Detroit Urban Bankers Association; February 22, 1991

Address & discussion; Men's Club Program; Scott Methodist Church; February 23, 1991

Address to students; Detroit Public Schools,

Washington Career Center; February 22, 1991

Address to students; Inkster Christian Academy; February 22, 1991

Eulogy of Mary Woods; Greater Grace Church; February 16, 1991

Introduction of Ben Carson, M.D.; program for young people co-sponsored by Detroit Board of Education & the Museum of African American History; February 8, 1991

Black Studies group; Center for African American Studies; University of Michigan—Ann Arbor; February 7, 1991

Black Students Seminar; guest speaker; Olivet College; February 6, 1991

"Mandela the Man;" NAACP meeting; Barth Hall; Detroit, Michigan; June 23, 1990

"The Underground Railroad;" class presentation; University of Michigan—Dearborn; June 14, 1990

"Striving for Excellence;" Career Day; William Robinson Elementary School; June 7, 1990

Pre-Med Students Discussion & Questions; Wayne State University; June 4, 1990

"Early History of Detroit;" Volunteers Meeting; Museum of African American History; May 15, 1990

"Careers in the 1990s;" Southeastern High School Career Day; May 9, 1990

"Tribute to Leroy Foster;" Leroy Foster Gallery; May 8, 1990

"Future Leadership;" Career Day; Denby High School; May 1, 1990

"Slavery;" class presentation; Wayne State University; April 5, 1990

Youth Dialogue; Detroit Urban League; Golightly Vocational School; March 21, 1990

"History of MAAH and its Contribution to the Community;" presentation and award; Museum of African American History; March 2, 1990

"Price of Leadership;" Renaissance High School; February 23, 1990

"Black Leaders;" Western Wayne Correctional
    Facility; Plymouth, Michigan; February 21, 1990

"Education in Alabama;" Redford Library; February
    19, 1990

"Mandela;" WQBH Radio Talk Show; February 19,
    1990

"Panama from the African American Perspective;"
    United Methodist Church; Southfield,
    Michigan; January 28, 1990

"Legacy of King;" Martin L. King Birthday
    Celebration; Museum of African American
    History; January 16, 1990

"Black History Makers of Tomorrow;" critiqued and
    scored essay contests; McDonald's Program;
    1988-1989

Exhibit Opening; Personal Collection on Paul
    Robeson; Detroit Pubic Library; November 20,
    1989-January 1990

"The Significance of a Black History Museum;"
    Museum of African American History; Wayne
    State University, College of Lifelong Learning;
    November 15, 1989

"Medical Ethics in a Technological Age;" Student
    National Medical Association, Inc.; Wayne State
    University; November 1989

"What Does the Future Hold for Our Daughters?"
    Fathers and Daughters Breakfast; Our Lady of
    Refuge Church; Orchard Lake, Michigan;
    November 12, 1989

"Hampton University's Role in Black Education in
    Alabama;" Hampton Alumni Midwest Regional
    Conference; Days Inn Hotel; Southfield,
    Michigan; October 21, 1989

"Will the Real Josiah Henson Stand Up!" The Josiah
    Henson Celebration of His Bicentennial; June
    17, 1989

Fiftieth Annual Alumni Reunion; Alabama State
    University; Montgomery, Alabama; May 13-14,
    1989

"The Role of the Church in the Fight for Freedom;"
    Second Anniversary of Womack Temple CME
    Church Usher Board; April 23, 1989

"A Study of the African American Museum of History;"

Monroe, Michigan Chapter of the NAACP; April 2, 1989

"Who Shall Tell the Story?" Black History Month; Trinity Community Presbyterian Church; February 26, 1989

"The Need for a More Cooperative Effort Between Africans and African Americans;" Fourth African Nite Program; African Association of Greater Flint, Inc.; Flint, Michigan; February 25, 1989

"The Role of the Museum of African American History in this Community;" Midwest Labor Institute; February 2, 1989

"The Need for Creative Writing;" Fifth Annual Literature and Writing Workshop; Highland Park Community College; April 5, 1988

"Medical Ethics and US Foreign Policy;" annual lecture; Alpha Omega Alpha Medical Honor Society; Meharry Medical College; Nashville, Tennessee; April 22, 1987

"The Underground Railroad in Michigan;" student assembly; Soumi College; Hancock, Michigan; April 1, 1987

"The Significance of Black History;" Greater Christ Baptist Church; Detroit, Michigan; February 22, 1987

"Everyone Needs to Study Black History;" Women's Conference of Christians and Jews; Detroit, Michigan; February 18, 1987

"Should Our Health Care Responsibilities End at Our National Borders?" keynote speech; Ninth British Virgin Islands Medical Conference; Tortola, BVI; February 2, 1987

"The Unlikely Collaboration Between Two Giants;" videotape and lecture on the five-year friendship between George Washington Carver and Henry Ford; University of Michigan—Dearborn; Dearborn, Michigan; January 27, 1987

"King's Quest for Non-Violence Extends to the Vietnam War;" Department of Public Health; Lansing, Michigan; January 21, 1987

"My Work with King at Selma, 1965;" student assembly; University of Michigan—Ann Arbor; January 19, 1987

"A Critical Look at South Africa;" The New Era Study
Club; Detroit, Michigan; 1986

"The Preventability of Teenage Pregnancy;" Seventh
Annual British Virgin Islands Medical
Conference; Tortola, BVI; February 9, 1985

"A Comparison of Obstetrical Care in an HMO with
that in a Fee-for-Service Setting;" Grenada,
Spain; 1984

"The Christian's Responsibility in a Violent Society;"
Men's Day Service; Trinity Presbyterian Church;
Detroit, Michigan; October 27, 1982

"Medicine in Cuba;" Detroit Medical Society; Detroit,
Michigan; September 15, 1982

"The Responsibilities of the Black Medical Student;"
National Medical Association Convention; Ann
Arbor, Michigan; March 13, 1982

"The Historic Role of the Black Church;" Black
History Month lecture; Ecumenical Council;
Inkster, Michigan; February 14, 1982

"Do We Have a Stake in Southern Africa?" Annual
Meeting of Black Graduates; University of
Michigan—Ann Arbor; September 27, 1980

"Que Ofrece El Futuro Los Afro-Americanos?" El
Segundo Congreso Internationalismo del
Cultura Negra; Panama City, Panama; March
1980

"Our Most Endangered Species—The Black Male
Leader;" Founder's Banquet; Nu Omega
Chapter; Omega Psi Phi Fraternity; Detroit,
Michigan; 1979

"An Approach to Cost Containment in Health Care;"
Family Practice Section, National Medical
Association Convention; Detroit, Michigan;
1979

Testimony on Teenage Pregnancy before the National
Commission on the International Year of the
Child; Detroit, Michigan; 1979

"Why Study Ethnic History?" State Conference of
Michigan Historical Society; Holland,
Michigan; 1977

"La Lucha del Hombre Negro Para Libertad en los
Estados Unidos;" El Primero Congreso de La
Cultura Negra de las Americas; Cali, Colombia;
1977

"Non-Organic Causes of Pelvic Pain;" Annual Meeting; National Medical Association; Los Angeles, California; 1977

"Modified, Manual Rotation of Abnormal Presentations of the Fetal Head;" Annual Meeting; National Medical Association; Nashville, Tennessee; 1976

"Robeson, Peace Advocate;" Annual Conference; National Association for the Study of African American Life and History; Chicago, Illinois; 1976

"Paul Robeson: Labor's Forgotten Champion;" Purdue University; West Lafayette, Indiana; 1976

"Paul Robeson and the UAW;" UAW Council Meeting; Black Lake; Onaway, Michigan; 1975

"Drug Abuse in Detroit;" National Conference of Mayors; San Diego, California; June 1974

"Paul Robeson, Labor Activist;" Rutgers University; New Jersey; 1973

"The Creation of an Afro-American Museum;" Agustana College; Rock Island, Illinois; 1972

FIELD WORK

Month-long study tour in Cuba, 1982

Tour of duty aboard SS Hope; Cartegena, Columbia; 1967

Civil rights duty; Bogalusa, Louisiana; summer 1965

In command of the first-aid station during the Siege of Selma; Selma, Alabama; March 1965

Medical survey of Dahomey (now Benin), West Africa, under auspices of US State Department; 1965

Medical survey of Liberia, Nigeria and Sierra Leone, under auspices of US State Department; 1964

HONORS & AWARDS

Lifetime Achievement Award; Detroit Medical Society; for Invaluable Service to Medicine; June 20, 1998

Graduation Keynote Address; A-Phillip Randolph Career & Technical Center; May 27, 1998

Special Guest; "History of Detroit's Museum;" Michigan State University Graduate Studies

Program; East Lansing, Michigan; April 17, 1998

Special Guest; Dr. Charles H. Wright Museum of African American History- Anniversary (one year at new site); April 17, 1998

Achievement Award; Eastern Michigan University Dept. of African American Studies; April 8, 1998

Special Guest; Carter Metropolitan CME Church; Youth Church & Youth Sunday School; March 22, 1998

Accommodation of Excellence Award; Detroit Medical Society Regional Conference of Detroit IV, National Medical Association; May 4, 1996

Dr. Robert Greenidge Award; Ulti-Med Luncheon & Book signing; March 13, 1996

Eugene Power Achievement Award; United Negro College Fund Dinner; Washetenaw County, Michigan; March 10, 1996

Citation; Bal African group; Detroit Institute of the Arts; June 1995

"Living the Dream" Award; Employees of Ameritech of Michigan; March 1995

Certificate of Congressional Recognition; Congresswoman Barbara Rose Collins, 15th Congressional District; February 28, 1995

Dr. Alain Locke Award; Friends of African Art; Detroit Institute of the Arts; December 3, 1994

Community Service Award; Detroit Club of the National Association of Negro Business and Professional Women's Clubs; University of Michigan—Dearborn; April 24, 1994

Award; The Foster Grandparents of Detroit; November 22, 1993

Magnificent Doctor Award; Detroit Medical Society and its Auxiliary; July 1993

Community Service Award; Afro-American Sports Hall of Fame and Gallery; June 1993

Fiftieth Year Award; Michigan State Medical Society; Southfield, Michigan; March 15, 1993

Arts Advocate Award; Wayne State University; March 11, 1993

Living History Hall of Fame Induction; Brewer Elementary School; Detroit, Michigan; February 25, 1993

Citizen of the Year; Founder's Banquet; Omega Psi
Phi Fraternity; November 16, 1991

Tribute in Black; Messiah Baptist Church; June 17,
1990

Quest Role Model Award; Cadillac School-Detroit;
May 17, 1990

Certificate of Appreciation-Career Day; Denby High
School-Detroit; May 1, 1990

Medical Service to the Community; Comprehensive
Health Services of Detroit; April 6, 1990

Outstanding Medical Service: a 40-year award;
Detroit Medical Society; March 27, 1990

Resolution of Legislators for 25 Years of Service to
Community; Legislature; State of Michigan;
March 17, 1990

Grant Service Award: 25th Anniversary; Museum of
African American History; March 17, 1990

Recognition for Paul Robeson "Detroiters Collect"
display; Michigan Center for the Book; Library
of Michigan; November 16, 1989

Outstanding Service to Summer Youth Employment
Program; Detroit Public Schools; 1989

Distinguished Award for Pioneering in the Arts; Fifth
Annual Literature & Writing Workshop; United
Black Artists, USA; April 5, 1989

St. Agnes Comm. Award; St. Agnes School; 1989

Appreciation for Contribution to Africa; African
Association of Greater Flint; February 25, 1989

Heritage Award; Ford Motor Company Employees;
February 24, 1989

Certificate of App. Service to Detroit; Pelham Middle
School; February 19, 1989

Distinguished Community Service; University of
Detroit Black Students' Association; July 23,
1988

Summit Award; Detroit Chamber of Commerce; June
23, 1988

Humanitarian Award; 100 Black Men of America; May
28, 1988

13th Annual Brotherhood Award; Bethel AME
Church; February 28, 1988

Certificate of Appreciation for Devoted & Invaluable
Service; African American Museums
Association; February 26, 1988

Roy Wilkins Award; NAACP; February 1988

Celebrating the Dream-25th Anniversary of King's 1963 Woodward Avenue March; Michigan Council of Human Rights; January 23, 1988

Michiganian of the Year; The Detroit News; January 17, 1988

Dedication to African American Culture; Kettering High School Family; 1988

Ossian Sweet Award; Association of Black Judges of Michigan; 1988-1989

Outstanding Leadership as Founder & Chairman of MAAH; Detroit Association of Women's Clubs; 1987

Salute You as Leader; Wayne County Community College Students and Faculty; June 10, 1987

Outstanding Contribution to the People of State of Michigan; Michigan Week Committee; May 20, 1987

Frederick Douglass Award; National Association of Business & Professional Women (New Metropolitan Detroit Club); May 9, 1987

Induction into Alpha Omega Alpha Honor Medical Society; Meharry Medical College; April 22, 1987

Distinguished Warrior Award; Detroit Urban League; March 29, 1987

Augustus J. Calloway, Jr. Distinguished Service Award; Michigan Bell Telephone Company; October 30, 1986

Outstanding Leadership; Comprehensive Health Service of Detroit; May 6, 1986

Resolution of Honor; Wayne County Commissioners; May 6, 1986

Ah! Men Award-Distinguished Personal Achievement-One of Detroit's Most Admired Men; Men of Second Baptist Church; July 19, 1986

Outstanding Physician Service; Detroit Medical Society; May 31, 1986

Ellen G. Martin Service Award for Humanitarian Service; Hutzel Hospital; 1986

Eleven Years of Outstanding Service Black Heritage; Comprehensive Health Services of Detroit; 1986

Image Award for Outstanding Service in Preserving;

Little Rock Baptist Church; 1986

Outstanding Physician's 40-Year Service Award; Detroit Medical Society Roast; 1986

Achievement as a Bridge-Builder; New Calvary Baptist Church; October 12, 1985

Appointed by Gov. Blanchard to Michigan's Sesquicentennial Commission; State of Michigan; 1985

Listed in Who's Who in the World; Marquis Listing; 1985

Education-Black Awareness of the Year Award; Minority Women Network Detroit Man Chapter; April 11, 1985

Work with African Medical Education Fund; Dunbar Hospital Historical Museum; 1984

In Appreciation for Outstanding Service; Detroit Memorial Hospital; 1984

Outstanding Effort on Behalf of Humanity; Peace Links - Women Against Nuclear War; October 8, 1984

Induction, International Heritage Hall of Fame; International Institute; Detroit, Michigan; June 5, 1984

Life-Long Contributions to People of Detroit to Establish a Museum; Michigan Association of Black Journalists; March 10, 1984

Afro-American History Award; E.B.W.C., Inc.; February 7, 1982

Community Service Award; Booker T. Washington Business Association; 1980

Certificate of Service; Detroit Renaissance Lions; 1975-1976

Outstanding Alumnus of Century; Alabama State University—Montgomery; 1974

Named in Who's Who in the Midwest; Marquis Listing; 1968

Service aboard S.S. Hope (Cartegena, Colombia); People to People Health Foundation; 1967

Certificate of Commendation; Michigan State Medical Society; 1967

Anniversary Award for Community Service; National Association of Negro Business & Professional Women Clubs, Inc. (Detroit Club); Michigan

State Medical Society; 1966

National Omega Man of the Year; Omega Psi Phi Fraternity; 1965

Physician of the Year Award; Detroit Medical Society; 1963

For Meritorious Service in His Profession and Civil and Human Rights; New Calvary Baptist Church; 1963

Alumni Achievement Award; Detroit Chapter of Alabama State College Alumni Association; 1953

MEDIA & PRODUCTIONS

Television

Mandela—Interviewed during week of June 25; Channel 50, For My People; Channel 50, Newsline; Channel 7, Up Front. On-air consultant for Channel 7 during Detroit visit of Winnie and Nelson Mandela; June 28, 1990

Another Ann Arbor—Television station WBSX, Channel 31, Ann Arbor; "Future of the Museum of African American History;" May 10, 1990

The U.S. Constitution and its Impact on African Americans—A 108-minute video-taped discussion with Judge Avern Cohn, Congressman George Crockett and Professors Wade McCree and Harold Norris. Collaboration with the University of Michigan¾Dearborn

Audio-Visual Profile of the Life of Charles H. Wright—An hour-long profile of the life of the founder of the Museum of African American History, done by Ike Krasner; 1987.

An Unlikely Collaboration Between Two Giants—A 35-minute video interview with Austin Curtis, George Washington Carver's former laboratory assistant, who describes the five-year friendship between Carver and Henry Ford; 1987.

Robeson at the Peace Arch Park—A two-hour TV interview with citizens of Seattle, Washington who participated in Paul Robeson's stand-off against the U.S. Immigration Service, 1952-1955. Made in the studios of the University of Washington¾Seattle; 1986

Segregation in Public Transportation—A half-hour discussion celebrating the 25th anniversary of the Montgomery Bus Boycott. Audio-visual Department at Wayne State University; 1981

Rosa Parks and the Montgomery Bus Boycott—An hour-long celebration of the 20th anniversary of the Montgomery Bus Boycott, Channel 62; 1975

Were You There?—An hour-long musical drama, modern version of the Easter sttory. Channel 56 (writer and producer); 1972-1976

Teenagers Look at Venereal Disease—An hour-long panel discussion with call-in questions. Channel 56; 1972

The Making of a Militant—A half-hour program explaining the origin of Paul Robeson's militancy; Channel 4; 1971

Swing Low, Sweet Chariot—A half-hour, Channel 2, presentation depicting African Americans escaping enslavement

Plays

"Were You There?" an original musical drama. Onstage, 1963, 1964 and 1966. Adapted to television in 1972

"The Caracas Gang;" Unpublished

Films, Executive Producer

"The Proper Technique for the Surgical Scrub;" training film for operating-room personnel; in collaboration with and distributed by Quality Clinical Laboratories; Detroit, Michigan; 1982

"The Bank is Open to You;" National Bank of Detroit; distributed by American Banker Association; 1969

"You Can Be a Doctor;" Detroit Medical Society; fifteen-minute color film distributed by McGraw Hill Publishers; 1968

Radio Productions

"The Voting Rights Law of 1965;" one-hour broadcast to encourage support for the Voting Rights Bill that was to expire in 1970, the year of the broadcast

"Rosa Parks and the Montgomery Bus Boycott;" A

one-hour radio review of that event on the fifteenth anniversary; 1970

"The Voice of the Century;" One-hour documentary on the life of Paul Robeson

Scientific Exhibit

"Teenage Pregnancy;" National Medical Convention; 1979

Books

The National Medical Association Demands Equal Opportunity: Nothing More, Nothing Less. Southfield, Michigan: Charro Book Company, Inc., July 1995

The Peace Advocacy of Paul Robeson. Highland Park, Michigan: Harlo Press, 1984

Robeson: Labor's Forgotten Champion. Detroit, Michigan: Balamp Publishers, 1975

The National Medical Association's Turbulent Third Quarter, 1945-1970. Unpublished

ELECTED POSITIONS

Chairman, Board of Directors: Museum of African American History, 1965-1989

President: Penn Center: Michigan Support Group, 1992-1996

Board of Trustees: Penn Center, South Carolina, 1991-1995

Board of Trustees: Dunbar Medical Project, Inc., 1979-1981

Board of Trustees: Hutzel Hospital, 1979-1984

Board of Trustees: University of Detroit, 1969-1976

Board of Trustees: WTVS, Channel 56, 1967-1977

Chairman, Board of Trustees: African Medical Education Fund, 1960-1985

JOURNALS, ARTICLES, PAPERS

"Mandela Controversy." *Detroit News,* June 3, 1991

"Dr. King Answered the Call and Chose the Path of Non-violence." *The Detroit News,* January 21, 1991

"Mandela's World Tour." *Detroit Free Press,* June 28, 1990

"The Unfinished Business of the Bantustans." *Michigan Chronicle,* June 28, 1990

"The Continuing Burden of Bantu Education."

Michigan Chronicle, June 21, 1990

"Hendrik F. Verwoerd-The Architect of Apartheid."
Michigan Chronicle, June 14, 1990

"Three Seconds with Mandela." *Michigan Chronicle,*
June 7, 1990

"We've Got to go to Montgomery." *Detroit News,*
March 6, 1990

"Panama Perspective." *Michigan Chronicle,* February
24, 1990

"Peace Advocacy of Nelson Mandela." *Michigan
Chronicle,* December 30, 1989

"Paul Robeson Pleas for Peace." *Detroit News,* April
7, 1989

"A Salute to Nelson Mandela on His 70th Birthday."
July 18, 1988

"The Separation of Powers: Checks and Balances of
the U.S. Constitution." (Statement for
Bicentennial of Federal Constitution, 1987).

"Paul Robeson in Detroit." Unisys Corporation;
Detroit, Michigan; 1986

"Opposition to the World Medical Assembly in South
Africa, 1985." *Journal of the National Medical
Association, 78,* 1, 1985

"Obstetric Care in a Health Maintenance
Organization and a Private Fee-for-Service
Practice: A Comparative Analysis." *American
Journal of OB/GYN, 149,* 8, 848-856: 1984

"Scrub Film." *OB/GYN News,* April 1-4, 1982

"Physicians Must be Reminded of Their Economic
Responsibilities." *Michigan Medicine,* July
1981

"Surgical Scrub Film Raises Afro-Med. Funds." *Health
Care News,* December 31, 1980

"An Approach to Cost Containment in Health Care."
*Journal of the National Medical Association,
72,* 11, 1119: 1980

""Our Most Endangered Species—The Black Male
Leader." *The Oracle (Omega Psi Phi),* Winter
1980

"The Prevention of Teenage Pregnancy—The Only
Answer." *Journal of the National Medical
Association, 72,* 1, 1980

"Low Drama in Obstetrics." *The Medical Center
News,* February 14, 1979

"Travesty on the Oath of Hippocrates." *Journal of the National Medical Association, 70,* 1978

"Non-Organic Causes of Pelvic Pain." *OB/GYN News, 12,* 19, October 1, 1977

"Media Unfair in Reporting Local Crime." *Michigan Chronicle,* October 9, 1976

"Paul Robeson: He Left a Legacy of Pride (eulogy)." *Michigan Chronicle,* February 21, 1976

"A Method for Shortening the Second Stage of Labor." *Obstetrics & Gynecology Observer,* 1976

"The Peekskill Affair." *Freedomways Magazine, 15,* 2, 1975, (2) *The Great Forerunner.* p. 278, New York: International Publishers, and (3) Berlin: Seven Seas Books, 1977. This excerpt taken from "Robeson: Labor's Forgotten Champion."

"Richard M. Nixon's Civil Rights Requiem." *The Michigan Chronicle,* January 20, 1973

"Cervical Cerclage." *Michigan Medicine, 68,* 19, October 1969

"Talent Recruitment Films." *Journal of the National Medical Association, 6,* 2, March 1969

"The Economic Factor in Incompetent Cervix." *Journal of the National Medical Association, 57,* 4, July 1965

"Some Unusual Complications of Carcinoma of the Cervix and Treatment." *Journal of the National Medical Association, 55,* 6, November 1963

"Between the Shoulders and the Cord." *Obstetrics & Gynecology, 15,* 1, January 1960

"Spontaneous Intraperitoneal Hemorrhage." *American Journal of Surgery, 88,* 4, October 1959

"Effects of Carbonic Anhydrase Inhibitors on the Course of Sickle Cell Disease." *AMA Archives of Internal Medicine, 104,* July 1959

"Variations in Weights in Multiple Gestation." *Journal of Michigan State Medical Society, 53,* 6, June 1954

"Penetrating Wounds of the Gravid Uterus." *American Journal of Obstetrics & Gynecology, 67,* 6, June 1954

"Pregnancy Following Pneumonectomy for Pulmonary Tuberculosis." *Harlem Hospital Bulletin, 6, 1,* January 1953